Somalia, A Country Study

Federal Research Division

Table of Contents

Somalia, a country study...1

    Federal Research Division...1

    FOREWORD...5

    Preface..6

    GEOGRAPHY...7

    ECONOMY...7

    GOVERNMENT AND POLITICS...9

    Introduction..10

    THE SOMALIS: THEIR ORIGINS, MIGRATIONS, AND SETTLEMENT....23

    Emergence of Adal..24

    The Somali Peninsula on the Eve of Imperial Partition..............................25

    SOMALIA...26

    FOREWORD..26

    Acknowledgments...27

    Preface..28

    COUNTRY PROFILE...29

    GEOGRAPHY...30

    SOCIETY...30

    ECONOMY...31

    TRANSPORTATION...33

    GOVERNMENT AND POLITICS...34

    NATIONAL SECURITY..35

    Introduction..36

    Chapter 1. Historical Setting..49

    THE SOMALIS: THEIR ORIGINS, MIGRATIONS, AND SETTLEMENT....50

    Coastal Towns..52

    Emergence of Adal..53

    Mogadishu and Its Banaadir Hinterlands..54

    The Somali Peninsula on the Eve of Imperial Partition..............................55

    The Majeerteen Sultanates...56

    IMPERIAL PARTITION...57

    Mahammad Abdille Hasau's Dervish Resistance to Colonial Occupation..........59

    Consolidation of Colonial Rule..59

    Somalia During World War II...60

    British Military Administration...61

Table of Contents

Somalia, a country study

Trusteeship and Protectorate: The Road to Independence.................................66

FROM INDEPENDENCE TO REVOLUTION..................................72

Problems of National Integration......................................72

Pan–Somalism...74

Foreign Relations, 1960–69.......................................76

The Husseen Government...78

The Igaal Government...80

Coup d'Etat...82

THE REVOLUTIONARY REGIME..................................83

Supreme Revolutionary Council....................................84

Challenges to the Regime...87

Siad Barre and Scientific Socialism.................................87

The Language and Literacy Issue...................................89

Creation of the Somali Revolutionary Socialist Party..................91

SOMALIA'S DIFFICULT DECADE, 1980–90..........................92

Siad Barre's Repressive Measures..................................95

Persecution of the Majeerteen.....................................97

Oppression of the Isaaq..97

Harrying of the Hawiye..98

Chapter 2. The Society and Its Environemnt.........................100

PHYSICAL SETTING..103

Climate..104

Terrain, Vegetation, and Drainage.................................105

POPULATION AND SETTLEMENT PATTERNS.......................108

THE SEGMENTARY SOCIAL ORDER..............................113

Samaal..116

Digil and Rahanwayn...118

Riverine and Coastal People of Non–Somali Origin..................121

Specialized Occupational Groups..................................123

Social Change...124

LINEAGE SEGMENTATION AND THE SOMALI CIVIL WAR.............132

RELIGIOUS LIFE..134

The Tenets of Islam..135

Religious Roles in Somali Islam..................................137

Table of Contents

Somalia, a country study

Religious Orders and the Cult of the Saints....................................137
Folk Islam and Indigenous Ritual...141
Islam in the Colonial Era and After..143
Rising Islamism..145
LANGUAGE AND EDUCATION...145
Education..147
HEALTH...151
REFUGEES...153
BREAKDOWN OF THE INFRASTRUCTURE..157
Chapter 3. The Economy...159
PASTORALISM AND COMMERCE IN HISTORICAL PERSPECTIVE.....159
THE COLONIAL ECONOMY...160
ECONOMIC DEVELOPMENT, 1960–69..163
SCIENTIFIC SOCIALISM, 1970–75..164
THE SOCIALIST REVOLUTION after 1975..168
FROM SCIENTIFIC SOCIALISM TO "IMF–ISM," 1981–90.....................169
NATURAL RESOURCES AND ECONOMIC INFRASTRUCTURE...........173
Energy...174
Transportation...175
Communications...177
THE "REAL" SOMALI ECONOMY IN THE 1980s...178
Export of Labor..178
Export of Livestock..179
Rural Subsistence Sector...179
Urban Subsistence and Government Employment....................................181
Undeveloped Sectors..183
Mining...183
Forestry...184
Fishing..184
Manufacturing..184
Foreign Trade..185
Chapter 4. Government and Politics...186
GOVERNMENT STRUCTURE...188
Constitution...191

Table of Contents

Somalia, a country study

Legislature...192
Local Government..193
Legal System...194
Courts..195
POLITICAL DYNAMICS..197
Opposition Movements..198
Politics of Reconciliation...200
Politics of Succession..202
Politics of Disintegration...204
MASS MEDIA...204
FOREIGN RELATIONS...205
Relations with Other African States...206
Relations with Arab Countries...208
Relations with the United States..209
Other Foreign Relations..210
Chapter 5. National Security..211
INTERNATIONAL SECURITY CONCERNS..212
Irredentism and the Changing Balance of Power....................................212
The Ogaden War: Performance and Implications of Defeat.....................215
Postwar Status of the Armed Forces..217
INTERNAL SECURITY CONCERNS..218
Government Security Policy..219
Sources of Opposition...220
HISTORY AND DEVELOPMENT OF THE ARMED FORCES................228
The Warrior Tradition and Development of a Modern Army....................229
The Armed Forces in National Life...233
The Military and the Government..233
The Military and the Economy..234
Mission, Organization, and Strength...235
Manpower, Training, and Conditions of Service......................................237
FOREIGN MILITARY ASSISTANCE..239
STATE SECURITY SERVICES...245
People's Militia..249
National Security Service...249

Table of Contents

Somalia, a country study

CRIMINAL JUSTICE..250

Penal System..250

Prison System..252

HUMAN RIGHTS..253

Somalia, a country study

Federal Research Division

Kessinger Publishing reprints thousands of hard–to–find books!

Visit us at http://www.kessinger.net

- FOREWORD
- Preface
- GEOGRAPHY
- ECONOMY
- GOVERNMENT AND POLITICS
- Introduction
- THE SOMALIS: THEIR ORIGINS, MIGRATIONS, AND SETTLEMENT
- Emergence of Adal
- The Somali Peninsula on the Eve of Imperial Partition
- SOMALIA
- FOREWORD
- Acknowledgments
- Preface
- COUNTRY PROFILE
- GEOGRAPHY
- SOCIETY
- ECONOMY
- TRANSPORTATION
- GOVERNMENT AND POLITICS
- NATIONAL SECURITY
- Introduction
- Chapter 1. Historical Setting
- THE SOMALIS: THEIR ORIGINS, MIGRATIONS, AND SETTLEMENT
- Coastal Towns
- Emergence of Adal
- Mogadishu and Its Banaadir Hinterlands
- The Somali Peninsula on the Eve of Imperial Partition

1

- The Majeerteen Sultanates
- IMPERIAL PARTITION
- Mahammad Abdille Hasau's Dervish Resistance to Colonial Occupation
- Consolidation of Colonial Rule
- Somalia During World War II
- British Military Administration
- Trusteeship and Protectorate: The Road to Independence
- FROM INDEPENDENCE TO REVOLUTION
- Problems of National Integration
- Pan–Somalism
- Foreign Relations, 1960–69
- The Husseen Government
- The Igaal Government
- Coup d'Etat
- THE REVOLUTIONARY REGIME
- Supreme Revolutionary Council
- Challenges to the Regime
- Siad Barre and Scientific Socialism
- The Language and Literacy Issue
- Creation of the Somali Revolutionary Socialist Party
- SOMALIA'S DIFFICULT DECADE, 1980–90
- Siad Barre's Repressive Measures
- Persecution of the Majeerteen
- Oppression of the Isaaq
- Harrying of the Hawiye
- Chapter 2. The Society and Its Environemnt
- PHYSICAL SETTING
- Climate
- Terrain, Vegetation, and Drainage
- POPULATION AND SETTLEMENT PATTERNS
- THE SEGMENTARY SOCIAL ORDER
- Samaal
- Digil and Rahanwayn
- Riverine and Coastal People of Non–Somali Origin
- Specialized Occupational Groups
- Social Change

- LINEAGE SEGMENTATION AND THE SOMALI CIVIL WAR
- RELIGIOUS LIFE
- The Tenets of Islam
- Religious Roles in Somali Islam
- Religious Orders and the Cult of the Saints
- Folk Islam and Indigenous Ritual
- Islam in the Colonial Era and After
- Rising Islamism
- LANGUAGE AND EDUCATION
- Education
- HEALTH
- REFUGEES
- BREAKDOWN OF THE INFRASTRUCTURE
- Chapter 3. The Economy
- PASTORALISM AND COMMERCE IN HISTORICAL PERSPECTIVE
- THE COLONIAL ECONOMY
- ECONOMIC DEVELOPMENT, 1960–69
- SCIENTIFIC SOCIALISM, 1970–75
- THE SOCIALIST REVOLUTION after 1975
- FROM SCIENTIFIC SOCIALISM TO "IMF–ISM," 1981–90
- NATURAL RESOURCES AND ECONOMIC INFRASTRUCTURE
- Energy
- Transportation
- Communications
- THE "REAL" SOMALI ECONOMY IN THE 1980s
- Export of Labor
- Export of Livestock
- Rural Subsistence Sector
- Urban Subsistence and Government Employment
- Undeveloped Sectors
- Mining
- Forestry
- Fishing
- Manufacturing
- Foreign Trade
- Chapter 4. Government and Politics

- GOVERNMENT STRUCTURE
- Constitution
- Legislature
- Local Government
- Legal System
- Courts
- POLITICAL DYNAMICS
- Opposition Movements
- Politics of Reconciliation
- Politics of Succession
- Politics of Disintegration
- MASS MEDIA
- FOREIGN RELATIONS
- Relations with Other African States
- Relations with Arab Countries
- Relations with the United States
- Other Foreign Relations
- Chapter 5. National Security
- INTERNATIONAL SECURITY CONCERNS
- Irredentism and the Changing Balance of Power
- The Ogaden War: Performance and Implications of Defeat
- Postwar Status of the Armed Forces
- INTERNAL SECURITY CONCERNS
- Government Security Policy
- Sources of Opposition
- HISTORY AND DEVELOPMENT OF THE ARMED FORCES
- The Warrior Tradition and Development of a Modern Army
- The Armed Forces in National Life
- The Military and the Government
- The Military and the Economy
- Mission, Organization, and Strength
- Manpower, Training, and Conditions of Service
- FOREIGN MILITARY ASSISTANCE
- STATE SECURITY SERVICES
- People's Militia
- National Security Service

- CRIMINAL JUSTICE
- Penal System
- Prison System
- HUMAN RIGHTS

FOREWORD

The five chapters that follow represent preliminary drafts of *Somalia: A Country Study*, to be published by the Federal Research Division of the Library of Congress. The revised edition of this publication is now in the editorial process and will appear in the first half of 1993. The finished work will contain an introduction that highlights major trends detailed in the individual chapters and brings Somalia's situation up to date. The book also will include maps, photographs, a glossary, and a bibliography.

Most books in the area handbook series deal with a particular foreign country, describing and analyzing its political, economic, social, and national security systems and institutions, and examining the interrelationships of those systems and the ways they are shaped by cultural factors. The authors seek to provide a basic understanding of the observed society, striving for a dynamic rather than a static portrayal. Particular attention is devoted to the people who make up the society, their origins, dominant beliefs and values, their common interests and the issues on which they are divided, the nature and extent of their involvement with national institutions, and their attitudes toward each other and toward their social system and political order.

Louis R. Mortimer
Chief
Federal Research Division
Library of Congress
Washington, D C. 20540

Preface

Like its predecessor, this study is an attempt to treat in a concise and objective manner the dominant historical, social, political, economic, and military aspects of contemporary Somali society. Sources of information included scholarly journals and monographs, official reports of government and international organizations, newspapers, and numerous periodicals. Chapter bibliographies appear at the end of the book; brief comments on some of the more valuable sources suggested as possible further reading appear at the end of each chapter. Measurements are given in the metric system; a conversion table is provided to assist those readers who are unfamiliar with metric measurements (see table 1, Appendix). A glossary is also included.

Place–names generally have been spelled in accordance with those established by the United States Board on Geographic Names and the Permanent Committee on Geographic Names for British Official Use, known as the BGN/PCGN system. The spelling of other proper names conforms to the current usage in the country or to the most authoritative available sources.

Because Somalia has been in a state of virtual anarchy since the fall of the regime of Mahammad Siad Barre in January 1991 (and, actually, to a considerable degree since the outbreak of civil war in the latter 1980s), the lack of functioning government institutions has meant that statistics tend to be unreliable or nonexistent.

Therefore, statistics cited in the text or tables in the appendix should be viewed with caution.

The arrival of United States military forces in Somalia as part of Operation Restore Hope in the latter part of 1992, together with forces from other United Nations member states, has resulted in detailed Western press coverage of Somalia. However, much background data continued to be lacking.

The body of the text reflects information available as of mid–1992. Certain other portions of the text, however, have been updated. The Introduction discusses significant events that have occurred since the completion of research, the Country Profile includes updated information as available, and the Bibliography includes recently published help feel to the reader.

GEOGRAPHY

Size: Land area 637,540 square kilometers; coastline 3,025 kilometers; sovereignty claimed over territorial waters up to 200 nautical miles.

Topography: Flat plateau surfaces and plains predominate; principal exception rugged east–west ranges in far north that include Shimbir Berris, highest point at 2,407 meters.

Climate and Hydrology: Continuously hot except at higher elevations in north; two wet seasons bring erratic rainfall, largely April to June and October and November, averaging under 500 millimeters in much of the country; droughts frequent; only Jubba River in somewhat wetter southwest has permanent water flow.

Shabeelle River, also in southwest, flows about seven months of year.

ECONOMY

Salient Features: Formerly socialist–oriented economy undergoing market–oriented structural adjustment until 1991. Stabilization and macroeconomic adjustment programs implemented during 1980s under auspices of international credit and aid agencies. Privatization of wholesale trade and financial sectors largely complete by 1991; economic growth sporadic and uneven across sectors. Most economic activity disrupted by breakdown of Somali state in 1991.

Agriculture, Livestock, Forestry, and Fisheries: Crop and livestock production, forestry, and fisheries, accounted for bulk of gross domestic product (GDP) in 1991; livestock predominant agricultural export, also important source of animal products (mostly milk) for internal markets and subsistence. Crop cultivation dominated by rural subsistence sector, which generated sufficient surpluses to sustain domestic informal markets and barter economy until 1990. Main crops: sorghum, corn; incipient production of mild narcotic qat suppressed by central government during mid–1980s. Small plantation sector dedicated primarily to export of bananas and sugarcane. Domestic grain supply supplemented by international food aid. Small forestry sector dominated by production for export of frankincense and myrrh. Fisheries production showed modest growth during 1980s but remained minor economic activity. Agricultural activity severely curtailed as result of drought and breakdown of Somali state in 1991.

Mining: Mining contribution to GDP negligible (.3 percent of GDP in 1988) despite substantial deposits of gypsumanhydrite , quartz and piezoquartz, uranium, and iron ore. Meerschaum sepiolite mined; gold deposits suspected but not confirmed.

Manufacturing: Small manufacturing sector, based primarily on processing of agricultural products, consisted of few large state enterprises, hundreds of medium–sized private firms, and thousands of small–scale informal operations. Largescale enterprises dedicated mainly to processing of sugar, milk, and hides and skins. Overall manufacturing output declined during 1980s as result of failure of inefficient state enterprises under market conditions. Manufacturing activity further curtailed by civil war and collapse of Somali state. By 1990 manufacturing ceased to play significant role in economy (about 5 percent of GDP).

Energy: Domestic wood, charcoal, and imported petroleum provided basic sources of energy; significant hydroelectric potential of Jubba River remained unexploited; four small–scale wind turbine generators operated in Mogadishu. Prior to civil war, eighty state–owned oil–fired and diesel power plants provided electricity to cities and towns. Refining capacity limited to one refinery. Foreign oil supplies erratic throughout 1980s. United Nations Development Programme hydrocarbon study in 1991 indicated good potential for oil and gas deposits in northern Somalia.

Foreign Trade: Exports consisted of agricultural raw materials and food products. Livestock and bananas principal exports, followed by hides and skins, fish and fish products, and myrrh. Trade balance remained negative throughout 1980s and early 1990s. Principal imports in descending order: food, transportation equipment, nonelectrical machinery, cement and building materials, and iron and steel. Italy and Arab states main destinations of exports; Italy main country of origin for imported Somali goods in 1990; other minor suppliers included Norway, Bahrain, and Britain.

Currency: Somali shilling. During 1980s currency alternated between fixed and floating rates; as of March 31, 1992, US$1 equaled 3,800 shillings.

GOVERNMENT AND POLITICS

Government Structure: Country nominally under interim provisional government established by Executive Committee of United Somali Congress (USC) and headed by provisional president Ali Mahdi Mahammad after fall of Mahammad Siad Barre. As of September 1991, country effectively under control of as many as twelve rival clans and subclans. Central government authority at Mogadishu challenged by Somali National Movement (SNM), which in June 1991 declared independent Republic of Somaliland in former territory of British Somaliland. Constitution of 1979 nominally in force pending new constitution proposed by provisional government. Constitutionally mandated national legislature known as People's Assembly inactive since January 1991.

Administrative Divisions: Prior to fall of Siad Barre regime in January 1991, sixteen administrative regions, each containing three to six districts, with exception of capital region which was subdivided into fifteen districts, for total of eighty–four districts. Local government authority vested in regional and district councils whose members were elected, but whose candidature approved by district–level government. High level of military participation in regional and district councils. Ministry of Local Government and Rural Development exercised authority over structure of local government. From 1991 onward, no effective government organization existed.

Politics: During 1980s authoritarian regime of President Mahammad Siad Barre abandoned policy of scientific socialism on Marxist–Leninist lines and implemented marketoriented structural reforms of economy, while consolidating personal political authority. Broad–based national opposition met escalating government repression and provoked armed revolt in 1988 led by USC and SNM. Civil war caused eventual defeat of government forces and exile of Siad Barre in January 1991. USC faction led by General Mahammad Faarah Aidid contested authority of USC Executive Committee to form interim government and established rival government in southern Mogadishu, compelling Mahammad's government to retreat to northern Mogadishu. As of January 1993, country effectively fragmented under control of as many as twelve contending clan–families and clans.

Judicial System: Four–tier court system—Supreme Court, courts of appeal, regional courts, and district courts—based on Western models. Separate National Security Courts operating outside ordinary legal system and under direct control of executive given broad jurisdiction over offenses defined by government as affecting state security, until abolished in October 1990. Unified penal and civil law codes introduced in late 1960s and early 1970s, but some features of Islamic law considered in civil matters.

Foreign Relations: Foreign relations characterized by tension with neighboring states and economic dependence on aid from Arab and Western nations. Relations with neighboring states gradually improved as irredentist claims dating from Ogaden War period (1977–78) formally abandoned during 1980s; relations with Ethiopia remained strained despite 1988 peace agreement resulting from mutual harboring of foreign guerilla forces and uncontrolled mass migration. Relations with Western nations and United States broadened after 1977 rift with Soviet Union; United States military and economic aid provided throughout 1980s but suspended in 1989 because of human rights violations by Siad Barre government. Recipient of financial support from conservative Arab oil states.

Introduction

Figure 1. Administrative Divisions of Somalia, 1992 President George Bush visits United States forces in Somalia, January 1, 1993.

THE PEOPLE WHO LIVE in present–day Somalia have an ancient history. The medieval Arabs called them Berberi, and archaeological evidence indicates that they had occupied the area known as the Horn of Africa by 100 A.D. and possibly earlier. By the eighteenth century, the Somalis—their name derives from Samaal, their eponymous ancestor—had developed pastoral nomadism and were followers of Islam. Their first contact with Islam is believed to have occurred when a group of persecuted Muslims from Arabia sought refuge in the region at the time of the Prophet Muhammad in the eighth century. Historically, the area was home to two peoples: pastoral and agropastoral groups living in the interior, with informal and varied political structures; and trading communities on the coast, such as Seylac and Berbera in the north and Merca and Mogadishu in the south, that developed administrative and legal systems based on the Muslim sharia.

Somalia, a country study

The Somalis or Samaal consist of six major clan–families. Four of the families are predominantly pastoral—the Dir, Daarood, Isaaq, and Hawiye (representing about 70 percent of Somalia's population)—and two are agricultural—the Digil and Rahanwayn (constituting about 20 percent of the population). The remainder of the population consists of urban dwellers and marginal non–Samaal groups, most of whom engage in trade or crafts and who historically have lacked political participation and the Samaal warrior tradition.

The Digil and the Rahanwayn are located mainly in the south in the area between the Jubba and Shabeelle rivers, the best agricultural area. The rest of the country consists primarily of arid plateaus and plains, with some rugged mountains in the north near the Gulf of Aden coast. Because of sparse rainfall, nomadic pastoralism has been the principal occupation of clan–families in much of the country.

Historically, Somalis have shown a fierce independence, an unwillingness to submit to authority, a strong clan consciousness, and conflict among clans and subclans despite their sharing a common language, religion, and pastoral customs. Clans are integral to Somali life. Clan consciousness has been described as centering around the struggle for recognition in all its forms—social, political, economic, and cultural rights and status. Despite this clan consciousness, the Somali community historically preserved its basic unity because of the relative homogeneity of the society.

Over the centuries, the Somali Peninsula and the East African coast were subject to various rulers, including the Omanis, the Zanzibaris, the sharifs of Mukha in present–day Yemen, and the Ottoman Turks. By 1885, there were five mini–Somalilands: the north central part controlled by the British; the east and southeast (mainly present–day Djibouti) controlled by the French; the south, controlled by the Italians; the Ogaden in the west controlled by Ethiopia; and the southwestern part that became a part of Kenya (known as the Northern Frontier District). This colonial control continued in various forms until Somalia gained its independence in 1960.

The British and Italians followed different courses in their colonial administration. The British regarded northern Somalia mainly as a source of livestock for Aden, the principal supply post en route to India through the Suez Canal, whereas the Italians developed plantation agriculture based bananas, citrus fruits, and sugarcane in southern Somalia. Between 1900 and 1920, while Italy and Britain were consolidating their colonial rule, a

Muslim resistance movement arose under Mahammad Abdille Hasan, whom the British called the Mad Mullah. Until he died in 1920, Abdille Hasan, a member of the Salihiyah brotherhood, and his followers constituted a dervish group that waged war originally against Ethiopia, and later against the British, seeking to regain the Ogaden for Somalis.

Early in World War II, Italy invaded British Somaliland and ejected the British. British forces retook the colony in 1941 and conquered Italian Somaliland and the Ogaden as well, placing all three areas under British military administration. The Potsdam Conference in 1945 decided not to return Italian Somaliland to Italy; ultimately, the matter was referred to the United Nations (UN) General Assembly, which decided in 1949 to make the southern area an Italian trust territory. Meanwhile, under pressure from its World War II allies, Britain returned the Ogaden to Ethiopia in 1948, to the dismay of Somalis because the majority of the inhabitants were Somalis.

Nationalism had been growing in Somalia, largely as a result of the efforts of salaried Somali colonial officials who constituted an urban petty bourgeoisie. In 1943 the first Somali political party, the Somali Youth Club, was created. In 1947 the group changed its name to the Somali Youth League (SYL) and adopted the goals of unifying all Somali territories and opposing clannishness. Partly in response to nationalist pressures, both the Italians and the British took steps to improve education and health facilities, spur economic development, and give Somalis some experience in the political process.

Somalia's independence in 1960 faced several obstacles. Economically, the country was obliged to rely on Italian and British subsidies; it also had to obtain other foreign loans to build an infrastructure and to create model farms and livestock improvement programs, all designed to increase exports. Other major obstacles included clan–family and subclan rivalries, the irredentist pressures to incorporate Somalis living in the various mini–Somalilands, and differences between residents of British and Italian Somaliland. These differences were of two main kinds: economic (pastoral nomadism with its tending of flocks as opposed to plantation agriculture) and political (northern Somalis were less experienced in administration and political participation than their counterparts in the south). Furthermore, the new Somali constitution did not include strategies designed to move citizens away from clan loyalties and toward national objectives. For example, the Iise clan of the Dir clan–family had devised a system by which the smallest clan was given a special role: that of providing the overall clan leader and also of being responsible for settling disputes. Such an approach could have served as a model for the

Western framers of the Somali constitution.

As a result of clan–family dissensions, one of the major objectives of the Somali government after independence became that of national integration. This objective was accompanied by the efforts of the first president, Abdirashiid Ali Shermaarke, to promote a Greater Somalia. In seeking to distance itself from its colonial past, the new government cultivated relations with the Soviet Union and Eastern Europe. Soviet influence prevailed, particularly in the armed forces, and later the German Democratic Republic (East Germany) established the National Security Service (NSS). The police force, however, was trained primarily by the Federal Republic of Germany (West Germany) and the United States. The 1969 elections for the National Assembly demonstrated the Somali characteristic of independence: sixty–four political parties participated, some of them as small as one man. The SYL, however, dominated the field. The elections revealed that various groups, especially the military, had become increasingly critical of government corruption and nepotism.

The October 1969 killing of President Shermaarke by one of his bodyguards led the army, which had previously avoided political participation, to take over under army commander Major General Mahammad Siad Barre. The new governing body, the Supreme Revolutionary Council (SRC), named Siad Barre president. Retroactively, to facilitate continued Soviet aid, the SRC indicated it was pursuing scientific socialism, although Somalia lacked the infrastructure appropriate to Marxist socialism. Among the new government's objectives were breaking up the old regions (administrative units) into smaller entities and resettling many of the nomads in farming and fishing cooperatives. The government also sought to promote nationalist and socialist goals by appointing "peacekeepers" to replace the traditional elders and by creating various committees in place of traditional clan groups. With reference to the legal system, Siad Barre eliminated codes that gave clans land, water, and grazing rights. He also abolished the Islamic payment of blood money *(diya)* for injuries. Presumably, all these steps were designed to break down the traditional clan structure and strengthen the personal control of Siad Barre, as well as to weaken the role of religious leaders.

Although Siad Barre proclaimed scientific socialism compatible with Islam, his regime attempted to reduce the influence, particularly in politics, of Muslim leaders. Historically, clans had relied on itinerant religious teachers and on religiously devout males, known as *wadaddo*, who generally were the only literate individuals and who often occupied judicial roles. These religious functions were supplemented by Sufi religious orders or brotherhoods, whose leaders were more learned than the *wadaddo*. The best known of the latter was Mahammad Abdille Hasan, the early twentieth– century leader of the revolt against the British. In the first half of the twentieth century, religious teachers provided most of Somali education through Quranic schools that gave minimal literacy instruction. A major difficulty was the absence of an agreed–upon orthography for the Somali language until the government decreed one in 1973. The government undertook a huge literacy campaign thereafter and established numerous primary schools, some secondary schools, and a university. As of 1990, Somalia had 4,600 university students.

Whereas in its early years the SRC devoted considerable attention to such fields as education and economics, later a major part of its activity related to the political sphere. Despite the SRC's denunciation of clannishness, the clans connected with Siad Barre and his family became sufficiently prominent to be dubbed the MOD (Mareehaan–Ogaden–Dulbahante—the name of Siad Barre's clan, his mother's clan, and his son–in– law's clan, respectively). Initially, the SRC outlawed political parties, but in 1976 Siad Barre dissolved the SRC (it was later revived) and created one national party, the Somali Revolutionary Socialist Party (SRSP). The party in practice occupied a largely ceremonial position; actual power remained with Siad Barre.

To entrench his personal rule and in an attempt to regain the Ogaden, Siad Barre launched the Ogaden War against Ethiopia in 1977. The war officially ended in 1978 but low–level conflict continued with border raids and skirmishes for years afterward. Somalia experienced defeat and the death of 8,000 men, the influx of about 650,000 ethnic Somali and Ethiopian Oromo refugees, and a severe drain on its economy. The economic drain was caused by the purchase of military matériel to replace equipment lost in the war—three–quarters of Somalia's armored units and one–half of its air force. Having lost its alliance with the Soviet Union, which shifted its support to Ethiopia during the war, Somalia sought military aid from the United States. The latter, following the fall of the shah of Iran in 1979, was eager to bolster defenses in the Persian Gulf–Indian Ocean area. As a result, in return for the United States provision of arms and military training in 1980 the United States and Somalia concluded a military access agreement by which the United States could use Somali ports and airfields in the event of a crisis. The expansion of its armed forces, which grew from 5,000 troops at independence to 65,000 in 1990, also sapped Somalia's economy; for example, 30 percent of the national budget went for the military in the mid–1980s.

To develop the economy, in the early years of his regime Siad Barre launched several development plans, created agricultural and fishing cooperatives, and began establishing food processing plants. Somalia's foreign debt, however, increased at a tremendous rate as a result of the 1977–78 Ogaden War. Unable to call on the Soviet Union for aid, the Siad Barre regime turned for economic aid to the West, to oil–producing Arab states such as Kuwait, Qatar, Saudi Arabia, and the United Arab Emirates, and to the World Bank (see Glossary).

The economic crisis forced Somalia to devalue its currency and to encourage privatization. Economic output from agriculture and manufacturing, however, showed little progress and in some cases declined, partly as a result of intermittent droughts. The country lacked any energy sources, apart from wood and charcoal, despite surveys that indicated the likelihood of oil offshore in the Gulf of Aden. Moreover, its transportation and communications networks were minimal. In addition to livestock and agricultural products, which have constituted the bulk of Somalia's exports, the country did have a number of undeveloped sectors, however.

Among the chief of these were forestry (myrrh and frankincense were among Somalia's exports), fishing, and mineral deposits, including uranium.

Following the Ogaden War, Siad Barre recognized that to gain Western support he needed to create a political system that would appear to restore many civil rights that had been eliminated by the military regime.

Accordingly, the constitution of 1979 provided for freedom of speech, religion, publication, and assembly, but these rights were subject to major qualifications. The constitution made the president both head of state and head of government, with broad powers to conduct foreign affairs, serve as commander in chief of the armed forces, appoint various ministers and leading officials, and dissolve the legislature. Members of a single–chamber legislature, the People's Assembly, served a five–year term, with the government drawing up official lists of candidates and the assembly occupying a largely symbolic position. On the local government level, Siad Barre had dissolved all elected bodies following the military coup and required that all candidates for election be approved by the central government. The constitution confirmed the National Security Courts introduced by Siad Barre; these courts had jurisdiction over numerous cases and supplemented the regular courts. Siad Barre appointed only military officers to the High

Court, thus bringing the judiciary under the executive.

Another result of the Ogaden War was the rise of several organized internal opposition movements. To counter them, Siad Barre undertook increasingly repressive measures, including measures that involved numerous human rights violations. After judging a number of Majeerteen members of the military guilty of a coup attempt in 1978, Siad Barre initiated a campaign against the clan–family, using the Red Berets, an elite unit that served as his bodyguard. Several Majeerteen colonels escaped and fled abroad, where in 1978 they formed the Somali Salvation Front, renamed in 1979 the Somali Salvation Democratic Front (SSDF). This was the first opposition movement dedicated to overthrowing the regime by force.

Siad Barre then turned on the Isaaq in the north, who were discontented because they felt inadequately represented in his government. Isaaq dissidents in London had formed the Somali National Movement (SNM)

in 1981 to topple Siad Barre's regime. In 1982 they transferred their headquarters to Dire Dawa, Ethiopia, from where they conducted guerrilla raids against Somali government–held territory. Siad Barre's campaign against the Isaaq was particularly bloody; it included the 1988 destruction by bombing of Hargeysa, Somalia's major northern city, causing the flight to neighboring countries of tens of thousands of refugees. Next, Siad Barre attacked the Hawiye in the central area around Mogadishu. The Hawiye had meanwhile formed their own opposition movement, the United Somali Congress (USC), which received support from the SNM.

Siad Barre thus progressively alienated an increasing number of clans, including some, such as the Ogaden, that originally had given him strong support. The Ogaden blamed him for Somalia's defeat in the Ogaden War and opposed his 1988 peace treaty and resumption of diplomatic relations with Ethiopia. As a result of Siad Barre's actions, many Ogaden officers deserted from the army and joined the Somali Patriotic Movement (SPM), an opposition group that had been formed in 1985 and that also received SNM support.

The various opposition groups waged relatively intense warfare against the national army during Siad Barre's final three years in office and gained control of extensive government areas: the SNM in the northwest, the USC in the center, and the SPM in the south. Africa

Watch reported that 50,000 unarmed civilians were killed in the course of Siad Barre's various reprisals against the Majeerteen, Isaaq, and Hawiye. Thousands more died of starvation resulting from the poisoning of waterwells and the slaughtering of cattle. In addition, hundreds of thousands sought refuge outside the country.

Following a July 1989 demonstration in Mogadishu in which about 450 persons were killed by government forces, leaders from various sectors of society, representing all clan–families, formed the Council for National Reconstruction and Salvation to press for political change. In May 1990, they published a manifesto calling for Siad Barre's resignation, the establishment of an interim government representing opposition movements, and a timetable for multiparty elections. Siad Barre ordered the arrest of the 114 signatories, but the security forces could only locate 45 persons. Foreign protests over their detention forced their release. Meanwhile, the opposition groups recognized the need to hold talks among themselves to coordinate strategy; time, however, did not allow mutual trust to develop.

Opposition forces defeated Siad Barre's regime on January 27, 1991. Long before the government collapsed, however, the armed forces, the police force, the People's Militia, government ministries, and institutions such as the People's Assembly, schools, and health facilities, for all practical purposes, had ceased to operate. Siad Barre fled Mogadishu, and, after a stay in Kenya, ultimately sought refuge in Nigeria. The USC announced the formation of a provisional government in February 1991, with Ali Mahdi Mahammad of the Hawiye clan–family as president and Umar Arteh Ghalib, of the Isaaq clan–family, as prime minister. However, former army commander General Mahammad Faarah Aidid opposed Mahammad's presidency and eventually split off to form his own USC faction. The provisional USC government created a Ministry of Constitutional Affairs charged with planning a constitutional convention and revising the constitution. Meanwhile, provisions of the constitution of 1979 that had not been specifically voided by the provisional government remained in force. The provisional government also announced its intention of restoring judicial independence.

The USC's establishment of a provisional government angered other opposition groups who felt they had not been consulted. In the subsequent clashes, the SSDF and the SPM aligned themselves against the USC. In the course of the fighting, control of various towns such as Chisimayu and Baidoa changed hands several times. A number of cease–fires were announced between early April 1991 and the latter part of 1992, but

17

none remained in effect long.

Meanwhile, in the north the SNM refused to participate in the unity talks proposed by the USC. In May 1991, the SNM proclaimed the Republic of Somaliland as an interim government, pending 1993 elections, and decreeing the sharia as its legal base. As of early 1993, the Republic of Somaliland had not been recognized by any foreign government. Moreover, the government has proved ineffective in establishing its authority throughout the region of former British Somaliland that it claims to control.

In the Mogadishu area, each of the opposition groups drew support from a particular clan and each resorted to arms to further its claims. The result was disintegration of government, civil society, and essential services by September 1991 if not earlier. Serious fighting in Mogadishu began in September 1991, intensified in November, and by the end of March 1992 was estimated by Africa Watch to have caused 14,000 deaths and 27,000 wounded. Mahammad, a member of the Abgaal clan of the Hawiye clan–family and leader of one USC faction that had a force of about 5,000 fighters, gained control of northern Mogadishu. He was challenged primarily by Faarah Aidid, of the Habar Gidir clan of the Hawiye, who led a USC faction of about 10,000 guerrillas that advocated cooperation with the SNM. During 1991 and 1992, outside parties, such as Djibouti, the League of Arab States, the Organization of African Unity, the Islamic Conference, and the United Nations made numerous unsuccessful attempts to end the fighting in Mogadishu.

The situation in the country as a whole deteriorated rapidly, as a result not only of the civil war but also of the drought in central and southern Somalia that left hundreds of thousands starving. By August 1992 Somali refugees were reliably estimated at 500,000 in Ethiopia, 300,000 in Kenya, 65,000 in Yemen, 15,000 in Djibouti, and about 100,000 in Europe. The civil war destroyed Somalia's infrastructure and brought all economic activities, apart from minimal subsistence agriculture, herding, and internal trade, to a virtual halt.

Following an official visit to Somalia in early August 1992 by Muhammad Sahnoun, the UN Special Representative, and Bernard Kouchner, the French minister of health and humanitarian affairs, an estimate was released that approximately one–fourth of the population, about 1.5 million people, was in danger of death by starvation—other estimates ran as high as one–third of the population. A United States Centers for Disease

Control study further showed that in the city of Baidoa at least 40 percent of the August 1992 population had died between August 9 and November 14; relief organizations estimated that as of September 25 percent of all Somali children under five years of age had died.

The problem of food distribution to the starving was aggravated by armed bandits, frequently under the influence of qat, a mild stimulant known to increase aggressiveness, that was grown in several areas of East Africa. These bandits, who recognized no authority except occasionally that of local warlords, looted warehouses in Mogadishu and other major centers as well as shipments of food to the interior. The rise of local warlords, who controlled the cities, including harbors and airports, as opposed to traditional clan leaders, clan councils, and clan−recruited militias in the hinterland, was a relatively new phenomenon in Somali society. Their rise has been attributed to the breakdown of central government authority and the lack of strong, well−organized opposition parties. The availability of vast quantities of arms in the country from earlier Soviet and United States arming of Somalia (between the early 1980s and mid− 1990, the United States provided Somalia with US$403 million in military aid), from the large caches of arms gained in gray and black markets, and from the cross−border trade, particularly in ammunition, as well as the military training that the Siad Barre regime required all school and college graduates and civil servants to undergo further facilitated the rise of warlords.

In response to this critical situation, UN secretary general Boutros−Ghali announced in early August that he would send UN soldiers to Somalia to protect food supplies. In mid−August United States president George Bush ordered a food air lift to Somalia. In implementation of his earlier pledge to protect food aid convoys, on August 28 Boutros−Ghali authorized sending 3,500 personnel in addition to a 500−man Pakistani force already authorized for Somalia.

After a number of delays resulting from the opposition of local warlords, on November 10 Pakistani units were allowed to take control of Mogadishu airport. Meanwhile, on November 21 the United States National Security Council decided to intervene in Somalia. It did so because of the scale of human disaster and the realization that the United States was the only nation perceived by Somalis and by the regional states as being in a position to maintain neutrality and with the ability to launch such a large−scale aid operation. The first United States military units in Operation Restore Hope arrived in Mogadishu on December 9. They were joined by elements of the French Foreign Legion from Djibouti with others from Belgium, Canada, Egypt, Italy, Saudi Arabia, and Turkey expected. To avoid contact with the foreign forces, Somali armed groups and their "technicals" (vehicles on which an automatic weapon had been mounted) began leaving Mogadishu, thus exacerbating security problems in the hinterland.

United States forces and those of their allies gradually branched out from the airport and harbor of Mogadishu to the surrounding area. In succession they secured the Soviet–built airport at Baledogle (halfway to Baidoa), Baidoa, and then Chisimayu, Baardheere, Oddur, Beledweyne, and Jalalaqsi. The plan entailed setting up food distribution centers in each of the major areas affected by the famine and bringing in large quantities of food so as to eliminate looting and hoarding. By doing so, the operation would ensure that food was no longer a "power chip," thereby eliminating the role of the warlords. As the provision of food to southern Somalia reached massive proportions, however, it became clear that as a result of the August rains and resultant domestic crop production, it would be necessary to sell some of the donated grain in local markets at a suitable price in order to safeguard the livelihood of local farmers in the hinterland.

The question of the security of food shipments proved a difficult one with respect to disarming the population.

The commander in chief of the United States Central Command, Marine General Joseph P. Hoar, announced on December 14 that the United States would not disarm Somalis because the carrying of arms was a political issue to be settled by Somalis. However, by January 7, 1993, after completing the first stage of Operation Restore Hope, United States forces began to pursue "technicals" and raid arms depots in order to safeguard the operation and protect United States and allied personnel and Somali civilians.

In the second stage of the operation, United States political officers also began coordinating town meetings in Mogadishu, Baidoa, Baardheere, and Chisimayu, encouraging Somalis to set up their own municipal institutions. Furthermore, United States military personnel cleared streets and restored municipal water systems. Observers noted that Somali women, who displayed a gift for reconciliation, were playing key roles in operating many of the food distribution centers established by nongovernmental organizations.

Meanwhile, on the political level, in an effort to further reconciliation, Aidid and Mahammad met several times, as arranged by former United States ambassador to Somalia Robert B. Oakley, who served as special presidential envoy. On December 28, the two Somalis led a peace march along the Green Line separating the two areas of Mogadishu controlled by their forces. Other factors complicating a political settlement were the control of Baardheere by Mahammad Siad Hersi Morgan, the son–in–law of Siad Barre and leader of the Somali National Front, a Mareehaan organization; and the control of Chisimayu by Colonel Ahmad Omar Jess, a leader allied with the SDM and the Southern Somali National Movement (SSNM). Jess was reliably reported to have killed between 100 and 200 individuals whom he regarded as potential enemies before United States forces reached Chisimayu.

As a symbol of support for United States forces and their efforts in Somalia, President Bush arrived on New Year's Eve for a one–day visit and received a warm welcome from Somalis. In contrast, the UN secretary general faced an angry reception from Somali crowds on January 3. The Somalis remembered Boutros– Ghali's former cordial relationship with Siad Barre when Boutros– Ghali served as Egyptian minister of foreign affairs. They also faulted the UN for its long inaction in relieving the starvation in Somalia; voluntary organizations, particularly the International Committee of the Red Cross, had proved more effective than the UN in sending food to Somalia and in setting up kitchens to feed hundreds of thousands daily. Despite this negative reception on January 4 the leaders of fourteen Somali factions attended meetings in Addis Ababa chaired by the UN secretary general at which the United States was represented. After considerable discussion, on January 15 the faction leaders signed a cease–fire agreement and a disarmament pact and called for a national reconciliation conference to be held in Addis Ababa on March 15. Despite the cease–fire, fighting and instability in Somalia continued to exist in late January.

Because of the number of foreign forces that had joined Operation Restore Hope—as of January 9 these numbered about 10,000—the first contingent of United States military personnel began to leave Somalia on January 19. Overall, United States forces were scheduled to remain at 25,000 in the immediate future. The long–term goal was to turn over the operation as rapidly as possible to a UN force; it was said that perhaps as many as 5,000 United States logistical, transportation, and engineering personnel might be assigned to the UN force.

With regard to Somalia's future, the role of Islamism, sometimes referred to as fundamentalism, concerned the United States and some of its allies. In the north, Islamic militants, who were well trained and armed and supplied with funds primarily by wealthy Saudis, had at one time controlled the town of Bender Cassim in the northeast but had been driven out by the SSDF. From Bender Cassim the Islamists spread westward into such SNM areas as Hargeysa. Although Islamic militants, known as the Somali Islamic Union or popularly as Ittihad (Union), had relatively few supporters in Somalia, their numbers appeared to be increasing somewhat.

In the latter months of 1992 they became active in Merca, the seaport south of Mogadishu, where they had sought an alliance with clan leaders in the SSNM, which was aligned with that section of the USC led by Faarah Aidid. Time would indicate whether the Islamists could prove effective in providing services that the government was not providing in such fields as education and health. If so, the likelihood of their gaining followers would increase greatly.

Other steps toward the creation of what President Bush termed a "secure environment" included a discussion held in mid–January between Aidid and Mahammad on reestablishing a police force. The police force had traditionally commanded respect in Somalia, and if such a force could be reconstituted initially in a number of regions but ultimately nationally, it would help diminish the power of the warlords and restore internal order.

It was also likely to strengthen the position of traditional clan elders. Such steps would be consonant with the apparent goal of the UN Security Council to create a national government in Somalia with sufficient authority to maintain security but one that allowed considerable autonomy to the various regions.

The situation with regard to the relationship of the self–proclaimed Republic of Somaliland in the north and the rest of Somalia in the south remained unclear. Most knowledgeable observers noted that as yet there was no effective government in the northern region that could negotiate with the remainder of Somalia. Therefore, in the near future the establishment of either a federation with Somalia or a unitary state combining the two as in the past was unlikely.

January 29, 1993 Helen Chapin Metz *Do NOT bookmark these search results.*

THE SOMALIS: THEIR ORIGINS, MIGRATIONS, AND SETTLEMENT

Shaykh Abdulaziz Mosque, ninth century, Mogadishu Courtesy R W S. Hudson A paucity of written historical evidence forces the student of early Somalia to depend on the findings of archeology, anthropology, historical linguistics, and related disciplines. Such evidence has provided insights that in some cases have refuted conventional explanations of the origins and evolution of the Somali people.

For example, where historians once believed that the Somalis originated on the Red Sea's western coast, or perhaps in southern Arabia, it now seems clear that the ancestral homeland of the Somalis, together with affiliated Cushite peoples, was in the highlands of southern Ethiopia, specifically in the lake regions.

Similarly, the once–common notion that the migration and settlement of early Mus,lims followers of the Prophet Muhammad on the Somali coast in the early centuries of Islam had a significant impact on the Somalis no longer enjoys much academic support. Scholars now recognize that the Arab factor—except for the Somalis' conversion to Islam—is marginal to understanding the Somali past. Furthermore, conventional wisdom once held that Somali migrations followed a north–to–south route; the reverse of this now appears to be nearer the truth.

Increasingly, evidence places the Somalis within a wide family of peoples called Eastern Cushites by modern linguists and described earlier in some instances as Hamites. From a broader cultural–linguistic perspective, the Cushite family belongs to a vast stock of languages and peoples considered Afro–Asiatic. Afro–Asiatic languages in turn include Cushitic (principally Somali, Oromo, and Afar), the Hausa language of Nigeria, and the Semitic languages of Arabic, Hebrew, and Amharic. Medieval Arabs referred to the Eastern Cushites as the Berberi.

In addition to the Somalis, the Cushites include the largely nomadic Afar (Danakil), who straddle the Great Rift Valley between Ethiopia and Djibouti; the Oromo, who have

23

played such a large role in Ethiopian history and in the 1990s constituted roughly one–half of the Ethiopian population and were also numerous in northern Kenya; the Reendille (Rendilli) of Kenya; and the Aweera (Boni) along the Lamu coast in Kenya. The Somalis belong to a subbranch of the Cushites, the Omo–Tana group, whose languages are almost mutually intelligible. The original home of the Omo–Tana group appears to have been on the Omo and Tana rivers, in an area extending from Lake Turkana in present–day northern Kenya to the Indian Ocean coast.

The Somalis form a subgroup of the Omo–Tana called Sam. Having split from the main stream of Cushite peoples about the first half of the first millennium B.C., the proto–Sam appear to have spread to the grazing plains of northern Kenya, where protoSam communities seem to have followed the Tana River and to have reached the Indian Ocean coast well before the first century A.D. On the coast, the proto–Sam splintered further; one group (the Boni) remained on the Lamu Archipelago, and the other moved northward to populate southern Somalia. There the group's members eventually developed a mixed economy based on farming and animal husbandry, a mode of life still common in southern Somalia. Members of the proto–Sam who came to occupy the Somali Peninsula were known as the so–called Samaale, or Somaal, a clear reference to the mythical father figure of the main Somali clan–families, whose name gave rise to the term *Somali*.

The Samaale again moved farther north in search of water and pasturelands. They swept into the vast Ogaden (Ogaadeen) plains, reaching the southern shore of the Red Sea by the first century A.D. German scholar Bernd Heine, who wrote in the 1970s on early Somali history, observed that the Samaale had occupied the entire Horn of Africa by approximately 100 A.D.

Emergence of Adal

In addition to southward migration, a second factor in Somali history from the fifteenth century onward was the emergence of centralized state systems. The most important of these in medieval times was Adal, whose influence at the height of its power and prosperity in the sixteenth century extended from Saylac, the capital, through the fertile valleys of the Jijiga and the Harer plateau to the Ethiopian highlands. Adal's fame derived not only from the prosperity and cosmopolitanism of its people, its architectural sophistication, graceful mosques, and high learning, but also from its conflicts with the expansionist Ethiopians. For hundreds of years before the fifteenth century, goodwill had existed between the dominant new civilization of Islam and the Christian neguses of Ethiopia. One tradition holds that Muhammad blessed Ethiopia and enjoined his disciples from ever conducting jihad (holy war) against the Christian kingdom in gratitude for the protection early Muslims had received from the Ethiopian negus. Whereas Muslim armies rapidly overran the more powerful empires of Persia and Byzantium soon after the birth of Islam, there was no jihad against Christian Ethiopia for centuries. The forbidding Ethiopian terrain of deep gorges, sharp escarpments, and perpendicular massifs that rise more than 4,500 meters also discouraged the Muslims from attempting a campaign of conquest against so inaccessible a kingdom.

Muslim–Christian relations soured during the reign of the aggressive Negus Yeshaq (ruled 1414–29). Forces of his rapidly expanding empire descended from the highlands to despoil Muslim settlements in the valley east of the ancient city of Harer. Having branded the Muslims "enemies of the Lord," Yeshaq invaded the Muslim Kingdom of Ifat in 1415. He crushed the armies of Ifat and put to flight in the wastes along the Gulf of Tadjoura (in present–day Djibouti) Ifat's king Saad ad Din. Yeshaq followed Saad ad Din to the island off the coast of Saylac (which still bears his name), where the Muslim king was killed. Yeshaq compelled the Muslims to offer tribute, and also ordered his singers to compose a gloating hymn of thanksgiving for his victory. In the hymn's lyrics, the word *Somali* appears for the first time in written record.

By the sixteenth century, the Muslims had recovered sufficiently to break through from the east into the central Ethiopian highlands. Led by the charismatic Imam Ahmad Guray (1506–43), the Muslims poured into Ethiopia, using scorched–earth tactics that decimated the population of the country. A Portuguese expedition led by Pedro da Gama, a son of Vasco da Gama who was looking for the Prester John of medieval European folklore—a Christian, African monarch of vast dominions—arrived from the sea and saved Ethiopia. The joint Portuguese–Ethiopian force used cannon to route the Muslims, whose imam died on the battlefield.

The Somali Peninsula on the Eve of Imperial Partition

In 1728 the last Portuguese foothold on the East African coast was dislodged from the great Mombasa castle of Fort Jesus. From then until the European "scramble" for African colonies in the 1880s, the Omanis exercised a shadowy authority over the Banaadir coast. Omani rule over the Somalis consisted for the most part of a token annual tribute payment and the presence of a resident qadi (Muslim judge) and a handful of *askaris* (territorial police).

Whereas the Banaadir coast was steadily drawn into the orbit of Zanzibari rulers, the northern coast, starting in the middle of the eighteenth century, passed under the sharifs of Mukha, who held their feeble authority on behalf of the declining Ottomans. The Mukha sharifs, much like the sultans of Zanzibar, satisfied themselves with a token yearly tribute collected for them by a native governor. In 1854–55 when Lieutenant Richard Burton of the British India navy frequented the northern Somali coast, he found a Somali governor, Haaji Shermaarke Ali Saalih of the Habar Yoonis clan of the Isaaq clan–family, exercising real power over Saylac and adjacent regions. By the time of Burton's arrival, once–mighty Saylac had only a tenuous influence over its environs. The city itself had degenerated into a rubble of mud and wattle huts, its water storage no longer working, its once formidable walls decayed beyond recognition, and its citizenry insulted and oppressed at will by tribesmen who periodically infested the city.

SOMALIA

A Country Study Unavailable *Ancient Arab tower near the old port, Mogadishu F* deral Research Division Library of Congress Edited by Helen Chapin Metz Research Completed May 1992 ***Do NOT bookmark these search results.***

Search results are stored in a TEMPORARY file for display purposes.

FOREWORD

The five chapters that follow represent preliminary drafts of *Somalia: A Country Study*, to be published by the Federal Research Division of the Library of Congress. The revised edition of this publication is now in the editorial process and will appear in the first half of 1993. The finished work will contain an introduction that highlights major trends detailed in the individual chapters and brings Somalia's situation up to date. The book also will include maps, photographs, a glossary, and a bibliography.

Most books in the area handbook series deal with a particular foreign country, describing and analyzing its political, economic, social, and national security systems and institutions, and examining the interrelationships of those systems and the ways they are shaped by cultural factors. The authors seek to provide a basic understanding of the observed society, striving for a dynamic rather than a static portrayal. Particular attention is devoted to the people who make up the society, their origins, dominant beliefs and values, their common interests and the issues on which they are divided, the nature and extent of their involvement with national institutions, and their attitudes toward each other and toward their social system and political order.

Louis R. Mortimer Chief Federal Research Division Library of Congress Washington, D C. 20540 *Do NOT bookmark these search results.*

Search results are stored in a TEMPORARY file for display purposes.

Acknowledgments

The authors wish to acknowledge the contributions of the following individuals who wrote the 1982 edition of *Somalia: A Country Study* : Robert Rinehart, Irving Kaplan, Donald P. Whitaker, Jean R. Tartter, and Frederick Ehrenreich. Their work provided the basis of the present volume, as well as substantial portions of the text.

The authors are grateful to individuals in various government agencies and private institutions who gave their time, research materials, and expertise to the production of this book. These individuals include Ralph K.

Benesch, who oversees the Country Studies—Area Handbook program for the Department of the Army.

Special thanks are owed to Thomas Ofcansky who assisted in providing data with which to update the various chapters. Graphics support was supplied by the firm of Greenhorne and O'Mara; Harriet R. Blood, who prepared the topography and drainage map; Carlyn Dawn Anderson, who designed the illustrations on the title pages of the chapters; and Wayne Horne, who designed the cover.

Special appreciation is due the Department of Defense for the use of January 1993 photographs from Operation Restore Hope. These pictures, taken by members of the United States Armed Forces with digitized cameras, were transmitted by satellite from Somalia directly to computers in the Pentagon; they represent a technological advance for on-the-scene photographic coverage.

The authors also wish to thank members of the Federal Research Division who contributed directly to the preparation of the manuscript. These people include Sandra W. Meditz, who reviewed all drafts and graphic material and served as liaison with the sponsoring agency; Tim L. Merrill, who assisted in preparing maps; LaVerle Berry who provided background area information; David P. Cabitto, who provided invaluable graphic assistance and supervised graphics production; and Marilyn L. Majeska, who managed editing and production. Also involved in preparing the text were editorial assistants Barbara Edgerton and Izella Watson.

Individual chapters were edited by Vincent Ercolano. Cissie Coy and Catherine Schwartzstein performed the final prepublication review, and Joan C. Cook compiled the index. The Library of Congress Composing Unit prepared the camera-ready copy, under the supervision of Peggy Pixley.

Preface

Like its predecessor, this study is an attempt to treat in a concise and objective manner the dominant historical, social, political, economic, and military aspects of contemporary Somali society. Sources of information included scholarly journals and monographs, official reports of government and international organizations, newspapers, and numerous periodicals. Chapter bibliographies appear at the end of the book; brief comments on some of the more valuable sources suggested as possible further reading appear at the end of each chapter. Measurements are given in the metric system; a conversion table is provided to assist those readers who are unfamiliar with metric measurements (see table 1, Appendix). A glossary is also included.

Place–names generally have been spelled in accordance with those established by the United States Board on Geographic Names and the Permanent Committee on Geographic Names for British Official Use, known as the BGN/PCGN system. The spelling of other proper names conforms to the current usage in the country or to the most authoritative available sources.

Because Somalia has been in a state of virtual anarchy since the fall of the regime of Mahammad Siad Barre in January 1991 (and, actually, to a considerable degree since the outbreak of civil war in the latter 1980s), the lack of functioning government institutions has meant that statistics tend to be unreliable or nonexistent.

Therefore, statistics cited in the text or tables in the appendix should be viewed with caution.

The arrival of United States military forces in Somalia as part of Operation Restore Hope in the latter part of 1992, together with forces from other United Nations member states, has resulted in detailed Western press coverage of Somalia. However, much background data continued to be lacking.

The body of the text reflects information available as of mid–1992. Certain other portions of the text, however, have been updated. The Introduction discusses significant events that have occurred since the completion of research, the Country Profile includes updated information as available, and the Bibliography includes recently published help feel to the reader.

COUNTRY PROFILE

Country Profile **COUNTRY** *Formal Name:* Somali Democratic Republic.

Short Form: Somalia.

Term for Citizen: Somali (pl., Somalis).

Capital: Mogadishu.

GEOGRAPHY

Size: Land area 637,540 square kilometers; coastline 3,025 kilometers; sovereignty claimed over territorial waters up to 200 nautical miles.

Topography: Flat plateau surfaces and plains predominate; principal exception rugged east–west ranges in far north that include Shimbir Berris, highest point at 2,407 meters.

Climate and Hydrology: Continuously hot except at higher elevations in north; two wet seasons bring erratic rainfall, largely April to June and October and November, averaging under 500 millimeters in much of the country; droughts frequent; only Jubba River in somewhat wetter southwest has permanent water flow.

Shabeelle River, also in southwest, flows about seven months of year.

SOCIETY

Population: Estimates vary; United Nations 1991 estimate shows population of 7.7 million not including Ethiopian refugees but other estimates place at 8.4 million in mid–1990. Until early 1990s, predominantly nomadic pastoralisto and seminomadic herders made up about three–fifths of total; cultivators about one–fifth; town dwellers (vast majority in Mogadishu) about one–fifth. Pattern of residency dramatically altered by civil war in late 1980s onward, raising urban population of Mogadishu to 2 million.

Languages: Somali (script officially introduced January 1973) predominates. Several dialects; Common Somali most widely used; Coastal Somali spoken on the Banaadir Coast; Central Somali spoken in the interriverine area. English and Italian used by relatively small proportion (less than 10 percent) of urban population. Somali and Italian used at university level; Somali used at all school levels below university.

Arabic used in religious contexts. Indigenous languages include various dialects of Afar and Boni.

Ethnic Groups: Overwhelming majority of nationals ethnic Somalis; and two agricultural clan–families (Digil and Rahanwayn). In 1991 centralized state disintegrated into its constituent lineages and clans.

Religion: Former Somali state officially Islamic; overwhelming majority of nationals Sunni Muslims (less than 1 percent Christian). Activist Islamism increasing in some areas.

Education and Literacy: Until 1991 modern public education offered free at all levels; nationally owned educational facilities closed after collapse of Somali state; school attendance grew rapidly in settled areas in 1970s; primary education extended to nomadic children in early 1980s. Literacy campaigns resulted in substantial increases in 1970s but less than government's estimate of 60 percent, with relapse among nomads by 1977; United Nations estimate shows 24 percent literacy rate in 1990.

Health: Improvement in numbers of health care personnel and facilities during 1970s offset by civil war, refugee burden, and failure to expand services beyond urban areas; weak modern medical infrastructure deteriorated dramatically after 1991 collapse of central government. High incidence of pulmonary tuberculosis, malaria, tetanus, parasitic and venereal infections, leprosy, and a variety of skin and eye ailments; relatively low incidence of human immunovirus (HIV) (less than 1 percent) through 1992; general health severely affected by widespread malnutrition and famine in 1992.

ECONOMY

Salient Features: Formerly socialist–oriented economy undergoing market–oriented structural adjustment until 1991. Stabilization and macroeconomic adjustment programs implemented during 1980s under auspices of international credit and aid agencies. Privatization of wholesale trade and financial sectors largely complete by 1991; economic growth sporadic and uneven across sectors. Most economic activity disrupted by breakdown of Somali state in 1991.

Agriculture, Livestock, Forestry, and Fisheries: Crop and livestock production, forestry, and fisheries, accounted for bulk of gross domestic product (GDP) in 1991; livestock predominant agricultural export, also important source of animal products (mostly milk) for internal markets and subsistence. Crop cultivation dominated by rural subsistence sector, which generated sufficient surpluses to sustain domestic informal markets and barter economy until 1990. Main crops: sorghum, corn; incipient production of mild narcotic qat suppressed by central government during mid–1980s. Small plantation sector dedicated primarily to export of bananas and sugarcane. Domestic grain supply supplemented by international food aid. Small forestry sector dominated by production for export of frankincense and myrrh. Fisheries production showed modest growth during 1980s but remained minor economic activity. Agricultural activity severely curtailed as result of drought and breakdown of Somali state in 1991.

Mining: Mining contribution to GDP negligible (.3 percent of GDP in 1988) despite substantial deposits of gypsumanhydrite , quartz and piezoquartz, uranium, and iron ore. Meerschaum sepiolite mined; gold deposits suspected but not confirmed.

Manufacturing: Small manufacturing sector, based primarily on processing of agricultural products, consisted of few large state enterprises, hundreds of medium–sized private firms, and thousands of small–scale informal operations. Largescale enterprises dedicated mainly to processing of sugar, milk, and hides and skins. Overall manufacturing output declined during 1980s as result of failure of inefficient state enterprises under market conditions. Manufacturing activity further curtailed by civil war and collapse of Somali state. By 1990 manufacturing ceased to play significant role in economy (about 5 percent of GDP).

Energy: Domestic wood, charcoal, and imported petroleum provided basic sources of energy; significant hydroelectric potential of Jubba River remained unexploited; four small–scale wind turbine generators operated in Mogadishu. Prior to civil war, eighty state–owned oil–fired and diesel power plants provided electricity to cities and towns. Refining capacity limited to one refinery. Foreign oil supplies erratic throughout 1980s. United Nations Development Programme hydrocarbon study in 1991 indicated good potential for oil and gas deposits in northern Somalia.

Foreign Trade: Exports consisted of agricultural raw materials and food products. Livestock and bananas principal exports, followed by hides and skins, fish and fish products, and myrrh. Trade balance remained negative throughout 1980s and early 1990s. Principal imports in descending order: food, transportation equipment, nonelectrical machinery, cement and building materials, and iron and steel. Italy and Arab states main destinations of exports; Italy main country of origin for imported Somali goods in 1990; other minor suppliers included Norway, Bahrain, and Britain.

Currency: Somali shilling. During 1980s currency alternated between fixed and floating rates; as of March 31, 1992, US$1 equaled 3,800 shillings.

TRANSPORTATION

Railroads: None.

Roads: One paved road extends from Berbera in north through Mogadishu to Chisimayu. Roads of all categories totaled 21,000 kilometers in 1990: 2,600 kilometers paved, 2,900 kilometers gravel; 15,500 kilometers improved earth (stretches frequently impassable in rainy seasons). Highway infrastructure insufficient to open up isolated areas or to link isolated regions.

Civil Aviation: Eight paved civilian airfields; fewer than twenty additional widely–scattered gravel airfields.

International airport at Mogadishu contains 4,500–meter runway. In 1990 domestic service linked Mogadishu with seven other Somali cities. Somali Airlines owned one Airbus 310 in 1989. No scheduled service existed in 1992.

Ports and Shipping: Four major ports: deepwater facilities at Berbera, Mogadishu, and Chisimayu; lighterage port at Merca; minor port at Maydh. Port modernization program launched in latter half of 1980s with United States aid significantly improved cargo handling capabilities at Chisimayu, and increased number of berths and deepened harbor at Berbera.

GOVERNMENT AND POLITICS

Government Structure: Country nominally under interim provisional government established by Executive Committee of United Somali Congress (USC) and headed by provisional president Ali Mahdi Mahammad after fall of Mahammad Siad Barre. As of September 1991, country effectively under control of as many as twelve rival clans and subclans. Central government authority at Mogadishu challenged by Somali National Movement (SNM), which in June 1991 declared independent Republic of Somaliland in former territory of British Somaliland. Constitution of 1979 nominally in force pending new constitution proposed by provisional government. Constitutionally mandated national legislature known as People's Assembly inactive since January 1991.

Administrative Divisions: Prior to fall of Siad Barre regime in January 1991, sixteen administrative regions, each containing three to six districts, with exception of capital region which was subdivided into fifteen districts, for total of eighty-four districts. Local government authority vested in regional and district councils whose members were elected, but whose candidature approved by district-level government. High level of military participation in regional and district councils. Ministry of Local Government and Rural Development exercised authority over structure of local government. From 1991 onward, no effective government organization existed.

Politics: During 1980s authoritarian regime of President Mahammad Siad Barre abandoned policy of scientific socialism on Marxist-Leninist lines and implemented marketoriented structural reforms of economy, while consolidating personal political authority. Broad-based national opposition met escalating government repression and provoked armed revolt in 1988 led by USC and SNM. Civil war caused eventual defeat of government forces and exile of Siad Barre in January 1991. USC faction led by General Mahammad Faarah Aidid contested authority of USC Executive Committee to form interim government and established rival government in southern Mogadishu, compelling Mahammad's government to retreat to northern Mogadishu. As of January 1993, country effectively fragmented under control of as many as twelve contending clan-families and clans.

Judicial System: Four-tier court system—Supreme Court, courts of appeal, regional courts, and district courts—based on Western models. Separate National Security Courts operating outside ordinary legal system and under direct control of executive given broad jurisdiction over offenses defined by government as affecting state security, until abolished in October 1990. Unified penal and civil law codes introduced in late 1960s and early 1970s, but some features of Islamic law considered in civil matters.

Foreign Relations: Foreign relations characterized by tension with neighboring states and economic dependence on aid from Arab and Western nations. Relations with neighboring states gradually improved as irredentist claims dating from Ogaden War period (1977–78) formally abandoned during 1980s; relations with Ethiopia remained strained despite 1988 peace agreement resulting from mutual harboring of foreign guerilla forces and uncontrolled mass migration. Relations with Western nations and United States broadened after 1977 rift with Soviet Union; United States military and economic aid provided throughout 1980s but suspended in 1989 because of human rights violations by Siad Barre government. Recipient of financial support from conservative Arab oil states.

NATIONAL SECURITY

Armed Forces: As of January 1991, Somali National Army and all related military and security forces disbanded; indeterminate elements reconstituted as clan militias and irregular regional forces.

Major Tactical Units: Until January 1991, Army ground forces organized into twelve divisions composed of four tank brigades, forty–five mechanized and infantry brigades, four commando brigades, one surface–to–air missile brigade, three field artillery brigades, thirty field battalions, and one air defense battalion. Poor serviceability of obsolete equipment of Soviet and United States origin. Somali Air Force organized into three fighter ground attack squadrons; three fighter squadrons; one counterinsurgency squadron; one transport squadron; and one helicopter squadron. None believed to be operational in 1992. Small, poorly equipped naval force not believed to be operational.

Major Military Suppliers: Exclusively supplied by Soviet Union until 1977 when Treaty of Friendship and Cooperation was terminated. Subsequently Somalia improved relations with United States and received average of US$36 to $US40 million per year of United States military assistance between 1983 and 1986.

Levels of military aid during 1980s insufficient to avert deterioration and collapse of Somali armed forces by 1991.

Military Costs: Military expenditures totaled about US$44.5 million annually for 1980–90 decade. Military procurement supported largely by foreign financial assistance and military aid.

Paramilitary and Internal Security Forces: Somali Police Force, People's Militia, and National Security Service disbanded as of January 1991.

Introduction

Figure 1. Administrative Divisions of Somalia, 1992 President George Bush visits United States forces in Somalia, January 1, 1993.

Courtesy Unidet States Department of Defense United Nations secretray general Boutros Boutros–Ghali inspects UN forces from Pakistan in mid–January 1993 Courtesy Unidet States Department of Defense Somali men unloading wheat outside Malaile, January 1993 Courtesy Unidet States Department of Defense Sorghum destined for Baidoa being unloaded from British C–130 Hercules aircraft, January 1993 Courtesy Unidet States Department of Defense Russian personnel unload some prefabricated roofs for shelters Courtesy Unidet States Department of Defense United States Marines escort UN food convoy,, January 1993 Courtesy Unidet States Department of Defense Somali villagers line up to receive food provided by UN Courtesy Unidet States Department of Defense Somalis wait near their water bottles, January 1993 Courtesy Unidet States Department of Defense Children gather along a wall in Mogadishu Courtesy Unidet States Department of Defense United States Navy doctor examines a Somali enfant, January 1993.

THE PEOPLE WHO LIVE in present–day Somalia have an ancient history. The medieval Arabs called them Berberi, and archaeological evidence indicates that they had occupied the area known as the Horn of Africa by 100 A.D. and possibly earlier. By the eighteenth century, the Somalis—their name derives from Samaal, their eponymous ancestor—had developed pastoral nomadism and were followers of Islam. Their first contact with Islam is believed to have occurred when a group of persecuted Muslims from Arabia sought refuge in the region at the time of the Prophet Muhammad in the eighth century. Historically, the area was home to two peoples: pastoral and agropastoral groups living in the interior, with informal and varied political structures; and trading communities on the coast, such as Seylac and Berbera in the north and Merca and Mogadishu in the south, that developed administrative and legal systems based on the Muslim sharia.

The Somalis or Samaal consist of six major clan–families. Four of the families are predominantly pastoral—the Dir, Daarood, Isaaq, and Hawiye (representing about 70 percent of Somalia's population)—and two are agricultural—the Digil and Rahanwayn (constituting about 20 percent of the population). The remainder of the population consists of urban dwellers and marginal non–Samaal groups, most of whom engage in trade or crafts and who historically have lacked political participation and the Samaal warrior tradition.

The Digil and the Rahanwayn are located mainly in the south in the area between the Jubba and Shabeelle rivers, the best agricultural area. The rest of the country consists primarily of arid plateaus and plains, with some rugged mountains in the north near the Gulf of Aden coast. Because of sparse rainfall, nomadic pastoralism has been the principal occupation of clan–families in much of the country.

Historically, Somalis have shown a fierce independence, an unwillingness to submit to authority, a strong clan consciousness, and conflict among clans and subclans despite their sharing a common language, religion, and pastoral customs. Clans are integral to Somali life. Clan consciousness has been described as centering around the struggle for recognition in all its forms—social, political, economic, and cultural rights and status. Despite this clan consciousness, the Somali community historically preserved its basic unity because of the relative homogeneity of the society.

Over the centuries, the Somali Peninsula and the East African coast were subject to various rulers, including the Omanis, the Zanzibaris, the sharifs of Mukha in present–day Yemen, and the Ottoman Turks. By 1885, there were five mini–Somalilands: the north central part controlled by the British; the east and southeast (mainly present–day Djibouti) controlled by the French; the south, controlled by the Italians; the Ogaden in the west controlled by Ethiopia; and the southwestern part that became a part of Kenya (known as the Northern Frontier District). This colonial control continued in various forms until Somalia gained its independence in 1960.

The British and Italians followed different courses in their colonial administration. The British regarded northern Somalia mainly as a source of livestock for Aden, the principal supply post en route to India through the Suez Canal, whereas the Italians developed plantation agriculture based bananas, citrus fruits, and sugarcane in southern Somalia. Between 1900 and 1920, while Italy and Britain were consolidating their colonial rule, a Muslim resistance movement arose under Mahammad Abdille Hasan, whom the British called the Mad Mullah. Until he died in 1920, Abdille Hasan, a member of the Salihiyah brotherhood, and his followers constituted a dervish group that waged war originally against Ethiopia, and later against the British, seeking to regain the Ogaden for Somalis.

Early in World War II, Italy invaded British Somaliland and ejected the British. British forces retook the colony in 1941 and conquered Italian Somaliland and the Ogaden as well, placing all three areas under British military administration. The Potsdam Conference in 1945 decided not to return Italian Somaliland to Italy; ultimately, the matter was referred to the United Nations (UN) General Assembly, which decided in 1949 to make the southern area an Italian trust territory. Meanwhile, under pressure from its World War II allies, Britain returned the Ogaden to Ethiopia in 1948, to the dismay of Somalis because the majority of the inhabitants were Somalis.

Nationalism had been growing in Somalia, largely as a result of the efforts of salaried Somali colonial officials who constituted an urban petty bourgeoisie. In 1943 the first Somali political party, the Somali Youth Club, was created. In 1947 the group changed its name to the Somali Youth League (SYL) and adopted the goals of unifying all Somali territories and opposing clannishness. Partly in response to nationalist pressures, both the Italians and the British took steps to improve education and health facilities, spur economic development, and give Somalis some experience in the political process.

Somalia's independence in 1960 faced several obstacles. Economically, the country was obliged to rely on Italian and British subsidies; it also had to obtain other foreign loans to build an infrastructure and to create model farms and livestock improvement programs, all designed to increase exports. Other major obstacles included clan–family and subclan rivalries, the irredentist pressures to incorporate Somalis living in the various mini–Somalilands, and differences between residents of British and Italian Somaliland.

These differences were of two main kinds: economic (pastoral nomadism with its tending of flocks as opposed to plantation agriculture) and political (northern Somalis were less experienced in administration and political participation than their counterparts in the south). Furthermore, the new Somali constitution did not include strategies designed to move citizens away from clan loyalties and toward national objectives. For example, the Iise clan of the Dir clan–family had devised a system by which the smallest clan was given a special role: that of providing the overall clan leader and also of being responsible for settling disputes. Such an approach could have served as a model for the Western framers of the Somali constitution.

As a result of clan–family dissensions, one of the major objectives of the Somali government after independence became that of national integration. This objective was accompanied by the efforts of the first president, Abdirashiid Ali Shermaarke, to promote a Greater Somalia. In seeking to distance itself from its colonial past, the new government cultivated relations with the Soviet Union and Eastern Europe. Soviet influence prevailed, particularly in the armed forces, and later the German Democratic Republic (East Germany) established the National Security Service (NSS). The police force, however, was trained primarily by the Federal Republic of Germany (West Germany) and the United States. The 1969 elections for the National Assembly demonstrated the Somali characteristic of independence: sixty–four political parties participated, some of them as small as one man. The SYL, however, dominated the field. The elections revealed that various groups, especially the military, had become increasingly critical of government corruption and nepotism.

The October 1969 killing of President Shermaarke by one of his bodyguards led the army, which had previously avoided political participation, to take over under army commander Major General Mahammad Siad Barre. The new governing body, the Supreme Revolutionary Council (SRC), named Siad Barre president. Retroactively, to facilitate continued Soviet aid, the SRC indicated it was pursuing scientific socialism, although Somalia lacked the infrastructure appropriate to Marxist socialism. Among the new government's objectives were breaking up the old regions (administrative units) into smaller entities and resettling many of the nomads in farming and fishing cooperatives. The government also sought to promote nationalist and socialist goals by appointing "peacekeepers" to replace the traditional elders and by creating various committees in place of traditional clan groups. With reference to the legal system, Siad Barre eliminated codes that gave clans land, water, and grazing rights. He also abolished the Islamic payment of blood money *(diya)* for injuries. Presumably, all these steps were designed to break down the traditional clan structure and strengthen the personal control of Siad Barre, as well as to weaken the role of religious leaders.

Although Siad Barre proclaimed scientific socialism compatible with Islam, his regime attempted to reduce the influence, particularly in politics, of Muslim leaders. Historically, clans had relied on itinerant religious teachers and on religiously devout males, known as *wadaddo*, who generally were the only literate individuals and who often occupied judicial roles. These religious functions were supplemented by Sufi religious orders or brotherhoods, whose leaders were more learned than the *wadaddo*. The best known of the latter was Mahammad Abdille Hasan, the early twentieth– century leader of the revolt against the British. In the first half of the twentieth century, religious teachers provided most of Somali education through Quranic schools that gave minimal literacy instruction. A major difficulty was the absence of an agreed–upon orthography for the Somali language until the government decreed one in 1973. The government undertook a huge literacy campaign thereafter and established numerous primary schools, some secondary schools, and a university. As of 1990, Somalia had 4,600 university students.

Whereas in its early years the SRC devoted considerable attention to such fields as education and economics, later a major part of its activity related to the political sphere. Despite the SRC's denunciation of clannishness, the clans connected with Siad Barre and his family became sufficiently prominent to be dubbed the MOD (Mareehaan–Ogaden–Dulbahante—the name of Siad Barre's clan, his mother's clan, and his son–in– law's clan, respectively). Initially, the SRC outlawed political parties, but in 1976 Siad Barre dissolved the SRC (it was later revived) and created one national party, the Somali Revolutionary Socialist Party (SRSP). The party in practice occupied a largely ceremonial position; actual power remained with Siad Barre.

To entrench his personal rule and in an attempt to regain the Ogaden, Siad Barre launched the Ogaden War against Ethiopia in 1977. The war officially ended in 1978 but low–level conflict continued with border raids and skirmishes for years afterward. Somalia experienced defeat and the death of 8,000 men, the influx of about 650,000 ethnic Somali and Ethiopian Oromo refugees, and a severe drain on its economy. The economic drain was caused by the purchase of military matériel to replace equipment lost in the war—three-quarters of Somalia's armored units and one–half of its air force. Having lost its alliance with the Soviet Union, which shifted its support to Ethiopia during the war, Somalia sought military aid from the United States. The latter, following the fall of the shah of Iran in 1979, was eager to bolster defenses in the Persian Gulf–Indian Ocean area. As a result, in return for the United States provision of arms and military training in 1980 the United States and Somalia concluded a military access agreement by which the United States could use Somali ports and airfields in the event of a crisis. The expansion of its armed forces, which grew from 5,000 troops at independence to 65,000 in 1990, also sapped Somalia's economy; for example, 30 percent of the national budget went for the military in the mid–1980s.

To develop the economy, in the early years of his regime Siad Barre launched several development plans, created agricultural and fishing cooperatives, and began establishing food processing plants. Somalia's foreign debt, however, increased at a tremendous rate as a result of the 1977–78 Ogaden War. Unable to call on the Soviet Union for aid, the Siad Barre regime turned for economic aid to the West, to oil–producing Arab states such as Kuwait, Qatar, Saudi Arabia, and the United Arab Emirates, and to the World Bank (see Glossary).

The economic crisis forced Somalia to devalue its currency and to encourage privatization. Economic output from agriculture and manufacturing, however, showed little progress and in some cases declined, partly as a result of intermittent droughts. The country lacked any energy sources, apart from wood and charcoal, despite surveys that indicated the likelihood of oil offshore in the Gulf of Aden. Moreover, its transportation and communications networks were minimal. In addition to livestock and agricultural products, which have constituted the bulk of Somalia's exports, the country did have a number of undeveloped sectors, however.

Among the chief of these were forestry (myrrh and frankincense were among Somalia's exports), fishing, and mineral deposits, including uranium.

Following the Ogaden War, Siad Barre recognized that to gain Western support he needed to create a political system that would appear to restore many civil rights that had been eliminated by the military regime.

Accordingly, the constitution of 1979 provided for freedom of speech, religion, publication, and assembly, but these rights were subject to major qualifications. The constitution made the president both head of state and head of government, with broad

41

powers to conduct foreign affairs, serve as commander in chief of the armed forces, appoint various ministers and leading officials, and dissolve the legislature. Members of a single–chamber legislature, the People's Assembly, served a five–year term, with the government drawing up official lists of candidates and the assembly occupying a largely symbolic position. On the local government level, Siad Barre had dissolved all elected bodies following the military coup and required that all candidates for election be approved by the central government. The constitution confirmed the National Security Courts introduced by Siad Barre; these courts had jurisdiction over numerous cases and supplemented the regular courts. Siad Barre appointed only military officers to the High Court, thus bringing the judiciary under the executive.

Another result of the Ogaden War was the rise of several organized internal opposition movements. To counter them, Siad Barre undertook increasingly repressive measures, including measures that involved numerous human rights violations. After judging a number of Majeerteen members of the military guilty of a coup attempt in 1978, Siad Barre initiated a campaign against the clan–family, using the Red Berets, an elite unit that served as his bodyguard. Several Majeerteen colonels escaped and fled abroad, where in 1978 they formed the Somali Salvation Front, renamed in 1979 the Somali Salvation Democratic Front (SSDF). This was the first opposition movement dedicated to overthrowing the regime by force.

Siad Barre then turned on the Isaaq in the north, who were discontented because they felt inadequately represented in his government. Isaaq dissidents in London had formed the Somali National Movement (SNM)

in 1981 to topple Siad Barre's regime. In 1982 they transferred their headquarters to Dire Dawa, Ethiopia, from where they conducted guerrilla raids against Somali government–held territory. Siad Barre's campaign against the Isaaq was particularly bloody; it included the 1988 destruction by bombing of Hargeysa, Somalia's major northern city, causing the flight to neighboring countries of tens of thousands of refugees. Next, Siad Barre attacked the Hawiye in the central area around Mogadishu. The Hawiye had meanwhile formed their own opposition movement, the United Somali Congress (USC), which received support from the SNM.

Siad Barre thus progressively alienated an increasing number of clans, including some, such as the Ogaden, that originally had given him strong support. The Ogaden blamed him for Somalia's defeat in the Ogaden War and opposed his 1988 peace treaty and resumption of diplomatic relations with Ethiopia. As a result of Siad Barre's actions, many Ogaden officers deserted from the army and joined the Somali Patriotic Movement (SPM), an opposition group that had been formed in 1985 and that also received SNM support.

The various opposition groups waged relatively intense warfare against the national army during Siad Barre's final three years in office and gained control of extensive government areas: the SNM in the northwest, the USC in the center, and the SPM in the south. Africa Watch reported that 50,000 unarmed civilians were killed in the course of Siad Barre's various reprisals against the Majeerteen, Isaaq, and Hawiye. Thousands more died of starvation resulting from the poisoning of waterwells and the slaughtering of cattle. In addition, hundreds of thousands sought refuge outside the country.

Following a July 1989 demonstration in Mogadishu in which about 450 persons were killed by government forces, leaders from various sectors of society, representing all clan–families, formed the Council for National Reconstruction and Salvation to press for political change. In May 1990, they published a manifesto calling for Siad Barre's resignation, the establishment of an interim government representing opposition movements, and a timetable for multiparty elections. Siad Barre ordered the arrest of the 114 signatories, but the security forces could only locate 45 persons. Foreign protests over their detention forced their release. Meanwhile, the opposition groups recognized the need to hold talks among themselves to coordinate strategy; time, however, did not allow mutual trust to develop.

Opposition forces defeated Siad Barre's regime on January 27, 1991. Long before the government collapsed, however, the armed forces, the police force, the People's Militia, government ministries, and institutions such as the People's Assembly, schools, and health facilities, for all practical purposes, had ceased to operate. Siad Barre fled Mogadishu, and, after a stay in Kenya, ultimately sought refuge in Nigeria. The USC announced the formation of a provisional government in February 1991, with Ali Mahdi Mahammad of the Hawiye clan–family as president and Umar Arteh Ghalib, of the Isaaq clan–family, as prime minister. However, former army commander General Mahammad Faarah Aidid opposed Mahammad's presidency and eventually split off to form his own USC faction. The provisional USC government created a Ministry of Constitutional Affairs charged with planning a constitutional convention and revising the constitution.

43

Meanwhile, provisions of the constitution of 1979 that had not been specifically voided by the provisional government remained in force. The provisional government also announced its intention of restoring judicial independence.

The USC's establishment of a provisional government angered other opposition groups who felt they had not been consulted. In the subsequent clashes, the SSDF and the SPM aligned themselves against the USC. In the course of the fighting, control of various towns such as Chisimayu and Baidoa changed hands several times. A number of cease–fires were announced between early April 1991 and the latter part of 1992, but none remained in effect long.

Meanwhile, in the north the SNM refused to participate in the unity talks proposed by the USC. In May 1991, the SNM proclaimed the Republic of Somaliland as an interim government, pending 1993 elections, and decreeing the sharia as its legal base. As of early 1993, the Republic of Somaliland had not been recognized by any foreign government. Moreover, the government has proved ineffective in establishing its authority throughout the region of former British Somaliland that it claims to control.

In the Mogadishu area, each of the opposition groups drew support from a particular clan and each resorted to arms to further its claims. The result was disintegration of government, civil society, and essential services by September 1991 if not earlier. Serious fighting in Mogadishu began in September 1991, intensified in November, and by the end of March 1992 was estimated by Africa Watch to have caused 14,000 deaths and 27,000 wounded. Mahammad, a member of the Abgaal clan of the Hawiye clan–family and leader of one USC faction that had a force of about 5,000 fighters, gained control of northern Mogadishu. He was challenged primarily by Faarah Aidid, of the Habar Gidir clan of the Hawiye, who led a USC faction of about 10,000 guerrillas that advocated cooperation with the SNM. During 1991 and 1992, outside parties, such as Djibouti, the League of Arab States, the Organization of African Unity, the Islamic Conference, and the United Nations made numerous unsuccessful attempts to end the fighting in Mogadishu.

The situation in the country as a whole deteriorated rapidly, as a result not only of the civil war but also of the drought in central and southern Somalia that left hundreds of thousands starving. By August 1992 Somali refugees were reliably estimated at 500,000 in Ethiopia, 300,000 in Kenya, 65,000 in Yemen, 15,000 in Djibouti, and about 100,000 in Europe. The civil war destroyed Somalia's infrastructure and brought all economic activities, apart from minimal subsistence agriculture, herding, and internal trade, to a virtual halt.

Following an official visit to Somalia in early August 1992 by Muhammad Sahnoun, the UN Special Representative, and Bernard Kouchner, the French minister of health and humanitarian affairs, an estimate was released that approximately one–fourth of the population, about 1.5 million people, was in danger of death by starvation—other estimates ran as high as one–third of the population. A United States Centers for Disease Control study further showed that in the city of Baidoa at least 40 percent of the August 1992 population had died between August 9 and November 14; relief organizations estimated that as of September 25 percent of all Somali children under five years of age had died.

The problem of food distribution to the starving was aggravated by armed bandits, frequently under the influence of qat, a mild stimulant known to increase aggressiveness, that was grown in several areas of East Africa. These bandits, who recognized no authority except occasionally that of local warlords, looted warehouses in Mogadishu and other major centers as well as shipments of food to the interior. The rise of local warlords, who controlled the cities, including harbors and airports, as opposed to traditional clan leaders, clan councils, and clan–recruited militias in the hinterland, was a relatively new phenomenon in Somali society. Their rise has been attributed to the breakdown of central government authority and the lack of strong, well–organized opposition parties. The availability of vast quantities of arms in the country from earlier Soviet and United States arming of Somalia (between the early 1980s and mid– 1990, the United States provided Somalia with US$403 million in military aid), from the large caches of arms gained in gray and black markets, and from the cross–border trade, particularly in ammunition, as well as the military training that the Siad Barre regime required all school and college graduates and civil servants to undergo further facilitated the rise of warlords.

In response to this critical situation, UN secretary general Boutros–Ghali announced in early August that he would send UN soldiers to Somalia to protect food supplies. In mid–August United States president George Bush ordered a food air lift to Somalia. In implementation of his earlier pledge to protect food aid convoys, on August 28 Boutros–Ghali authorized sending 3,500 personnel in addition to a 500–man Pakistani force already authorized for Somalia.

After a number of delays resulting from the opposition of local warlords, on November 10 Pakistani units were allowed to take control of Mogadishu airport. Meanwhile, on November 21 the United States National Security Council decided to intervene in Somalia. It did so because of the scale of human disaster and the realization that the United States was the only nation perceived by Somalis and by the regional states as being in a position to maintain neutrality and with the ability to launch such a large-scale aid operation. The first United States military units in Operation Restore Hope arrived in Mogadishu on December 9. They were joined by elements of the French Foreign Legion from Djibouti with others from Belgium, Canada, Egypt, Italy, Saudi Arabia, and Turkey expected. To avoid contact with the foreign forces, Somali armed groups and their "technicals" (vehicles on which an automatic weapon had been mounted) began leaving Mogadishu, thus exacerbating security problems in the hinterland.

United States forces and those of their allies gradually branched out from the airport and harbor of Mogadishu to the surrounding area. In succession they secured the Soviet–built airport at Baledogle (halfway to Baidoa), Baidoa, and then Chisimayu, Baardheere, Oddur, Beledweyne, and Jalalaqsi. The plan entailed setting up food distribution centers in each of the major areas affected by the famine and bringing in large quantities of food so as to eliminate looting and hoarding. By doing so, the operation would ensure that food was no longer a "power chip," thereby eliminating the role of the warlords. As the provision of food to southern Somalia reached massive proportions, however, it became clear that as a result of the August rains and resultant domestic crop production, it would be necessary to sell some of the donated grain in local markets at a suitable price in order to safeguard the livelihood of local farmers in the hinterland.

The question of the security of food shipments proved a difficult one with respect to disarming the population.

The commander in chief of the United States Central Command, Marine General Joseph P. Hoar, announced on December 14 that the United States would not disarm Somalis because the carrying of arms was a political issue to be settled by Somalis. However, by January 7, 1993, after completing the first stage of Operation Restore Hope, United States forces began to pursue "technicals" and raid arms depots in order to safeguard the operation and protect United States and allied personnel and Somali civilians.

In the second stage of the operation, United States political officers also began coordinating town meetings in Mogadishu, Baidoa, Baardheere, and Chisimayu, encouraging Somalis to set up their own municipal institutions. Furthermore, United States military personnel cleared streets and restored municipal water systems. Observers noted that Somali women, who displayed a gift for reconciliation, were playing key roles in operating many of the food distribution centers established by nongovernmental organizations.

Meanwhile, on the political level, in an effort to further reconciliation, Aidid and Mahammad met several times, as arranged by former United States ambassador to Somalia Robert B. Oakley, who served as special presidential envoy. On December 28, the two Somalis led a peace march along the Green Line separating the two areas of Mogadishu controlled by their forces. Other factors complicating a political settlement were the control of Baardheere by Mahammad Siad Hersi Morgan, the son–in–law of Siad Barre and leader of the Somali National Front, a Mareehaan organization; and the control of Chisimayu by Colonel Ahmad Omar Jess, a leader allied with the SDM and the Southern Somali National Movement (SSNM). Jess was reliably reported to have killed between 100 and 200 individuals whom he regarded as potential enemies before United States forces reached Chisimayu.

As a symbol of support for United States forces and their efforts in Somalia, President Bush arrived on New Year's Eve for a one–day visit and received a warm welcome from Somalis. In contrast, the UN secretary general faced an angry reception from Somali crowds on January 3. The Somalis remembered Boutros– Ghali's former cordial relationship with Siad Barre when Boutros– Ghali served as Egyptian minister of foreign affairs. They also faulted the UN for its long inaction in relieving the starvation in Somalia; voluntary organizations, particularly the International Committee of the Red Cross, had proved more effective than the UN in sending food to Somalia and in setting up kitchens to feed hundreds of thousands daily. Despite this negative reception on January 4 the leaders of fourteen Somali factions attended meetings in Addis Ababa chaired by the UN secretary general at which the United States was represented. After considerable discussion, on January 15 the faction leaders signed a cease–fire agreement and a disarmament pact and called for a national reconciliation conference to be held in Addis Ababa on March 15. Despite the cease–fire, fighting and instability in Somalia continued to exist in late January.

Because of the number of foreign forces that had joined Operation Restore Hope—as of January 9 these numbered about 10,000—the first contingent of United States military personnel began to leave Somalia on January 19. Overall, United States forces were scheduled to remain at 25,000 in the immediate future. The long–term goal was to turn over the operation as rapidly as possible to a UN force; it was said that perhaps as many as 5,000 United States logistical, transportation, and engineering personnel might be assigned to the UN force.

With regard to Somalia's future, the role of Islamism, sometimes referred to as fundamentalism, concerned the United States and some of its allies. In the north, Islamic militants, who were well trained and armed and supplied with funds primarily by wealthy Saudis, had at one time controlled the town of Bender Cassim in the northeast but had been driven out by the SSDF. From Bender Cassim the Islamists spread westward into such SNM areas as Hargeysa. Although Islamic militants, known as the Somali Islamic Union or popularly as Ittihad (Union), had relatively few supporters in Somalia, their numbers appeared to be increasing somewhat.

In the latter months of 1992 they became active in Merca, the seaport south of Mogadishu, where they had sought an alliance with clan leaders in the SSNM, which was aligned with that section of the USC led by Faarah Aidid. Time would indicate whether the Islamists could prove effective in providing services that the government was not providing in such fields as education and health. If so, the likelihood of their gaining followers would increase greatly.

Other steps toward the creation of what President Bush termed a "secure environment" included a discussion held in mid–January between Aidid and Mahammad on reestablishing a police force. The police force had traditionally commanded respect in Somalia, and if such a force could be reconstituted initially in a number of regions but ultimately nationally, it would help diminish the power of the warlords and restore internal order.

It was also likely to strengthen the position of traditional clan elders. Such steps would be consonant with the apparent goal of the UN Security Council to create a national government in Somalia with sufficient authority to maintain security but one that allowed considerable autonomy to the various regions.

The situation with regard to the relationship of the self–proclaimed Republic of Somaliland in the north and the rest of Somalia in the south remained unclear. Most knowledgeable observers noted that as yet there was no effective government in the northern region that could negotiate with the remainder of Somalia. Therefore, in the near future the establishment of either a federation with Somalia or a unitary state combining the two as in the past was unlikely.

January 29, 1993 Helen Chapin Metz **Do NOT bookmark these search results.**

Search results are stored in a TEMPORARY file for display purposes.

Chapter 1. Historical Setting

Shaykh Abdulaziz Mosque, one of Mogadishu's oldest historical structures L CATED IN THE HORN OF AFRICA, adjacent to the Arabian Peninsula, Somalia is steeped in thousands of years of history. The ancient Egyptians spoke of it as "God's Land" (the Land of Punt). Chinese merchants frequented the Somali coast in the tenth and fourteenth centuries and, according to tradition, returned home with giraffes, leopards, and tortoises to add color and variety to the imperial menagerie. Greek merchant ships and medieval Arab dhows plied the Somali coast; for them it formed the eastern fringe of Bilad as Sudan, "the Land of the Blacks." More specifically, medieval Arabs referred to the Somalis, along with related peoples, as the Berberi.

By the eighteenth century, the Somalis essentially had developed their present way of life, which is based on pastoral nomadism and the Islamic faith. During the colonial period (approximately 1891 to 1960), the Somalis were separated into five mini–Somalilands: British Somaliland (north central); French Somaliland (east and southeast); Italian Somaliland (south); Ethiopian Somaliland (the Ogaden); and, what came to be called the Northern Frontier District (NFD) of Kenya. In 1960 Italian Somaliland and British Somaliland were merged into a single independent state, the Somali Republic. In its first nine years the Somali state, although plagued by territorial disputes with Ethiopia and Kenya, and by difficulties in integrating the dual legacy of

Italian and British administrations, remained a model of democratic governance in Africa; governments were regularly voted into and out of office. Taking advantage of the widespread public bitterness and cynicism attendant upon the rigged elections of early 1969, Major General Mahammad Siad Barre seized power on October 21, 1969, in a bloodless coup. Over the next twenty–one years Siad Barre established a military dictatorship that divided and oppressed the Somalis. Siad Barre maintained control of the social system by playing off clan against clan until the country became riven with interclan strife and bloodshed. Siad Barre's regime came to a disastrous end in early 1991 with the collapse of the Somali state. In the regime's place emerged armed clan militias fighting one another for political power. Siad Barre fled the capital on January 27, 1991, into the safety of his Mareehaan clan's territory in southern Somalia.

THE SOMALIS: THEIR ORIGINS, MIGRATIONS, AND SETTLEMENT

Shaykh Abdulaziz Mosque, ninth century, Mogadishu Courtesy R W S. Hudson A paucity of written historical evidence forces the student of early Somalia to depend on the findings of archeology, anthropology, historical linguistics, and related disciplines. Such evidence has provided insights that in some cases have refuted conventional explanations of the origins and evolution of the Somali people.

For example, where historians once believed that the Somalis originated on the Red Sea's western coast, or perhaps in southern Arabia, it now seems clear that the ancestral homeland of the Somalis, together with affiliated Cushite peoples, was in the highlands of southern Ethiopia, specifically in the lake regions.

Similarly, the once–common notion that the migration and settlement of early Mus,lims followers of the Prophet Muhammad on the Somali coast in the early centuries of Islam had a significant impact on the Somalis no longer enjoys much academic support. Scholars now recognize that the Arab factor—except for the Somalis' conversion to Islam—is marginal to understanding the Somali past. Furthermore, conventional wisdom once held that Somali migrations followed a north–to–south route; the reverse of this now appears to be nearer the truth.

Increasingly, evidence places the Somalis within a wide family of peoples called Eastern Cushites by modern linguists and described earlier in some instances as Hamites. From a broader cultural–linguistic perspective, the Cushite family belongs to a vast stock of languages and peoples considered Afro–Asiatic. Afro–Asiatic languages in turn include Cushitic (principally Somali, Oromo, and Afar), the Hausa language of Nigeria, and the Semitic languages of Arabic, Hebrew, and Amharic. Medieval Arabs referred to the Eastern Cushites as the Berberi.

In addition to the Somalis, the Cushites include the largely nomadic Afar (Danakil), who straddle the Great Rift Valley between Ethiopia and Djibouti; the Oromo, who have played such a large role in Ethiopian history and in the 1990s constituted roughly one–half of the Ethiopian population and were also numerous in northern Kenya; the Reendille (Rendilli) of Kenya; and the Aweera (Boni) along the Lamu coast in Kenya. The Somalis belong to a subbranch of the Cushites, the Omo–Tana group, whose languages are almost mutually intelligible. The original home of the Omo–Tana group appears to have been on the Omo and Tana rivers, in an area extending from Lake Turkana in present–day northern Kenya to the Indian Ocean coast.

The Somalis form a subgroup of the Omo–Tana called Sam. Having split from the main stream of Cushite peoples about the first half of the first millennium B.C., the proto–Sam appear to have spread to the grazing plains of northern Kenya, where protoSam communities seem to have followed the Tana River and to have reached the Indian Ocean coast well before the first century A.D. On the coast, the proto–Sam splintered further; one group (the Boni) remained on the Lamu Archipelago, and the other moved northward to populate southern Somalia. There the group's members eventually developed a mixed economy based on farming and animal husbandry, a mode of life still common in southern Somalia. Members of the proto–Sam who came to occupy the Somali Peninsula were known as the so–called Samaale, or Somaal, a clear reference to the mythical father figure of the main Somali clan–families, whose name gave rise to the term *Somali*.

The Samaale again moved farther north in search of water and pasturelands. They swept into the vast Ogaden (Ogaadeen) plains, reaching the southern shore of the Red Sea by the first century A.D. German scholar Bernd Heine, who wrote in the 1970s on early Somali history, observed that the Samaale had occupied the entire Horn of Africa by approximately 100 A.D.

Coastal Towns

The expansion into the peninsula as far as the Red Sea and Indian Ocean put the Somalis in sustained contact with Persian and Arab immigrants who had established a series of settlements along the coast. From the eighth to the tenth centuries, Persian and Arab traders were already engaged in lucrative commerce from enclaves along the Red Sea and Indian Ocean as far south as the coast of present–day Kenya. The most significant enclave was the renowned medieval emporium of Saylac on the Gulf of Aden. In the sixteenth century, Saylac became the principal outlet for trade in coffee, gold, ostrich feathers, civet, and Ethiopian slaves bound for the Middle East, China, and India. Over time Saylac emerged as the center of Muslim culture and learning, famed for its schools and mosques. Eventually it became the capital of the medieval state of Adal, which in the sixteenth century fought off Christian Ethiopian domination of the highlands. Between 1560 and 1660, Ethiopian expeditions repeatedly harried Saylac, which sank into decay. Berbera replaced Saylac as the northern hub of Islamic influence in the Horn of Africa. By the middle of the sixteenth century, Saylac and Berbera had become dependencies of the sharifs of Mocha and in the seventeenth century passed to the Ottoman Turks, who exercised authority over them through locally recruited Somali governors.

The history of commercial and intellectual contact between the inhabitants of the Arabian and Somali coasts may help explain the Somalia's connection with the Prophet Muhammad. Early in the Prophet's ministry, a band of persecuted Muslims had, with the Prophet's encouragement, fled across the Red Sea into the Horn of Africa. There the Muslim's were afforded protection by the Ethiopian negus, or king. Thus, Islam may have been introduced into the Horn of Africa well before the faith took root in its Arabian native soil. The large–scale conversion of the Somalis had to await the arrival in the eleventh, twelfth, and thirteenth centuries of Muslim patriarchs, in particular, the renowned Shaykh Daarood Jabarti and Shaykh Isahaaq, or Isaaq.

Daarood married Doombira Dir, the daughter of a local patriarch. Their issue gave rise to the confederacy that forms the largest clan–family (see Glossary) in Somalia, the Daarood. For his part, Shaykh Isaaq founded the numerous Isaaq clan–family in northern Somalia. Along with the clan (see Glossary) system of lineages (see Glossary), the Arabian shaykhs probably introduced into Somalia the patriarchal ethos and patrilineal genealogy typical of Indo–Europeans, and gradually replaced the indigenous Somali social organization, which, like that of many other African societies, may have been matrilineal (see The Segmentary Social Order , ch. 2).

Islam's penetration of the Somali coast, along with the immigration of Arabian elements, inspired a second great population movement reversing the flow of migration from northward to southward. This massive movement, which ultimately took the Somalis to the banks of the Tana River and to the fertile plains of Harear, in Ethiopia, commenced in the thirteenth century and continued to the nineteenth century. At that point, European interlopers appeared on the East African scene, ending Somali migration onto the East African plateau.

Emergence of Adal

In addition to southward migration, a second factor in Somali history from the fifteenth century onward was the emergence of centralized state systems. The most important of these in medieval times was Adal, whose influence at the height of its power and prosperity in the sixteenth century extended from Saylac, the capital, through the fertile valleys of the Jijiga and the Harer plateau to the Ethiopian highlands. Adal's fame derived not only from the prosperity and cosmopolitanism of its people, its architectural sophistication, graceful mosques, and high learning, but also from its conflicts with the expansionist Ethiopians. For hundreds of years before the fifteenth century, goodwill had existed between the dominant new civilization of Islam and the Christian neguses of Ethiopia. One tradition holds that Muhammad blessed Ethiopia and enjoined his disciples from ever conducting jihad (holy war) against the Christian kingdom in gratitude for the protection early Muslims had received from the Ethiopian negus. Whereas Muslim armies rapidly overran the more powerful empires of Persia and Byzantium soon after the birth of Islam, there was no jihad against Christian Ethiopia for centuries. The forbidding Ethiopian terrain of deep gorges, sharp escarpments, and perpendicular massifs that rise more than 4,500 meters also discouraged the Muslims from attempting a campaign of conquest against so inaccessible a kingdom.

Muslim–Christian relations soured during the reign of the aggressive Negus Yeshaq (ruled 1414–29). Forces of his rapidly expanding empire descended from the highlands to despoil Muslim settlements in the valley east of the ancient city of Harer. Having branded the Muslims "enemies of the Lord," Yeshaq invaded the Muslim Kingdom of Ifat in 1415. He crushed the armies of Ifat and put to flight in the wastes along the Gulf of Tadjoura (in present–day Djibouti) Ifat's king Saad ad Din. Yeshaq followed Saad ad Din to the island off the coast of Saylac (which still bears his name), where the Muslim king was killed. Yeshaq compelled the Muslims to offer tribute, and also ordered his singers to compose a gloating hymn of thanksgiving for his victory. In the hymn's lyrics, the word *Somali* appears for the first time in written record.

By the sixteenth century, the Muslims had recovered sufficiently to break through from the east into the central Ethiopian highlands. Led by the charismatic Imam Ahmad Guray (1506–43), the Muslims poured into Ethiopia, using scorched–earth tactics that decimated the population of the country. A Portuguese expedition led by Pedro da Gama, a son of Vasco da Gama who was looking for the Prester John of medieval European folklore—a Christian, African monarch of vast dominions—arrived from the sea and saved Ethiopia. The joint Portuguese–Ethiopian force used cannon to route the Muslims, whose imam died on the battlefield.

Mogadishu and Its Banaadir Hinterlands

In the eighteenth and nineteenth centuries, the southern city of Mogadishu became Somalia's most important city. Mogadishu, Merca, and Baraawe, had been major Somali coastal towns in medieval times. Their origins are unknown, but by the fourteenth century travelers were mentioning the three towns more and more as important centers of urban ease and learning. Mogadishu, the largest and most prosperous, dates back at least to the ninth century, when Persian and Arabian immigrants intermingled with Somali elements to produce a distinctive hybrid culture. The meaning of Mogadishu's name is uncertain. Some render it as a Somali version of the Arabic "maqad shah," or "imperial seat of the shah," thus hinting at a Persian role in the city's founding.

Others consider it a Somali mispronunciation of the Swahili "mwyu wa" (last northern city), raising the possibility of its being the northernmost of the chain of Swahili city–states on the East African coast.

Whatever its origin, Mogadishu was at the zenith of its prosperity when the well–known Arab traveler Ibn Batuta appeared on the Somali coast in 1331. Ibn Batuta describes "Maqdashu" as "an exceedingly large city"

with merchants who exported to Egypt and elsewhere the excellent cloth made in the city.

Through commerce, proselytization, and political influence, Mogadishu and other coastal commercial towns influenced the Banaadir hinterlands (the rural areas outlying Mogadishu) in the fifteenth and sixteenth centuries. Evidence of that influence was the increasing Islamization of the interior by sufis (Muslim mystics)

who emigrated upcountry, where they settled among the nomads, married local women, and brought Islam to temper the random violence of the inhabitants.

By the end of the sixteenth century, the locus of intercommunication shifted upland to the well–watered region between the Shabeelle and Jubba rivers. Evidence of the shift of initiative from the coast to the interior may be found in the rise between 1550 and 1650 of the Ujuuraan (also seen as Ajuuraan) state, which prospered on the lower reaches of the interriverine region under the clan of the Gareen. The considerable power of the Ujuuraan state was not diminished until the Portuguese penetration of the East African coast in the seventeenth and eighteenth centuries. Among Somali towns and cities, only Mogadishu successfully resisted the repeated depredations of the Portuguese.

The Somali Peninsula on the Eve of Imperial Partition

In 1728 the last Portuguese foothold on the East African coast was dislodged from the great Mombasa castle of Fort Jesus. From then until the European "scramble" for African colonies in the 1880s, the Omanis exercised a shadowy authority over the Banaadir coast. Omani rule over the Somalis consisted for the most part of a token annual tribute payment and the presence of a resident qadi (Muslim judge) and a handful of *askaris* (territorial police).

Whereas the Banaadir coast was steadily drawn into the orbit of Zanzibari rulers, the northern coast, starting in the middle of the eighteenth century, passed under the sharifs of Mukha, who held their feeble authority on behalf of the declining Ottomans. The Mukha sharifs, much like the sultans of Zanzibar, satisfied themselves with a token yearly tribute collected for them by a native governor. In 1854–55 when Lieutenant Richard Burton of the British India navy frequented the northern Somali coast, he found a Somali governor, Haaji Shermaarke Ali Saalih of the Habar Yoonis clan of the Isaaq clan–family, exercising real power over Saylac and adjacent regions. By the time of Burton's arrival, once–mighty Saylac had only a tenuous influence over its environs. The city itself had degenerated into a rubble of mud and wattle huts, its water storage no longer working, its once formidable walls decayed beyond recognition, and its citizenry insulted and oppressed at will by tribesmen who periodically infested the city.

The Majeerteen Sultanates

Farther east on the Majeerteen (Bari) coast, by the middle of the nineteenth century two tiny kingdoms emerged that would play a significant political role on the Somali Peninsula prior to colonization. These were the Majeerteen Sultanate of Boqor Ismaan Mahamuud, and that of his kinsman Sultan Yuusuf Ali Keenadiid of Hobyo (Obbia). The Majeerteen Sultanate originated in the mideighteenth century, but only came into its own in the nineteenth century with the reign of the resourceful Boqor Ismaan Mahamuud. Ismaan Mahamuud's kingdom benefited from British subsidies (for protecting the British naval crews that were shipwrecked periodically on the Somali coast) and from a liberal trade policy that facilitated a flourishing commerce in livestock, ostrich feathers, and gum arabic. While acknowledging a vague vassalage to the British, the sultan kept his desert kingdom free until well after 1800.

Boqor Ismaan Mahamuud's sultanate was nearly destroyed in the middle of the nineteenth century by a power struggle between him and his young, ambitious cousin, Keenadiid. Nearly five years of destructive civil war passed before Boqor Ismaan Mahamuud managed to stave off the challenge of the young upstart, who was finally driven into exile in Arabia. A decade later, in the 1870s, Keenadiid returned from Arabia with a score of Hadhrami musketeers and a band of devoted lieutenants. With their help, he carved out the small kingdom of Hobyo after conquering the local Hawiye clans. Both kingdoms, however, were gradually absorbed by the extension into southern Somalia of Italian colonial rule in the last quarter of the nineteenth century.

IMPERIAL PARTITION

Figure 2. Colonial Boundaries, 1891–1960 Italian triumphal arch, Mogadishu Courtesy R W S. Hudson Old port gate, Mogadishu Courtesy R W S. Hudson The last quarter of the nineteenth century saw political developments that transformed the Somali Peninsula.

During this period, the Somalis became the subjects of state systems under the flags of Britain, France, Italy, Egypt, and Ethiopia. The new rulers had various motives for colonization. Britain sought to gain control of the northern Somali coast as a source of mutton and other livestock products for its naval port of Aden in present–day Yemen. As a result of the growing importance of the Red Sea to British operations in the East, Aden was regarded as indispensable to the defense of British India. British occupation of the northern Somali coast began in earnest in February 1884, when Major A. Hunter arrived at Berbera to negotiate treaties of friendship and protection with numerous Somali clans. Hunter arranged to have British vice consuls installed in Berbera, Bullaxaar, and Saylac.

The French, having been evicted from Egypt by the British, wished to establish a coaling station on the Red Sea coast to strengthen naval links with their Indochina colonies. The French were also eager to bisect Britain's vaunted Cairo to Cape Town zone of influence with an east to west expansion across Africa. France extended its foothold on the Afar coast partly to counter the high duties that the British authorities imposed on French goods in Obock. A French protectorate was proclaimed under the governorship of Léonce Lagarde, who played a prominent role in extending French influence into the Horn of Africa.

Recently unified, Italy was inexperienced at imperial power plays. It was therefore content to stake out a territory whenever it could do so without confronting another colonial power. In southern Somalia, better known as the Banaadir coast, Italy was the main colonizer, but the extension of Italian influence was painstakingly slow owing to parliamentary lack of enthusiasm for overseas territory. Italy acquired its first possession in southern Somalia in 1888 when the Sultan of Hobyo, Keenadiid, agreed to Italian "protection."

In the same year, Vincenzo Filonardi, Italy's architect of imperialism in southern

Somalia, demanded a similar arrangement from the Majeerteen Sultanate of Ismaan Mahamuud. In 1889 both sultans, suspicious of each other, consented to place their lands under Italian protection. Italy then notified the signatory powers of the Berlin West Africa Conference of 1884–85 of its southeastern Somali protectorate (see fig. 2). Later, Italy seized the Banaadir coast proper, which had long been under the tenuous authority of the Zanzibaris, to form the colony of Italian Somaliland. Chisimayu Region, which passed to the British as a result of their protectorate over the Zanzibaris, was ceded to Italy in 1925 to complete Italian tenure over southern Somalia.

The catalyst for imperial tenure over Somali territory was Egypt under its ambitious ruler, Khedive Ismail. In the last quarter of the nineteenth century, this Ottoman vassal sought to carve out for Egypt a swath of territory in the Horn of Africa. However, the Sudanese anti–Egyptian Mahdist revolt that broke out in 1884 shattered the khedive's plan for imperial aggrandizement. The Egyptians needed British help to evacuate their troops marooned in Sudan and on the Somali coast.

What the European colonialists failed to foresee was that the biggest threat to their imperial ambitions in the Horn of Africa would come from an emerging regional power, the Ethiopia of Emperor Menelik II. Emperor Menelik II not only managed to defend Ethiopia against European encroachment, but also succeeded in competing with the Europeans for the Somali–inhabited territories that he claimed as part of Ethiopia.

Between 1887 and 1897, Menelik II successfully extended Ethiopian rule over the long independent Muslim Emirate of Harer and over western Somalia (better known as the Ogaden). Thus, by the turn of the century, the Somali Peninsula, one of the most culturally homogeneous regions of Africa, was divided into British Somaliland, French Somaliland, Italian Somaliland, Ethiopian Somaliland (the Ogaden), and what came to be called the Northern Frontier District (NFD) of Kenya.

Although the officials of the three European powers often lacked funds, they nevertheless managed to establish the rudimentary organs of colonial administration. Moreover, because they controlled the port outlets, they could levy taxes on livestock to obtain the necessary funds to administer their respective Somali territories. In contrast, Ethiopia was largely a feudal state with a subsistence economy that required its army of occupation to live off the land. Thus, Ethiopian armies repeatedly despoiled the Ogaden in the last two decades of the nineteenth century.

Mahammad Abdille Hasau's Dervish Resistance to Colonial Occupation

Given the frequency and virulence of the Ethiopian raids, it was natural that the first pan–Somali or Greater Somalia effort against colonial occupation, and for unification of all areas populated by Somalis into one country, should have been directed at Ethiopians rather than at the Europeans; the effort was spearheaded by the Somali dervish resistance movement. The dervishes followed Mahammad Abdille Hasan of the puritanical Salihiyah *tariqa* (religious order or brotherhood). His ability as an orator and a poet (much–valued skills in Somali society) won him many disciples, especially among his own Dulbahante and Ogaden clans (both of the Daarood clan–family). The British dismissed Hasan as a religious fanatic, calling him the "Mad Mullah."

They underestimated his following, however, because from 1899 to 1920, the dervishes conducted a war of resistance against the Ethiopians and British, a struggle that devastated the Somali Peninsula and resulted in the death of an estimated one–third of northern Somalia's population and the near destruction of its economy.

One of the longest and bloodiest conflicts in the annals of sub–Saharan resistance to alien encroachment, the dervish uprising was not quelled until 1920 with the death of Hasan, who became a hero of Somali nationalism. Deploying a Royal Air Force squadron recently returned from action in combat in World War I, the British delivered the decisive blow with a devastating aerial bombardment of the dervish capital at Taleex in northern Somalia.

Consolidation of Colonial Rule

The two decades between 1900 and 1920 were a period of colonial consolidation. However, of the colonial powers that had divided the Somalis, only Italy developed a comprehensive administrative plan for its colony.

The Italians intended to plant a colony of settlers and commercial entrepreneurs in the region between the Shabeelle and Jubba rivers in southern Somalia. The motivation was threefold: to "relieve population pressure at home," to offer the "civilizing Roman mission" to the Somalis, and to increase Italian prestige through overseas colonization. Initiated by Governor Carletti (1906–10), Italy's colonial program received further impetus by the introduction of fascist ideology and economic planning in the 1920s, particularly during the administration of Governor Cesare Maria de Vecchi de Val Cismon. Large–scale development projects were launched, including a system of plantations on which citrus fruits, primarily bananas, and sugarcane, were grown. Sugarcane fields in Giohar and numerous banana plantations around the town of Jannaale on the Shabeelle River, and at the southern mouth of the Jubba River near Chisimayu, helped transform southern Somalia's economy.

In contrast to the Italian colony, British Somaliland stayed a neglected backwater. Daunted by the diversion of substantial development funds to the suppression of the dervish insurrection and by the "wild" character of the anarchic Somali pastoralists, Britain used its colony as little more than a supplier of meat products to Aden.

This policy had a tragic effect on the future unity and stability of independent Somalia. When the two former colonies merged to form the Somali Republic in 1960, the north lagged far behind the south in economic infrastructure and skilled labor. As a result, southerners gradually came to dominate the new state's economic and political life—a hegemony that bred a sense of betrayal and bitterness among northerners.

Somalia During World War II

Italy's 1935 attack on Ethiopia led to a temporary Somali reunification. After Italian premier Benito Mussolini's armies marched into Ethiopia and toppled Emperor Haile Selassie, the Italians seized British Somaliland. During their occupation (1940–41), the Italians reamalgamated the Ogaden with southern and northern Somalilands, uniting for the first time in forty years all the Somali clans that had been arbitrarily separated by the Anglo–Italo–Ethiopian boundaries. The elimination of these artificial boundaries and the unification of the Somali Peninsula enabled the Italians to set prices and impose taxes and to issue a common currency for the entire area. These actions helped move the Somali economy from traditional exchange in kind to a monetarized system.

Thousands of Italians, either veterans of the Ethiopian conquest or new emigrants, poured into Somalia, especially into the interriverine region. Although colonization was designed to entrench the white conquerors, many Somalis did not fare badly under Italian rule during this period. Some, such as the Haaji Diiriye and Yuusuf Igaal families, accumulated considerable fortunes. One indicator of the Somali sense of relative wellbeing may have been the absence of any major anti–Italian revolt during Italy's occupation.

At the onset of World War II, Italian holdings in East Africa included southern Somalia, Ethiopia, and Eritrea.

Italy subsequently invaded northern Somalia and ejected the British from the Horn of Africa. The Italian victory turned out to be short–lived, however. In March 1941, the British counterattacked and reoccupied northern Somalia, from which they launched their lightning campaign to retake the whole region from Italy and restore Emperor Haile Selassie to his throne. The British then placed southern Somalia and the Ogaden under a military administration.

British Military Administration

Following Italy's defeat, the British established military administrations in what had been British Somaliland, Italian Somaliland, and Ethiopian Somaliland. Thus, all Somali–inhabited territories—with the exception of French Somaliland and Kenya's Northern Frontier District (NFD)—were for the second time brought under a single tenure. No integrated administrative structure for the Somali areas was established, however, and under intense pressure from Haile Selassie, Britain agreed to return the Ogaden to Ethiopian jurisdiction. A military governor, aided by a handful of military officers, took over the work of the colonial civil service. In what had been Italian Somaliland, a similar military administration, headed by a military commander, was established.

The principal concern of the British administration during World War II and subsequently was to reestablish order. Accordingly, the Somaliland Camel Corps (local levies raised during the dervish disturbances) was reorganized and later disbanded. This effort resulted in the creation of five battalions known as the Somaliland Scouts, (Ilalos), which absorbed former irregular units (see The Warrior Tradition and Development of a Modern Army , ch. 5). The British disbanded the Italian security units in the south and raised a new army, the Somalia Gendarmerie, commanded by British officers, to police the occupied territory.

Originally, many of the rank and file of the gendarmerie were *askaris* from Kenya and Uganda who had served under British officers. The gendarmerie was gradually transformed into an indigenous force through the infusion of local recruits who were trained in a new police academy created by the British military administration. Somalia was full of Italian military stragglers, so the security services of the northern and southern protectorates collaborated in rounding them up. The greater security challenge for the British during World War II and immediately after was to disarm the Somalis who had taken advantage of the windfall in arms brought about by the war. Also, Ethiopia had organized Somali bandits to infest the British side so as to discourage continued British occupation of the Ogaden. Ethiopia also armed clan militias and encouraged them to cross into the British zone and cause bloodshed.

Despite its distracting security problems, the British military forces that administered the two Somali protectorates from 1941 to 1949 effected greater social and political changes than had their predecessors.

Britain's wartime requirement that the protectorate be self–supporting was modified after 1945, and the appropriation of new funds for the north created a burst of development. To signal the start of a new policy of increased attention to control of the interior, the capital was transferred from Berbera, a hot coastal town, to Hargeysa, whose location on the inland plateau offered the incidental benefit of a more hospitable climate.

Although the civil service remained inadequate to staff the expanding administration, efforts were made to establish health and veterinary services, to improve agriculture in the Gabiley–Boorama agricultural corridor northwest of Hargeysa, to increase the water supply to pastoralists by digging more bore wells, and to introduce secular elementary schools where previously only Quranic schools had existed. The judiciary was reorganized as a dual court system combining elements from the Somali *heer* (traditional jurisprudence), Islamic sharia or religious law, and British common law.

Somalia, a country study

In Italian Somaliland, the British improved working conditions for Somali agricultural laborers, doubled the size of the elementary school system, and allowed Somalis to staff the lower stratum of the civil service and gendarmerie. Additionally, military administrators opened the political process for Somalis, replacing Italian–appointed chiefs with clan–elected bodies, as well as district and regional councils whose purpose was to advise the military administration.

Military officials could not govern without the Italian civilians who constituted the experienced civil service.

The British military also recognized that Italian technocrats would be needed to keep the economy going.

Only Italians deemed to be security risks were interned or excluded from the new system. In early 1943, Italians were permitted to organize political associations. A host of Italian organizations of varying ideologies sprang up to challenge British rule, to compete politically with Somalis and Arabs (the latter being politically significant only in the urban areas, particularly the towns of Mogadishu, Merca, and Baraawe), and to agitate, sometimes violently, for the return of the colony to Italian rule. Faced with growing Italian political pressure, inimical to continued British tenure and to Somali aspirations for independence, the Somalis and the British came to see each other as allies. The situation prompted British colonial officials to encourage the Somalis to organize politically; the result was the first modern Somali political party, the Somali Youth Club (SYC), established in Mogadishu in 1943.

To empower the new party, the British allowed the better educated police and civil servants to join it, thus relaxing Britain's traditional policy of separating the civil service from leadership, if not membership, in political parties. The SYC expanded rapidly and boasted 25,000 card–carrying members by 1946. In 1947 it renamed itself the Somali Youth League (SYL) and began to open offices not only in the two British–run Somalilands but also in Ethiopia's Ogaden and in the NFD of Kenya. The SYL's stated objectives were to unify all Somali territories, including the NFD and the Ogaden; to create opportunities for universal modern education; to develop the Somali language by a standard national orthography; to safeguard Somali interests; and to oppose the restoration of Italian rule. SYL policy banned clannishness so that the thirteen founding members, although representing four of Somalia's six major clans, refused to disclose their ethnic identities. A second political body sprang up, originally calling itself the Patriotic Benefit Union but later renaming itself the Hisbia Digil Mirifle (HDM), representing the two interriverine clans of Digil and Mirifle. The HDM allegedly cooperated with the Italians and accepted significant Italian financial backing in its struggle against the SYL. Although the SYL enjoyed considerable popular support from northerners, the principal parties in British Somaliland were the Somali National League (SNL), mainly associated with the Isaaq clan–family, and the United Somali Party (USP), which had the support of the Dir (Gadabursi and Issa) and Daarood (Dulbahante and Warsangali) clan–families.

Although southern Somalia legally was an Italian colony, in 1945 the Potsdam Conference decided not to return to Italy the African territory it had seized during the war. The disposition of Somalia therefore fell to the Allied Council of Foreign Ministers, which assigned a four–power commission consisting of Britain, France, the Soviet Union, and the United States to decide Somalia's future. The British suggested that all the Somalis should be placed under a single administration, preferably British, but the other powers accused Britain of imperial machinations.

In January 1948, commission representatives arrived in Mogadishu to learn the aspirations of the Somalis.

The SYL requested and obtained permission from the military administration to organize a massive demonstration to show the commission delegates the strength of popular demand for independence. When the SYL held its rally, a counter demonstration led by Italian elements came out to voice pro– Italian sentiment and to attempt to discredit the SYL before the commission. A riot erupted in which fifty–one Italians and twenty–four Somalis were killed. Despite the confusion, the commission proceeded with its hearings and seemed favorably impressed by the proposal the SYL presented: to reunite all Somalis and to place Somalia under a ten–year trusteeship overseen by an international body that would lead the country to independence.

The commission heard two other plans. One was offered by the HDM, which departed from its pro–Italian stance to present an agenda similar to that of the SYL, but which included a request that the trusteeship period last thirty years. The other was put forward by a combination of Italian and Somali groups petitioning for the return of Italian rule.

The commission recommended a plan similar to that of the SYL, but the Allied Council of Foreign Ministers, under the influence of conflicting diplomatic interests, failed to reach consensus on the way to guide the country to independence. France favored the colony's return to Italy; Britain favored a formula much like that of the SYL, but the British plan was thwarted by the United States and the Soviet Union, which accused Britain of seeking imperial gains at the expense of Ethiopian and Italian interests. Britain was unwilling to quarrel with its erstwhile allies over Somali well–being and the SYL plan was withdrawn. Meanwhile, Ethiopia strongly pressured Britain through the United States, which was anxious to accommodate Emperor Haile Selassie in return for his promise to offer the United States a military base in Ethiopia. For its part, the Soviet Union preferred to reinstate Italian tenure, mainly because of the growing communist influence on Italian domestic politics.

Under United States and Soviet prodding, Britain returned the Ogaden to Ethiopia in 1948 over massive Somali protests. The action shattered Somali nationalist aspirations for Greater Somalia, but the shock was softened by the payment of considerable war reparations—or "bribes," as the Somalis characterized them—to Ogaden clan chiefs. In 1949 many grazing areas in the hinterlands also were returned to Ethiopia, but Britain gained Ethiopian permission to station British liaison officers in the Reserved Areas, areas frequented by British– protected Somali clans. The liaison officers moved about with the British–protected clans that frequented the Haud pasturelands for six months of the year. The liaison officers protected the pastoralists from Ethiopian "tax collectors"—armed bands that Ethiopia frequently sent to the Ogaden, both to demonstrate its sovereignty and to defray administrative costs by seizing Somali livestock.

Meanwhile, because of disagreements among commission members over the disposition of Somalia, the Allied Council of Foreign Ministers referred the matter to the United Nations (UN) General Assembly. In November 1949, the General Assembly voted to make southern Somalia a trust territory to be placed under Italian control for ten years, following which it would become independent. The General Assembly stipulated that under no circumstance should Italian rule over the colony extend beyond 1960. The General Assembly seems to have been persuaded by the argument that Italy, because of its experience and economic interests, was best suited to administer southern Somalia. Thus, the SYL's vehement opposition to the reimposition of Italian rule fell on deaf ears at the UN.

Trusteeship and Protectorate: The Road to Independence

The conditional return of Italian administration to southern Somalia gave the new trust territory several unique advantages compared with other African colonies. To the extent that Italy held the territory by UN mandate, the trusteeship provisions gave the Somalis the opportunity to gain experience in political education and self–government. These were advantages that British Somaliland, which was to be incorporated into the new Somali state, did not have. Although in the 1950s British colonial officials attempted, through various development efforts, to make up for past neglect, the protectorate stagnated. The disparity between the two territories in economic development and political experience would cause serious difficulties when it came time to integrate the two parts.

The UN agreement established the Italian Trusteeship Administration (Amministrazione Fiduciaria Italiana della Somalia—AFIS) to prepare southern Somalia for independence over a ten–year period. Under the agreement, a UN Advisory Council based in Mogadishu observed the AFIS and reported its progress to the UN Trusteeship Council. The agreement required the new administration to develop the colony's political institutions, to expand the educational system, to improve the economic infrastructure, and to give the indigenous people freedom of the press and the right to dissent. These political and civil guarantees did not make for smooth Italo–Somali relations. Seen by the Italians as the source of nationalist sentiment and activity, the SYL distrusted the new administration, suspecting it of having a hidden colonial agenda. SYL fears were exacerbated when the AFIS, soon after taking control, proceeded to jail some SYL members and to fire others from their civil service posts. The SYL responded with protests, civil disobedience, and representations to the UN Advisory Council. The council intervened to arbitrate the disputes and to encourage the two sides to collaborate. The conflict simmered for three years (1950–53) until new economic and political initiatives provided a channel for the energies of Somali nationalists.

The centerpiece of the initiatives was a series of seven–year development programs introduced in 1954.

Drawing on development blueprints provided by the United States Agency for

International Cooperation (AIC; later the United States Agency for International Development—AID) and the UN Development Programme, the Italian administration initiated plans to stimulate local agriculture, to improve the infrastructure, and to expand educational facilities. Exports, responding to these stimuli, trebled from 1954 to 1960. Despite these improvements, an acute balance of payments deficit persisted, and the administration had to rely on foreign grants and Italian subsidies to balance the budget.

Development efforts in education were more successful. Between 1952 and 1957, student enrollment at the elementary and secondary levels doubled. In 1957 there were 2,000 students receiving secondary, technical, and university education in Italian Somaliland and through scholarship programs in China, Egypt, and Italy.

Another program offered night–school adult literacy instruction and provided further training to civil servants.

However, these programs were severely handicapped by the absence of a standard script and a written national language. Arabic, Italian, and English served as media of instruction in the various schools; this linguistic plurality created a Tower of Babel.

Progress was made throughout the 1950s in fostering political institutions. In accordance with a UN resolution, in 1950 the Italians had established in Italian Somaliland an advisory body known as the Territorial Council, which took an active part in discussions of proposed AFIS legislation. Composed of thirty–five members, the council came to be dominated by representatives of political parties such as the SYL and HDM.

Acting as a nascent parliament, the Territorial Council gained experience not only in procedural matters but also in legislative debates on the political, economic, and social problems that would face future Somali governments. For its part the AFIS, by working closely with the council, won legitimacy in Somali eyes.

There were other forums, besides the Territorial Council, in which Somalis gained executive and legislative experience. These included the forty–eight–member Municipal Council introduced in 1950, whose members dealt with urban planning, public services, and, after 1956, fiscal and budgetary matters. Rural councils handled tribal and local problems such as conflicts over grazing grounds and access to water and pasturelands.

However, the effectiveness of the rural councils was undermined by the wanderings of the nomads as they searched for water wells and pastures, a circumstance that made stable political organizations difficult to sustain. Thus, the UN Advisory Council's plans to use the rural councils as bridges to development turned out to be untenable, a situation that enabled AFIS–appointed district commissioners to become the focus of power and political action.

Territory–wide elections were first held in southern Somalia in 1956. Although ten parties fielded candidates to select representatives to a new seventy–seat Legislative Assembly that replaced the Territorial Council, only the SYL (which won forty– three seats) and HDM (which won thirteen seats) gained significant percentages of the sixty seats that the Somalis contested. The remaining ten seats were reserved for Indians, Arabs, and other non–Somalia. Abdullaahi Iise, leader of the SYL in the assembly, became the first prime minister of a government composed of five ministerial posts, all held by Somalis. The new assembly assumed responsibility for domestic affairs, although the governor as representative of the Italian government and as the most senior official of the AFIS retained the "power of absolute veto" as well as the authority to rule by emergency decree should the need arise. Moreover, until 1958 the AFIS continued to control important areas such as foreign relations, external finance, defense, and public order.

The term of office of the Iise government was four years (1956–60)—a trial period that enabled the nascent southern Somali administration to shape the terms under which it was to gain its independence. This period was the most stable in modern Somali politics. The government's outlook was modernist and, once the Somalis become convinced that Italy would not attempt to postpone independence, pro–Italian. The franchise was extended to women in 1958, and nationalization at all levels of administration from district commissioner to provincial governor proceeded apace. Attempts were made to suppress clannishness and to raise the status of women and of groups holding lowly occupations. The future promised hope: the moral support of global anticolonial forces, the active backing of the UN, and the goodwill of the Western powers, including Italy.

The southern Somali government's principal tasks were to increase economic self–sufficiency and to find external sources of financial assistance that would replace the support Italy would withdraw after independence. Another major concern was to frame the constitution that would take effect once Somalia became independent. The writers of this document faced two sensitive issues: the form of government—federalist or unitary—the new nation would adopt, and nationalist aspirations concerning Greater Somalia. The first issue was of great interest to the HDM, whose supporters mainly were cultivators from the well–watered region between the Shabeelle and Jubba rivers and who represented about 30 percent of the population. The HDM wanted a federal form of government. This preference derived from concerns about dominance by the SYL, which was supported by pastoral clans that accounted for 60 percent of the population (Daarood and Hawiye; see Samaal , ch. 2). Not surprisingly, the SYL advocated a unitary form of government, arguing that federalism would encourage clannishness and social strife. In the end, political and numerical strength enabled the SYL to prevail.

The delicate issue of Greater Somalia, whose recreation would entail the detachment from Ethiopia, Djibouti, and Kenya of Somali–inhabited areas, presented Somali leaders with a dilemma: they wanted peace with their neighbors, but making claims on their territory was certain to provoke hostility. Led by Haaji Mahammad Husseen, the SYL radical wing wanted to include in the constitution an article calling for the unification of the Somali nation "by all means necessary." In the end, the moderate majority prevailed in modifying the wording to demand "reunification of the dismembered nation by peaceful means."

During the four–year transition to independence, conflicts over unresolved economic and political issues took the form of intraparty squabbling within the dominant SYL rather than interparty competition, as Daarood and Hawiye party stalwarts banded into factions. The Daarood accused Iise's government of being under Italian influence and the Hawiye countered with a charge of clannishness in the Daarood ranks. Husseen's radical faction continued to charge Iise's government with being too close to the West, and to Italy in particular, and of doing little to realize the national goal of reconstituting Greater Somalia. Despite his rift with prime minister Iise, Husseen, who had headed the party in the early years, was again elected SYL president in July 1957. But his agenda of looser ties with the West and closer relations with the Arab world clashed with the policies of Iise and of Aadan Abdullah Usmaan, the parliamentary leader who would become the first president of independent Somalia. Husseen inveighed against "reactionaries in government," a thinly veiled reference to Iise and Usmaan. The latter two responded by expelling Husseen and his supporters from the SYL. Having lost the power struggle, Husseen created a militant new party, the Greater Somali League (GSL). Although Husseen's firebrand politics continued to worry the SYL leadership, he never managed to cut deeply into the party's constituency.

The SYL won the 1958 municipal elections in the Italian trust territory, in part because it had begun to succeed in attracting important Rahanwayn clan elements like Abdulqaadir Soppe, who formerly had supported the HDM. Its growing appeal put the SYL in a commanding position going into the pre–independence election campaigns for the National Assembly of the Republic, a new body that replaced the two legislative assemblies of British and Italian Somaliland. The National Assembly had been enlarged to contain ninety seats for southern representatives and thirty– three for northern representatives. The HDM and the GSL accused the SYL of tampering with the election process and decided to boycott the elections.

Consequently, the SYL garnered sixty–one uncontested seats by default, in addition to the twenty seats contested and won by the party. The new government formed in 1959 was headed by incumbent prime minister Iise. The expanded SYL gave representation to virtually all the major clans in the south. Although efforts were made to distribute the fifteen cabinet posts among the contending clan–families, a political tug–of–war within the party continued between conservatives from the religious communities and modernists such as Abdirashiid Ali Shermaarke.

Meanwhile, in British Somaliland the civilian colonial administration attempted to expand educational opportunities in the protectorate. The number of Somalis qualifying for administrative posts remained negligible, however. The protectorate had experienced little economic or infrastructural development apart from the digging of more bore wells and the establishment of agricultural and veterinary services to benefit animal and plant husbandry. Comprehensive geological surveys failed to uncover exploitable mineral resources.

Politically, although the SYL opened branches in the north and the SNL continued to expand its membership, neither party could mobilize grass–roots support. This changed in 1954, when the last British liaison officers withdrew from the Reserved Areas—parts of the Ogaden and the Haud in which the British were given temporary administrative rights, in accordance with a 1942 military convention between Britain and Ethiopian emperor in exile Haile Selassie. This move conformed with Britain's agreement with Ethiopia confirming the latter's title deeds to the Haud under the 1897 treaty that granted Ethiopia full jurisdiction over the region. The British colonial administrators of the area were, however, embarrassed by what they saw as Britain's betrayal of the trust put in it by Somali clans who were to be protected against Ethiopian raids.

The Somalis responded with dismay to the ceding of the Haud to Ethiopia. A new party named the National United Front (NUF), supported by the SNL and the SYL, arose under the leadership of a Somali civil servant, Michael Mariano, a prominent veteran of the SYL's formative years. Remarkably, for the militantly Muslim country, the man selected to lead the nationalist struggle for the return of the Haud, was a Christian. NUF representatives visited London and the UN seeking to have the Haud issue brought before the world community, in particular the International Court of Justice. Britain attempted unsuccessfully to purchase the Haud from Ethiopia. Ethiopia responded with a counterprotest laying claim to all Somali territories, including the British and Italian Somalilands, as part of historical Ethiopia—territories, Haile Selassie claimed, seized by the European powers during a period of Ethiopian weakness. The Europeans were reluctant to press new territorial demands on Haile Selassie and did little to help the Somalis recover the Haud.

Political protests forced Britain in 1956 to introduce representative government in its protectorate and to accept the eventual unification of British Somaliland with southern Somalia. Accordingly, in 1957 a Legislative Council was established, composed of six members appointed by the governor to represent the principal clan–families. The council was expanded the following year to consist of twelve elected members, two appointees, and fifteen senior elders and notables chosen as ex officio members. The electoral procedure in the north followed that in the south, with elections in urban areas conducted by secret ballot and in the countryside by acclamation in clan assemblies. In 1960 the first elections contested along party lines resulted in a victory for the SNL and its affiliate the USP, the two winning between them all but one of the thirty–three seats in the new Legislative Assembly. The remaining seat was won by Mariano, the NUF's defeat clearly attributable to his Christian affiliation, which his political opponents had made a prominent campaign issue.

Following the election, Mahammad Ibrahim Igaal was chosen as prime minister to lead a four–man government.

Popular demand compelled the leaders of the two territories to proceed with plans for immediate unification.

The British government acquiesced to the force of Somali nationalist public opinion and agreed to terminate its rule of Somaliland in 1960 in time for the protectorate to merge with the trust territory on the independence date already fixed by the UN commission. In April 1960, leaders of the two territories met in Mogadishu and agreed to form a unitary state. An elected president was to be head of state. Full executive powers would be held by a prime minister answerable to an elected National Assembly of 123 members representing the two territories. Accordingly, British Somaliland received its independence on June 26, 1960, and united with the trust territory to establish the Somali Republic on July 1, 1960. The legislature appointed Usmaan president; he in turn appointed Shermaarke the first prime minister. Shermaarke formed a coalition government dominated by the SYL but supported by the two clan–based northern parties, the SNL and the USC. Usmaan's appointment as president was ratified a year later in a national referendum.

FROM INDEPENDENCE TO REVOLUTION

Old fort, used as museum, Mogadishu Courtesy R W S. Hudson D ring the nine–year period of parliamentary democracy that followed Somali independence, freedom of expression was widely regarded as being derived from the traditional right of every man to be heard. The national ideal professed by Somalis was one of political and legal equality in which historical Somali values and acquired Western practices appeared to coincide. Politics was viewed as a realm not limited to one profession, clan, or class, but open to all male members of society. The role of women, however, was more limited. Women had voted in Italian Somaliland since the municipal elections in 1958. In May 1963, by an assembly margin of 52 to 42, suffrage was extended to women in former British Somaliland as well. Politics was at once the Somalis' most practiced art and favorite sport. The most desired possession of most nomads was a radio, which was used to keep informed on political news. The level of political participation often surpassed that in many Western democracies.

Problems of National Integration

Although unified as a single nation at independence, the south and the north were, from an institutional perspective, two separate countries. Italy and Britain had left the two with separate administrative, legal, and education systems in which affairs were conducted according to different procedures and in different languages. Police, taxes, and the exchange rates of their respective currencies also differed. Their educated elites had divergent interests, and economic contacts between the two regions were virtually nonexistent. In 1960 the UN created the Consultative Commission for Integration, an international board headed by UN official Paolo Contini, to guide the gradual merger of the new country's legal systems and institutions and to reconcile the differences between them. (In 1964 the Consultative Commission for Legislation succeeded this body. Composed of Somalis, it took up its predecessor's work under the chairmanship of Mariano.) But many southerners believed that, because of experience gained under the Italian trusteeship, theirs was the better prepared of the two regions for self–government. Northern political, administrative, and commercial elites were reluctant to recognize that they now had to deal with Mogadishu.

At independence, the northern region had two functioning political parties: the SNL, representing the Isaaq clan–family that constituted a numerical majority there; and the USP, supported largely by the Dir and the Daarood. In a unified Somalia, however, the Isaaq were a small minority, whereas the northern Daarood joined members of their clan–family from the south in the SYL. The Dir, having few kinsmen in the south, were pulled on the one hand by traditional ties to the Hawiye and on the other hand by common regional sympathies to the Isaaq. The southern opposition party, the GSL, pro–Arab and militantly panSomali , attracted the support of the SNL and the USP against the SYL, which had adopted a moderate stand before independence.

Northern misgivings about being too tightly harnessed to the south were demonstrated by the voting pattern in the June 1961 referendum on the constitution, which was in effect Somalia's first national election. Although the draft was overwhelmingly approved in the south, it was supported by less than 50 percent of the northern electorate.

Dissatisfaction at the distribution of power among the clanfamilies and between the two regions boiled over in December 1961, when a group of British–trained junior army officers in the north rebelled in reaction to the posting of higher ranking southern officers (who had been trained by the Italians for police duties) to command their units. The ringleaders urged a separation of north and south. Northern noncommissioned officers arrested the rebels, but discontent in the north persisted.

In early 1962, GSL leader Husseen, seeking in part to exploit northern dissatisfaction, attempted to form an amalgamated party, known as the Somali Democratic Union (SDU). It enrolled northern elements, some of which were displeased with the northern SNL representatives in the coalition government. Husseen's attempt failed. In May 1962, however, Igaal and another northern SNL minister resigned from the cabinet and took many SNL followers with them into a new party, the Somali National Congress (SNC), which won widespread northern support. The new party also gained support in the south when it was joined by an SYL faction composed predominantly of Hawiye. This move gave the country three truly national political parties and further served to blur north–south differences.

Pan–Somalism

Despite the difficulties encountered in integrating north and south, the most important political issue in postindependence Somali politics was the unification of all areas populated by Somalis into one country—a concept identified as pan–Somalism, or Greater Somalia. Politicians assumed that this issue dominated popular opinion and that any government would fall if it did not demonstrate a militant attitude toward neighboring countries occupying Somali territory.

Preoccupation with Greater Somalia shaped the character of the country's newly formed institutions and led to the build–up of the Somali military and ultimately to the war with Ethiopia and fighting in the NFD in Kenya.

By law the exact size of the National Assembly was not established in order to facilitate the inclusion of representatives of the contested areas after unification. The national flag featured a five–pointed star whose points represented those areas claimed as part of the Somali nation—the former Italian and British territories, the Ogaden, Djibouti, and the NFD. Moreover, the preamble to the constitution approved in 1961 included the statement, "The Somali Republic promotes by legal and peaceful means, the union of the territories." The constitution also provided that all ethnic Somalis, no matter where they resided, were citizens of the republic.

The Somalis did not claim sovereignty over adjacent territories, but rather demanded that

Somalis living in them be granted the right to self–determination. Somali leaders asserted that they would be satisfied only when their fellow Somalis outside the republic had the opportunity to decide for themselves what their status would be.

At the 1961 London talks on the future of Kenya, Somali representatives from the NFD demanded that Britain arrange for the NFD's separation before Kenya was granted independence. The British government appointed a commission to ascertain popular opinion in the NFD on the question. Its investigation indicated that separation from Kenya was almost unanimously supported by the Somalis and their fellow nomadic pastoralists, the Oromo. These two peoples, it was noted, represented a majority of the NFD's population.

Despite Somali diplomatic activity, the colonial government in Kenya did not act on the commission's findings. British officials believed that the federal format then proposed in the Kenyan constitution would provide a solution through the degree of autonomy it allowed the predominantly Somali region within the federal system. This solution did not diminish Somali demands for unification, however, and the modicum of federalism disappeared after Kenya's government opted for a centralized constitution in 1964.

The denial of Somali claims led to growing hostility between the Kenyan government and Somalis in the NFD. Adapting easily to life as *shiftas*, or bandits, the Somalis conducted a guerrilla campaign against the police and army for more than four years between 1960 and 1964. The Somali government officially denied Kenya's charges that the guerrillas were trained in Somalia, equipped there with Soviet arms, and directed from Mogadishu. But it could not deny that the Voice of Somalia radio influenced the level of guerrilla activity by means of its broadcasts beamed into Kenya.

Somalia refused to acknowledge in particular the validity of the Anglo–Ethiopian Treaty of 1954 recognizing Ethiopia's claim to the Haud or, in general, the relevance of treaties defining Somali–Ethiopian borders.

Somalia's position was based on three points: first, that the treaties disregarded agreements made with the clans that had put them under British protection; second, that the Somalis were not consulted on the terms of the treaties and in fact had not been informed of their existence; and third, that such treaties violated the self–determination principle.

Incidents began to occur in the Haud within six months after Somali independence. At first the incidents were confined to minor clashes between Ethiopian police and armed parties of Somali nomads, usually resulting from traditional provocations such as smuggling, livestock rustling, and tax collecting, rather than irredentist agitation. Their actual causes aside, these incidents tended to be viewed in Somalia as expressions of Somali nationalism. Hostilities grew steadily, eventually involving small-scale actions between Somali and Ethiopian armed forces along the border. In February 1964, armed conflict erupted along the Somali–Ethiopian frontier, and Ethiopian aircraft raided targets in Somalia. Hostilities ended in April through the mediation of Sudan, acting under the auspices of the Organization of African Unity (OAU). Under the terms of the cease-fire, a joint commission was established to examine the causes of frontier incidents, and a demilitarized zone ten to fifteen kilometers wide was established on either side of the border. At least temporarily, further military confrontations were prevented.

Ethiopia and Kenya concluded a mutual defense pact in 1964 in response to what both countries perceived as a continuing threat from Somalia. This pact was renewed in 1980 and again on August 28, 1987, calling for the coordination of the armed forces of both states in the event of an attack by Somalia. Most OAU members were alienated by Somali irredentism and feared that if Somalia were successful in detaching the Somali–populated portions of Kenya and Ethiopia, the example might inspire their own restive minorities divided by frontiers imposed during the colonial period. In addition, in making its irredentist claims, the Somalis had challenged two of Africa's leading elder statesmen, President Jomo Kenyatta of Kenya and Emperor Haile Selassie of Ethiopia.

Foreign Relations, 1960–69

Somalia's government was in the hands of leaders who were favorably disposed toward the Western democracies, particularly Italy and Britain, in whose political traditions many of them had been educated.

Nevertheless, as a reflection of its desire to demonstrate self–reliance and nonalignment, the Somali government established ties with the Soviet Union and China soon after independence.

The growth of Soviet influence in Somalia dated from 1962, when Moscow agreed to provide loans to finance the training and equipping of the armed forces. By the late 1960s, about 300 Soviet military personnel were serving as advisers to the Somali forces, whose inventories had been stocked almost entirely with equipment of East European manufacture (see Foreign Military Assistance , ch. 5). During the same period, about 500 Somalis received military training in the Soviet Union. As a result of their contact with Soviet personnel, some Somali military officers developed a Marxist perspective on important issues that contrasted with the democratic outlook of most of the country's civilian leaders.

The Soviet Union also provided nonmilitary assistance, including technical training scholarships, printing presses, broadcasting equipment for the government, and agricultural and industrial development aid. By 1969 considerable nonmilitary assistance had also been provided by China. Such projects included the construction of hospitals and factories and in the 1970s of the major north–south road.

Somalia's relations with Italy after independence remained good, and Italian influence continued in the modernized sectors of social and cultural affairs. Although their number had dropped to about 3,000 by 1965, the Italians residing in Somalia still dominated many of the country's economic activities. Italian economic assistance during the 1960s totaled more than a quarter of all the nonmilitary foreign aid received, and Italy was an important market for Somali goods, particularly food crops produced on the large, Italian–owned commercial farms in the river valleys. Italy's sponsorship enabled Somalia to become an associate of the European Economic Community (EEC), which formed another source of economic and technical aid and assured preferential status for Somali exports in West European markets.

In contrast to the cordial relations maintained with Italy, Somalia severed diplomatic ties to Britain in 1962 to protest British support of Kenya's position on the NFD. Somalia's relations with France were likewise strained because of opposition to the French presence in the Territory of the Afars and Issas (formerly French Somaliland, later independent Djibouti). Meanwhile, the Federal Republic of Germany (West Germany)

provided Somalia with a moderate amount of aid, most notably sharing with Italy and the United States the task of training the police force. The Somali government purposely sought a variety of foreign sponsors to instruct its security forces, and Western–trained police were seen as counterbalancing the Soviet–trained military. Likewise, the division of training missions was believed to reduce dependence on either the West or the communist countries to meet Somali security needs (see Somalia Police Force , ch. 5).

Throughout the 1960s, the United States supplied nonmilitary aid to Somalia, a large proportion of it in the form of grants. But the image of the United States in the eyes of most Somalis was influenced more by its support for Ethiopia than by any assistance to Somalia. The large scale of United States military aid to Ethiopia was particularly resented. Although aid to that country had begun long before the Somali–Ethiopian conflict and was based on other considerations, the Somalis' attitude remained unchanged as long as the United States continued to train and equip a hostile neighbor.

The Husseen Government

Countrywide municipal elections, in which the SYL won 74 percent of the seats, occurred in November 1963.

These were followed in March 1964 by the country's first postindependence national elections. Again the SYL triumphed, winning 69 out of 123 parliamentary seats. The party's true margin of victory was even greater, as the fifty–four seats won by the opposition were divided among a number of small parties.

After the 1964 National Assembly election in March, a crisis occurred that left Somalia without a government until the beginning of September. President Usmaan, who was empowered to propose the candidate for prime minister after an election or the fall of a government, chose Abdirizaaq Haaji Husseen as his nominee instead of the incumbent, Shermaarke, who had the endorsement of the SYL party leadership. Shermaarke had been prime minister for the four previous years, and Usmaan decided that new leadership might be able to introduce fresh ideas for solving national problems.

In drawing up a Council of Ministers for presentation to the National Assembly, the nominee for prime minister chose candidates on the basis of ability and without regard to place of origin. But Husseen's choices strained intraparty relations and broke the unwritten rules that there be clan and regional balance. For instance, only two members of Shermaarke's cabinet were to be retained, and the number of posts in northern hands was to be increased from two to five.

The SYL's governing Central Committee and its parliamentary groups became split. Husseen had been a party member since 1944 and had participated in the two previous Shermaarke cabinets. His primary appeal was to younger and more educated party members. Several political leaders who had been left out of the cabinet joined the supporters of Shermaarke to form an opposition group within the party. As a result, the Husseen faction sought support among non–SYL members of the National Assembly.

Although the disagreements primarily involved personal or group political ambitions, the debate leading to the initial vote of confidence centered on the issue of Greater Somalia. Both Usmaan and prime minister–designate Husseen wanted to give priority to the country's internal economic and social problems.

Although Husseen had supported militant pan–Somalism, he was portrayed as willing to accept the continued sovereignty of Ethiopia and Kenya over Somali areas.

The proposed cabinet failed to be affirmed by a margin of two votes. Seven National Assembly members, including Shermaarke, abstained, while forty–eight members of the SYL voted for Husseen and thirty–three opposed him. Despite the apparent split in the SYL, it continued to attract recruits from other parties. In the first three months after the election, seventeen members of the parliamentary opposition resigned from their parties to join the SYL.

Usmaan ignored the results of the vote and again nominated Husseen as prime minister. After intraparty negotiation, which included the reinstatement of four party officials expelled for voting against him, Husseen presented a second cabinet list to the National Assembly that included all but one of his earlier nominees.

However, the proposed new cabinet contained three additional ministerial positions filled by men chosen to mollify opposition factions. The new cabinet was approved with the support of all but a handful of SYL National Assembly members. Husseen remained in office until the presidential elections of June 1967.

The 1967 presidential elections, conducted by a secret poll of National Assembly members, pitted former prime minister Shermaarke against Usmaan. Again the central issue was moderation versus militancy on the pan–Somali question. Usmaan, through Husseen, had stressed priority for internal development. Shermaarke, who had served as prime minister when pan–Somalism was at its height, was elected president of the republic.

The Igaal Government

The new president nominated as prime minister Mahammad Ibrahim Igaal, who raised cabinet membership from thirteen to fifteen members and included representatives of every major clanfamily , as well as some members of the rival SNC. In August 1967, the National Assembly confirmed his appointment without serious opposition. Although the new prime minister had supported Shermaarke in the presidential election, he was a northerner and had led a 1962 defection of the northern SNL assembly members from the government. He had also been closely involved in the founding of the SNC but, with many other northern members of that group, had rejoined the SYL after the 1964 elections.

A more important difference between Shermaarke and Igaal, other than their past affiliations, was the new prime minister's moderate position on pan–Somali issues and his desire for improved relations with other African countries. In these areas, he was allied with the "modernists" in the government, parliament, and administration who favored redirecting the nation's energies from confrontation with its neighbors to combating social and economic ills. Although many of his domestic policies seemed more in line with those of the previous administration, Igaal continued to hold the confidence of both Shermaarke and the National Assembly during the eighteen months preceding the March 1969 national elections.

Igaal's policy of regional détente resulted in improved relations with Ethiopia and Kenya. The prime minister did not relinquish Somalia's territorial claims, but he hoped to create an atmosphere in which the issue could be peacefully negotiated. In September 1968, Somalia and Ethiopia agreed to establish commercial air and telecommunication links. The termination of the state of emergency in the border regions, which had been declared by Ethiopia in February 1964, permitted the resumption of free access by Somali pastoralists to their traditional grazing lands and the reopening of the road across Ethiopian territory between Mogadishu and Hargeysa. With foreign affairs a less consuming issue, the government's energy and the country's meager resources could now be applied more effectively to the challenges of internal development. However, the relaxation of tensions had an unanticipated effect. The conflict with its neighbors had promoted Somalia's internal political cohesion and solidified public opinion at all levels on at least one issue. As tension from that source subsided, old cleavages based on clan rivalries became more prominent.

The March 1969 elections were the first to combine voting for municipal and National Assembly posts.

Sixty–four parties contested the elections. Only the SYL, however, presented candidates in every election district, in many cases without opposition. Eight other parties presented lists of candidates for national offices in most districts. Of the remaining fifty–five parties, only twenty–four gained representation in the assembly, but all of these were disbanded almost immediately when their fifty members joined the SYL.

Both the plethora of parties and the defection to the majority party were typical of Somali parliamentary elections. To register for elective office, a candidate merely needed either the support of 500 voters or the sponsorship of his clan, expressed through a vote of its traditional assembly. After registering, the office seeker then attempted to become the official candidate of a political party. Failing this, he would remain on the ballot as an individual contestant. Voting was by party list, which could make a candidate a one–person party. (This practice explained not only the proliferation of small parties but also the transient nature of party support.) Many candidates affiliated with a major party only long enough to use its symbol in the election campaign and, if elected, abandoned it for the winning side as soon as the National Assembly met. Thus, by the end of May 1969 the SYL parliamentary cohort had swelled from 73 to 109.

In addition, the eleven SNC members had formed a coalition with the SYL, which held 120 of the 123 seats in the National Assembly. A few of these 120 left the SYL after the composition of Igaal's cabinet became clear and after the announcement of his program, both of which were bound to displease some who had joined only to be on the winning side. Offered a huge list of candidates, the almost 900,000 voters in 1969 took delight in defeating incumbents. Of the incumbent deputies, 77 out of 123 were not returned (including 8 out of 18 members of the previous cabinet), but these figures did not unequivocally demonstrate dissatisfaction with the government. Statistically, they were nearly identical with the results of the 1964 election, and, given the profusion of parties and the system of proportional representation, a clear sense of public opinion could not be obtained solely on the basis of the election results. The fact that a single party—the SYL—dominated the field implied neither stability nor solidarity. Anthropologist I M. Lewis has noted that the SYL government was a very heterogeneous group with diverging personal and lineage interests.

Candidates who had lost seats in the assembly and those who had supported them were frustrated and angry.

A number of charges were made of government election fraud, at least some firmly founded. Discontent was exacerbated when the Supreme Court, under its newly appointed president, declined to accept jurisdiction over election petitions, although it had accepted such jurisdiction on an earlier occasion.

Neither the president nor the prime minister seemed particularly concerned about official corruption and nepotism. Although these practices were conceivably normal in a society based on kinship, some were bitter over their prevalence in the National Assembly, where it seemed that deputies ignored their constituents in trading votes for personal gain.

Among those most dissatisfied with the government were intellectuals and members of the armed forces and police. (General Mahammad Abshir, the chief of police, had resigned just before the elections after refusing to permit police vehicles to transport SYL voters to the polls.) Of these dissatisfied groups, the most significant element was the military, which since 1961 had remained outside politics. It had done so partly because the government had not called upon it for support and partly because, unlike most other African armed forces, the Somali National Army had a genuine external mission in which it was supported by all Somalis—that of protecting the borders with Ethiopia and Kenya.

Coup d'Etat

The stage was set for a coup d'état, but the event that precipitated the coup was unplanned. On October 15, 1969, a bodyguard killed president Shermaarke while prime minister Igaal was out of the country. (The assassin, a member of a lineage said to have been badly treated by the president, was subsequently tried and executed by the revolutionary government.) Igaal returned to Mogadishu to arrange for the selection of a new president by the National Assembly. His choice was, like Shermaarke, a member of the Daarood clan–family (Igaal was an Isaaq). Government critics, particularly a group of army officers, saw no hope for improving the country's situation by this means. On October 21, 1969, when it became apparent that the assembly would support Igaal's choice, army units took over strategic points in Mogadishu and rounded up government officials and other prominent political figures. The police cooperated with the army.

Although not regarded as the author of the military takeover, army commander Major General Mahammad Siad Barre assumed leadership of the officers who deposed the civilian government. The new governing body, the Supreme Revolutionary Council (SRC), installed Siad Barre as its president. The SRC arrested and detained at the presidential palace leading members of the democratic regime, including Igaal. The SRC banned political parties, abolished the National Assembly, and suspended the constitution. The new regime's goals included an end to "tribalism, nepotism, corruption, and misrule." Existing treaties were to be honored, but national liberation movements and Somali unification were to be supported. The country was renamed the Somali Democratic Republic.

THE REVOLUTIONARY REGIME

Statue of socialist workers, Mogadishu, erected in the 1970s Courtesy Hiram A. Ruiz The military coup that ended the democratic regime retroactively defined its action as a Marxist revolution not only instituting a new political order but also proposing the radical transformation of Somali society through the application of "scientific socialism." Despite the presence of Soviet advisers with the armed forces, no evidence indicated that the coup was Soviet–inspired. SRC members included officers ranging in rank from major general (Siad Barre and Jaama Ali Qoorsheel) to captain, but the young Soviet–trained junior officers—versed in Marx and Lenin—who had encouraged the coup were excluded from important positions in the revolutionary regime.

The SRC, which was synonymous with the new government, reorganized the country's political and legal institutions, formulated a guiding ideology based on the Quran as well as on Marx, and purged civilian officials who were not susceptible to "reeducation." The influence of lineage groups at all levels and elitism in public life based on clan affiliation were targeted for eradication. Eventually, Siad Barre emerged as Somalia's strongman, spokesman for its revolution, and leader of its government. In 1971 he announced the regime's intention to phase out military rule after the establishment of a political party whose central committee ultimately would supersede the SRC as a policy–and decision–making body.

Supreme Revolutionary Council

The SRC also gave priority to rapid economic and social development through "crash programs," efficient and responsive government, and creation of a standard written form of Somali as the country's single official language. The regime pledged continuance of regional détente in its foreign relations without relinquishing Somali claims to disputed territories.

The SRC's domestic program, known as the First Charter of the Revolution, appeared in 1969. Along with Law Number 1, an enabling instrument promulgated on the day of the military takeover, the First Charter provided the institutional and ideological framework of the new regime. Law Number 1 assigned to the SRC all functions previously performed by the president, the National Assembly, and the Council of Ministers, as well as many duties of the courts. The role of the twenty–five–member military junta was that of an executive committee that made decisions and had responsibility to formulate and execute policy. Actions were based on majority vote, but deliberations rarely were published. SRC members met in specialized committees to oversee government operations in given areas. A subordinate fourteen–man secretariat—the Council of the Secretaries of State (CSS)— functioned as a cabinet and was responsible for day–to–day government operation, although it lacked political power. The CSS consisted largely of civilians, but until 1974 several key ministries were headed by military officers who were concurrently members of the SRC. Existing legislation from the previous democratic government remained in force unless specifically abrogated by the SRC, usually on the grounds that it was "incompatible...with the spirit of the Revolution." In February 1970, the democratic constitution of 1960, suspended at the time of the coup, was repealed by the SRC under powers conferred by Law Number 1.

Although the SRC monopolized executive and legislative authority, Siad Barre filled a number of executive posts: titular head of state, chairman of the CSS (and thereby head of government), commander in chief of the armed forces, and president of the SRC. His titles were of less importance, however, than was his personal authority, to which most SRC members deferred, and his ability to manipulate the clans.

Military and police officers, including some SRC members, headed government agencies and public institutions to supervise economic development, financial management, trade, communications, and public utilities. Military officers replaced civilian district and regional officials. Meanwhile, civil servants attended reorientation courses that combined professional training with political indoctrination, and those found to be incompetent or politically unreliable were fired. A mass dismissal of civil servants in 1974, however, was dictated in part by economic pressures.

The legal system functioned after the coup, subject to modification. In 1970 special tribunals, the National Security Courts (NSC), were set up as the judicial arm of the SRC. Using a military attorney as prosecutor, the courts operated outside the ordinary legal system as watchdogs against activities considered to be counterrevolutionary. The first cases that the courts dealt with involved Shermaarke's assassination and charges of corruption leveled by the SRC against members of the democratic regime. The NSC subsequently heard cases with and without political content. A uniform civil code introduced in 1973 replaced predecessor laws inherited from the Italians and British and also imposed restrictions on the activities of sharia courts. The new regime subsequently extended the death penalty and prison sentences to individual offenders, formally eliminating collective responsibility through the payment of *diya* (see Glossary) or blood money (see Courts , ch. 4).

The SRC also overhauled local government, breaking up the old regions into smaller units as part of a long–range decentralization program intended to destroy the influence of the traditional clan assemblies and, in the government's words, to bring government "closer to the people." Local councils, composed of military administrators and representatives appointed by the SRC, were established under the Ministry of Interior at the regional, district, and village levels to advise the government on local conditions and to expedite its directives. Other institutional innovations included the organization (under Soviet direction) of the National Security Service (NSS), directed initially at halting the flow of professionals and dissidents out of the country and at counteracting attempts to settle disputes among the clans by traditional means. The newly formed Ministry of Information and National Guidance set up local political education bureaus to carry the government's message to the people and used Somalia's print and broadcast media for the "success of the socialist, revolutionary road." A censorship board, appointed by the ministry, tailored information to SRC guidelines.

The SRC took its toughest political stance in the campaign to break down the solidarity of the lineage groups.

Tribalism was condemned as the most serious impediment to national unity. Siad Barre denounced tribalism in a wider context as a "disease" obstructing development not only in Somalia, but also throughout the Third World. The government meted out prison terms and fines for a broad category of proscribed activities classified as tribalism. Traditional headmen, whom the democratic government had paid a stipend, were replaced by reliable local dignitaries known as "peacekeepers" (*nabod doan*), appointed by Mogadishu to represent government interests. Community identification rather than lineage affiliation was forcefully advocated at orientation centers set up in every district as the foci of local political and social activity. For example, the SRC decreed that all marriage ceremonies should occur at an orientation center. Siad Barre presided over these ceremonies from time to time and contrasted the benefits of socialism to the evils he associated with tribalism.

To increase production and control over the nomads, the government resettled 140,000 nomadic pastoralists in farming communities and in coastal towns, where the erstwhile herders were encouraged to engage in agriculture and fishing. By dispersing the nomads and severing their ties with the land to which specific clans made collective claim, the government may also have undercut clan solidarity. In many instances, real improvement in the living conditions of resettled nomads was evident, but despite government efforts to eliminate it, clan consciousness as well as a desire to return to the nomadic life persisted. Concurrent SRC attempts to improve the status of Somali women were unpopular in a traditional Muslim society, despite Siad Barre's argument that such reforms were consonant with Islamic principles.

Challenges to the Regime

The SRC announced on two occasions that it had discovered plotters in the act of initiating coup attempts.

Both instances involved SRC members. In April 1970, Qoorsheel, the first vice president, was arrested and charged with treason. Qoorsheel represented the more conservative police and army elements and thus opposed the socialist orientation of the majority of SRC members. He was convicted of treason in a trial before the National Security Court and sentenced to a prison term.

In May 1971, the second vice president, Major General Mahammad Ainanche, and a fellow SRC member, Soviet–trained Lieutenant Colonel Salah Gaveire Kedie, who had served as head of the Ministry of Defense and later as secretary of state for communications, were arrested along with several other army officers for plotting Siad Barre's assassination. The conspirators, who had sought the support of clans that had lost influence in the 1969 overthrow of the democratic regime, appeared to have been motivated by personal rivalries rather than by ideology. Accused of conspiring to assassinate the president, the two key figures in the plot and another army officer were executed after a lengthy trial.

By 1974 the SRC felt sufficiently secure to release Qoorsheel and most of the leaders of the democratic regime who had been detained since the 1969 coup. Igaal and four other former ministers were excepted from the amnesty, however, and were sentenced to long prison terms. Igaal received thirty years for embezzlement and conspiracy against the state.

Siad Barre and Scientific Socialism

Somalia's adherence to socialism became official on the first anniversary of the military coup when Siad Barre proclaimed that Somalia was a socialist state, despite the fact that the country had no history of class conflict in the Marxist sense. For purposes of Marxist analysis, therefore, tribalism was equated with class in a society struggling to liberate itself from distinctions imposed by lineage group affiliation. At the time, Siad Barre explained that the official ideology consisted of three elements: his own conception of community development based on the principle of self–reliance, a form of socialism based on Marxist principles, and Islam. These were subsumed under "scientific socialism," although such a definition was at variance with the Soviet and Chinese models to which reference was frequently made.

The theoretical underpinning of the state ideology combined aspects of the Quran with the influences of Marx, Lenin, Mao, and Mussolini, but Siad Barre was pragmatic in its application. "Socialism is not a religion," he explained; "It is a political principle" to organize government and manage production. Somalia's alignment with communist states, coupled with its proclaimed adherence to scientific socialism, led to frequent accusations that the country had become a Soviet satellite. For all the rhetoric extolling scientific socialism, however, genuine Marxist sympathies were not deep–rooted in Somalia. But the ideology was acknowledged—partly in view of the country's economic and military dependence on the Soviet Union—as the most convenient peg on which to hang a revolution introduced through a military coup that had supplanted a Western–oriented parliamentary democracy.

More important than Marxist ideology to the popular acceptance of the revolutionary regime in the early 1970s were the personal power of Siad Barre and the image he projected. Styled the "Victorious Leader"

(Guulwaadde), Siad Barre fostered the growth of a personality cult. Portraits of him in the company of Marx and Lenin festooned the streets on public occasions. The epigrams, exhortations, and advice of the paternalistic leader who had synthesized Marx with Islam and had found a uniquely Somali path to socialist revolution were widely distributed in Siad Barre's little blue–and–white book. Despite the revolutionary regime's intention to stamp out the clan politics, the government was commonly referred to by the code name MOD. This acronym stood for Mareehaan (Siad Barre's clan), Ogaden (the clan of Siad Barre's mother), and Dulbahante (the clan of Siad Barre son–in–law Colonel Ahmad Sulaymaan Abdullah, who headed the NSS).

These were the three clans whose members formed the government's inner circle. In 1975, for example, ten of the twenty members of the SRC were from the Daarood clan–family, of which these three clans were a part; the Digil and Rahanwayn, the sedentary interriverine clan–families, were totally unrepresented. L brary of Congress Country Studies *Do NOT bookmark these search results.*

Search results are stored in a TEMPORARY file for display purposes.

The Language and Literacy Issue

One of the principal objectives of the revolutionary regime was the adoption of a standard orthography of the Somali language. Such a system would enable the government to make Somali the country's official language.

Since independence Italian and English had served as the languages of administration and instruction in Somalia's schools. A11 government documents had been published in the two European languages. Indeed, it had been considered necessary that certain civil service posts of national importance be held by two officials, one proficient in English and the other in Italian. During the Husseen and Igaal governments, when a number of English–speaking northerners were put in prominent positions, English had dominated Italian in official circles and had even begun to replace it as a medium of instruction in southern schools. Arabic—or a heavily arabized Somali—also had been widely used in cultural and commercial areas and in Islamic schools and courts. Religious traditionalists and supporters of Somalia's integration into the Arab world had advocated that Arabic be adopted as the official language, with Somali as a vernacular.

A few months after independence, the Somali Language Committee was appointed to investigate the best means of writing Somali. The committee considered nine scripts, including Arabic, Latin, and various indigenous scripts. Its report, issued in 1962, favored the Latin script, which the committee regarded as the best suited to represent the phonemic structure of Somali and flexible enough to be adjusted for the dialects.

Facility with a Latin system, moreover, offered obvious advantages to those who sought higher education outside the country. Modern printing equipment would also be more easily and reasonably available for Latin type. Existing Somali grammars prepared by foreign scholars, although outdated for modern teaching methods, would give some initial advantage in the preparation of teaching materials. Disagreement had been so intense among opposing factions, however, that no action was taken to adopt a standard script, although successive governments continued to reiterate their intention to resolve the issue.

On coming to power, the SRC made clear that it viewed the official use of foreign languages, of which only a relatively small fraction of the population had an adequate working knowledge, as a threat to national unity, contributing to the stratification of society on the basis of language. In 1971 the SRC revived the Somali Language Committee and instructed it to prepare textbooks for schools and adult education programs, a national grammar, and a new Somali dictionary. However, no decision was made at the time concerning the use of a particular script, and each member of the committee worked in the one with which he was familiar.

The understanding was that, upon adoption of a standard script, all materials would be immediately transcribed.

On the third anniversary of the 1969 coup, the SRC announced that a Latin script had been adopted as the standard script to be used throughout Somalia beginning January 1, 1973. As a prerequisite for continued government service, all officials were given three months (later extended to six months) to learn the new script and to become proficient in it. During 1973 educational material written in the standard orthography was introduced in elementary schools and by 1975 was also being used in secondary and higher education.

Somalia's literacy rate was estimated at only 5 percent in 1972. After adopting the new script, the SRC launched a "cultural revolution" aimed at making the entire population literate in two years. The first part of the massive literacy campaign was carried out in a series of three–month sessions in urban and rural sedentary areas and reportedly resulted in several hundred thousand people learning to read and write. As many as 8,000 teachers were recruited, mostly among government employees and members of the armed forces, to conduct the program.

The campaign in settled areas was followed by preparations for a major effort among the nomads that got underway in August 1974. The program in the countryside was carried out by more than 20,000 teachers, half of whom were secondary school students whose classes were suspended for the duration of the school year.

The rural program also compelled a privileged class of urban youth to share the hardships of the nomadic pastoralists. Although affected by the onset of a severe drought, the program appeared to have achieved substantial results in the field in a short period of time (see Language and Education , ch. 2). Nevertheless, the UN estimate of Somalia's literacy rate in 1990 was only 24 percent.

Creation of the Somali Revolutionary Socialist Party

One of the SRC's first acts was to prohibit the existence of any political association. Under Soviet pressure to create a communist party structure to replace Somalia's military regime, Siad Barre had announced as early as 1971 the SRC's intention to establish a one–party state. The SRC already had begun organizing what was described as a "vanguard of the revolution" composed of members of a socialist elite drawn from the military and the civilian sectors. The National Public Relations Office (retitled the National Political Office in 1973)

was formed to propagate scientific socialism with the support of the Ministry of Information and National Guidance through orientation centers that had been built around the country, generally as local selfhelp projects.

The SRC convened a congress of the Somali Revolutionary Socialist Party (SRSP) in June 1976 and voted to establish the Supreme Council as the new party's central committee. The council included the nineteen officers who composed the SRC, in addition to civilian advisers, heads of ministries, and other public figures.

Civilians accounted for a majority of the Supreme Council's seventy–three members. On July 1, 1976, the SRC dissolved itself, formally vesting power over the government in the SRSP under the direction of the Supreme Council.

In theory the SRSP's creation marked the end of military rule, but in practice real power over the party and the government remained with the small group of military officers who had been most influential in the SRC.

Decision–making power resided with the new party's politburo, a select committee of the

Supreme Council that was composed of five former SRC members, including Siad Barre and his son–in–law, NSS chief Abdullah. Siad Barre was also secretary general of the SRSP, as well as chairman of the Council of Ministers, which had replaced the CSS in 1981. Military influence in the new government increased with the assignment of former SRC members to additional ministerial posts. The MOD circle also had wide representation on the Supreme Council and in other party organs. Upon the establishment of the SRSP, the National Political Office was abolished; local party leadership assumed its functions.

SOMALIA'S DIFFICULT DECADE, 1980–90

Entrenching Siad Barre's Personal Rule

The Ogaden War of 1977–78 between Somalia and Ethiopia and the consequent refugee influx forced Somalia to depend for its economic survival on humanitarian handouts (see The Ogaden War: Performance and Implications of Defeat , ch. 5). Domestically, the lost war produced a national mood of depression.

Organized opposition groups began to emerge, and in dealing with them Siad Barre intensified his political repression, using jailings, torture, and summary executions of dissidents and collective punishment of clans thought to have engaged in organized resistance.

Siad Barre's new Western friends, especially the United States, which had replaced the Soviet Union as the main user of the naval facilities at Berbera, turned out to be reluctant allies. Although prepared to help the Siad Barre regime economically through direct grants, World Bank (see Glossary)–sponsored loans, and relaxed International Monetary Fund (IMF—see Glossary) regulations, the United States hesitated to offer Somalia more military aid than was essential to maintain internal security. The amount of United States military and economic aid to the regime was US$34 million in 1984; by 1987 this amount had dwindled to about US$8.7 million, a fraction of the regime's requested allocation of US$47 million (see Foreign Military Assistance , ch. 5). Western countries were also pressuring the regime to liberalize economic and political life and to renounce historical Somali claims on territory in Kenya and Ethiopia. In response, Siad Barre held parliamentary elections in December 1979. A "people's parliament" was elected, all of whose members belonged to the government party, the SRSP. Following the elections,

Siad Barre again reshuffled the cabinet, abolishing the positions of his three vice presidents. This action was followed by another reshuffling in October 1980 in which the old Supreme Revolutionary Council was revived. The move resulted in three parallel and overlapping bureaucratic structures within one administration: the party's politburo, which exercised executive powers through its Central Committee, the Council of Minsters, and the SRC. The resulting confusion of functions within the administration left decision making solely in Siad Barre's hands.

In February 1982, Siad Barre visited the United States. He had responded to growing domestic criticism by releasing from detention two leading political prisoners of conscience, former premier Igaal and former police commander Abshir, both of whom had languished in prison since 1969. On June 7, 1982, apparently wishing to prove that he alone ruled Somalia, ordered the arrest of seventeen prominent politicians. This development shook the "old establishment" because the arrests included Mahammad Aadan Shaykh, a prominent Mareehaan politician, detained for the second time; Umar Haaji Masala, chief of staff of the military, also a Mareehaan; and a former vice president and a former foreign minister. At the time of detention, one official was a member of the politburo; the others were members of the Central Committee of the SRSP. The jailing of these prominent figures created an atmosphere of fear, and alienated the Isaaq, Majeerteen, and Hawiye clans, whose disaffection and consequent armed resistance were to lead to the toppling of the Siad Barre regime.

The regime's insecurity was considerably increased by repeated forays across the Somali border in the Mudug (central) and Boorama (northwest) areas by a combination of Somali dissidents and Ethiopian army units. In mid–July 1982, Somali dissidents with Ethiopian air support invaded Somalia in the center, threatening to split the country in two. The invaders managed to capture the Somali border towns of Balumbale and Galdogob, northwest of the Mudug regional capital of Galcaio. Siad Barre's regime declared a state of emergency in the war zone and appealed for Western aid to help repel the invasion. The United States government responded by speeding deliveries of light arms already promised. In addition, the initially pledged US$45 million in economic and military aid was increased to US$80 million. The new arms were not used to repel the Ethiopians, however, but to repress Siad Barre's domestic opponents.

Although the Siad Barre regime received some verbal support at the League of Arab States (Arab League) summit conference in September 1982, and Somali units participated in war games with the United States Rapid Deployment Force in Berbera, the revolutionary government's position continued to erode. In December 1984, Siad Barre sought to broaden his political base by amending the constitution. One amendment extended the president's term from six to seven years. Another amendment stipulated that the president was to be elected by universal suffrage (Siad Barre always received 99 percent of the vote in such elections) rather than by the National Assembly. The assembly rubber–stamped these amendments, thereby presiding over its own disenfranchisement.

On the diplomatic front, the regime undertook some fence mending. An accord was signed with Kenya in December 1984 in which Somalia "permanently" renounced its historical territorial claims, and relations between the two countries thereafter began to improve. This diplomatic gain was offset, however, by the "scandal" of South African foreign minister Roelof "Pik" Botha's secret visit to Mogadishu the same month, in which South Africa promised arms to Somalia in return for landing rights for South African Airways.

Complicating matters for the regime, at the end of 1984 the Western Somali Liberation Front (WSLF) (a guerrilla organizaton based in Ethiopia seeking to free the Ogaden and unite it with Somalia) announced a temporary halt in military operations against Ethiopia. This decision was impelled by the drought then ravaging the Ogaden and by a serious split within the WSLF, a number of whose leaders claimed that their struggle for selfdetermination had been used by Mogadishu to advance its expansionist policies. These elements said they now favored autonomy based on a federal union with Ethiopia. This development removed Siad Barre's option to foment anti–Ethiopian activity in the Ogaden in retaliation for Ethiopian aid to domestic opponents of his regime.

To overcome its diplomatic isolation, Somalia resumed relations with Libya in April 1985. Recognition had been withdrawn in 1977 in response to Libyan support of Ethiopia during the Ogaden War. Also in early 1985 Somalia participated in a meeting of EEC and UN officials with the foreign ministers of several northeast African states to discuss regional cooperation under a planned new authority, the Inter–Governmental Authority on Drought and Development (IGADD). Formed in January 1986 and headquartered in Djibouti, IGADD brought together Djibouti, Ethiopia, Kenya, Sudan, and Uganda in addition to Somalia. In January 1986, under the auspices of IGADD, Siad Barre met Ethiopian leader Mengistu Haile–Mariam in Djibouti to discuss the "provisional" administrative line (the undemarcated boundary) between Ethiopia and Somalia.

They agreed to hold further meetings, which took place on and off throughout 1986–87. Although Siad Barre and Mengistu agreed to exchange prisoners taken in the Ogaden War and to cease aiding each other's domestic opponents, these plans were never implemented. In August 1986, Somalia held joint military exercises with the United States.

Diplomatic setbacks also occurred in 1986, however. In September, Somali foreign minister Abdirahmaan Jaama Barre, the president's brother, accused the Somali Service of the British Broadcasting Corporation of anti–Somali propaganda. The charge precipitated a diplomatic rift with Britain. The regime also entered into a dispute with Amnesty International, which charged the Somali regime with blatant violations of human rights.

Wholesale human rights violations documented by Amnesty International, and subsequently by Africa Watch, prompted the United States Congress by 1987 to make deep cuts in aid to Somalia (see Relations with the United States , ch. 4).

Economically, the regime was repeatedly pressured between 1983 and 1987 by the IMF, the United Nations Development Programme, and the World Bank to liberalize its economy. Specifically, Somalia was urged to create a free market system and to devalue the Somali shilling (for value of the shilling—see Glossary) so that its official rate would reflect its true value (see From Scientific Socialism to "IMF–ism," 1981–90 , ch. 3).

Siad Barre's Repressive Measures

Faced with shrinking popularity and an armed and organized domestic resistance, Siad Barre unleashed a reign of terror against the Majeerteen, the Hawiye, and the Isaaq, carried out by the Red Berets (Duub Cas), a dreaded elite unit recruited from among the president's Mareehaan clansmen. Thus, by the beginning of 1986 Siad Barre's grip on power seemed secure, despite the host of problems facing the regime. The president received a severe blow from an unexpected quarter, however. On the evening of May 23, he was severely injured in an automobile accident. Astonishingly, although at the time he was in his early seventies and suffered from chronic diabetes, Siad Barre recovered sufficiently to resume the reins of government following a month's recuperation. But the accident unleashed a power struggle among senior army commandants, elements of the president's Mareehaan clan, and related factions, whose infighting practically brought the country to a standstill. Broadly, two groups contended for power: a constitutional faction and a clan faction.

The constitutional faction was led by the senior vice president, Brigadier General Mahammad Ali Samantar; the second vice president, Major General Husseen Kulmiye; and generals Ahmad Sulaymaan Abdullah and Ahmad Mahamuud Faarah. The four, together with president Siad Barre, constituted the politburo of the SRSP.

Opposed to the constitutional group were elements from the president's Mareehaan clan, especially members of his immediate family, including his brother, Abdirahmaan Jaama Barre; the president's son, Colonel Masleh Siad, and the formidable Mama Khadiija, Siad Barre's senior wife. By some accounts, Mama Khadiija ran her own intelligence network, had well-placed political contacts, and oversaw a large group who had prospered under her patronage.

In November 1986, the dreaded Red Berets unleashed a campaign of terror and intimidation on a frightened citizenry. Meanwhile, the ministries atrophied and the army's officer corps was purged of competent career officers on suspicion of insufficient loyalty to the president. In addition, ministers and bureaucrats plundered what was left of the national treasury after it had been repeatedly skimmed by the top family.

The same month, the SRSP held its third congress. The Central Committee was reshuffled and the president was nominated as the only candidate for another seven-year term. Thus, with a weak opposition divided along clan lines, which he skillfully exploited, Siad Barre seemed invulnerable well into 1988. The regime might have lingered indefinitely but for the wholesale disaffection engendered by the genocidal policies carried out against important lineages of Somali kinship groupings. These actions were waged first against the Majeerteen clan (of the Daarood clan-family), then against the Isaaq clans of the north, and finally against the Hawiye, who occupied the strategic central area of the country, which included the capital. The disaffection of the Hawiye and their subsequent organized armed resistance eventually caused the regime's downfall.

Persecution of the Majeerteen

In the aftermath of the Ogaden debacle, a group of disgruntled army officers attempted a coup d'état against the regime in April 1978. Their leader was Colonel Mahammad Shaykh Usmaan, a member of the Majeerteen clan. The coup failed and seventeen alleged ringleaders, including Usmaan, were summarily executed. All but one of the executed were of the Majeerteen clan. One of the plotters, Lieutenant Colonel Abdillaahi Yuusuf Ahmad, a Majeerteen, escaped to Ethiopia and founded an anti–Siad Barre organization initially called the Somali Salvation Front (SSDF; later the Somali Salvation Democratic Front, SSDF) (see Sources of Opposition , ch. 5). During their preeminence in the civilian regimes, the Majeerteen had alienated other clans. Thus, when Siad Barre sent the Red Berets against the Majeerteen in Mudug Region, other clans declined to support them.

The Red Berets systematically smashed the small reservoirs in the area around Galcaio so as to deny water to the Umar Mahamuud Majeerteen sublineages and their herds. In May and June 1979, more than 2,000 Umar Mahamuud, the Majeerteen sublineage of Colonel Ahmad, died of thirst in the waterless area northeast of Galcaio, Garoowe, and Jerriiban. In Galcaio, members of the Victory Pioneers, the urban militia notorious for harassing civilians, raped large numbers of Majeerteen women. In addition, the clan lost an estimated 50,000 camels, 10,000 cattle, and 100,000 sheep and goats.

Oppression of the Isaaq

The Isaaq as a clan–family occupy the northern portion of the country. Three major cities are predominantly, if not exclusively, Isaaq: Hargeysa, the second largest city in Somalia until it was razed during disturbances in 1988; Burao in the interior, also destroyed by the military; and the port of Berbera.

Formed in London on April 6, 1981, by 400 to 500 Isaaq emigrés, the Somali National Movement (SNM) remained an Isaaq clan–family organization dedicated to ridding the country of Siad Barre. The Isaaq felt deprived both as a clan and as a region, and Isaaq outbursts against the central government had occurred sporadically since independence. The SNM launched a military campaign in 1988, capturing Burao on May 27 and part of Hargeysa on May 31. Government forces bombarded the towns heavily in June, forcing the SNM to withdraw and causing more than 300,000 Isaaq to flee to Ethiopia.

The military regime conducted savage reprisals against the Isaaq. The same methods were used as against the Majeerteen— destruction of water wells and grazing grounds and raping of women. An estimated 5,000 Isaaq were killed between May 27 and the end of December 1988. About 4,000 died in the fighting, but 1,000, including women and children, were alleged to have been bayoneted to death.

Harrying of the Hawiye

The Hawiye occupy the south central portions of Somalia (see Samaal , ch. 2). The capital of Mogadishu is located in the country of the Abgaal, a Hawiye subclan. In numbers the Hawiye in Somalia are roughly comparable to the Isaaq, occupying a distant second place to the Daarood clans. Southern Somalia's first prime minister during the UN trusteeship period, Abdullaahi Iise, was a Hawiye; so was the trust territory's first president, Aadan Abdullah Usmaan. The first commander of the Somali army, General Daauud, was also a Hawiye. Although the Hawiye had not held any major office since independence, they had occupied important administrative positions in the bureaucracy and in the top army command.

In the late 1980s, disaffection with the regime set in among the Hawiye who felt increasingly marginalized in the Siad Barre regime. From the town of Beledweyne in the central valley of the Shabeelle River to Buulobarde, to Giohar, and in Mogadishu, the clan was subjected to ruthless assault. Government atrocities inflicted on the Hawiye were considered comparable in scale to those against the Majeerteen and Isaaq. By undertaking this assault on the Hawiye, Siad Barre committed a fatal error. By the end of 1990, he still controlled the capital and adjacent regions but by alienating the Hawiye, Siad Barre turned his last stronghold into enemy territory.

Faced with saboteurs by day and sniper fire by night, Siad Barre ordered remaining units of the badly demoralized Red Berets to massacre civilians. By 1989 torture and murder became the order of the day in Mogadishu. On July 9, 1989, Somalia's Italian–born Roman Catholic bishop, Salvatore Colombo, was gunned down in his church in Mogadishu by an unknown assassin. The order to murder the bishop, an outspoken critic of the regime, was widely believed to have had come from the presidential palace.

On the heels of the bishop's murder came the infamous July 14 massacre, when the Red Berets slaughtered 450 Muslims demonstrating against the arrest of their spiritual leaders. More than 2,000 were seriously injured. On July 15, forty–seven people, mainly from the Isaaq clan, were taken to Jasiira Beach west of the city and summarily executed. The July massacres prompted a shift in United States policy as the United States began to distance itself from Siad Barre.

With the loss of United States support, the regime grew more desperate. An anti–Siad Barre demonstration on July 6, 1990, at a soccer match in the main stadium deteriorated into a riot, causing Siad Barre's bodyguard to panic and open fire on the demonstrators. At least sixty–five people were killed. A week later, while the city reeled from the impact of what came to be called the Stadia Corna Affair, Siad Barre sentenced to death 46 prominent members of the Manifesto Group, a body of 114 notables who had signed a petition in May calling for elections and improved human rights. During the contrived trial that resulted in the death sentences, demonstrators surrounded the court and activity in the city came to a virtual halt. On July 13, a shaken Siad Barre dropped the charges against the accused. As the city celebrated victory, Siad Barre, conceding defeat for the first time in twenty years, retreated into his bunker at the military barracks near the airport to save himself from the people's wrath.

* * * Little literature exists on the history of Somalia. In his monumental three–volume work, *Somalia: Scritti Vari Editi ed Inediti*, Enrico Cerulli provided the research on which most subsequent writers have relied. I M.

Lewis, the prolific dean of English–speaking Somalists, offers a valuable survey in *A Modern History of Somalia*, revised and updated in 1988 to cover the 1970s and early 1980s. With *The Shaping of Somali Society*, Lee Cassanelli has produced the first book–length study of precolonial Somali history.

An excellent reference work is Margaret Castagno's *Historical Dictionary of Somalia*. Robert Hess's *Italian Colonialism in Somalia* offers a detailed review of the Italian colonial period in the south.

Douglas Jardine's *Mad Mullah of Somali Land* remains the classic biography of Sayyid Mahammad Abdille Hasan, the mystic, poet, and warrior leader of the Somali dervish anticolonial movement. Said S. Samatar's *Oral Poetry and Somali Nationalism* analyzes Mahammad Abdille's poetry and assesses his nationalist and literary contributions to the Somali heritage. I M. Lewis's *A Pastoral Democracy* and David Laitin's *Politics, Language, and Thought: The Somali Experience* stand as invaluable contributions to an understanding of the social and cultural aspects of Somali history. The origins and growth of Somali nationalist sentiment and political struggles are treated in Saadia Touval's *Somali Nationalism*.

Somali irredentism is treated in historical context by John Drysdale's *The Somali Dispute*. Tom Farer's *War Clouds on the Horn of Africa* deals with the same subject from a vantage point less sympathetic to Somali revolutionaries. I M. Lewis draws on his great knowledge of Somali society and politics to analyze the background and initial consequences of the military coup in the "The Politics of the 1969 Somali Coup,"

whereas David Laitin considers the ongoing development of the coup in "Somalia's Military Government and Scientific Socialism." Both pieces appear in *Socialism in Sub–Saharan Africa*.

Laitin and Samatar's *Somalia: Nation in Search of a State* provides a detailed analysis of the degeneration of the Somali revolution into a brutal dictatorship. Samatar's *Somalia: A Nation in Turmoil*, published as the Minority Rights Group Report by the London–based organization in August 1991, treats Siad Barre's reign of terror, his precipitous fall from power, and the collapse of the Somali state into separate regions ruled by clan–affiliated political groups. (For further information and complete citations, see Bibliography.)

Chapter 2. The Society and Its Environemnt

Somali nomad, symbol of the country's predominantly pastoral life ThE SOMALIS ARE A

Somalia, a country study

CULTURALLY, linguistically, and religiously homogeneous people, who are divided along clan lines and sparsely scattered over a harsh, dry land. There are significant distinctions among sectors of the population, related in part to variations in means of livelihood. In the early 1990s, roughly 60 percent of an estimated population of more than 8.4 million were still nomadic pastoralists or seminomadic herders, subject to the vicissitudes of an arid climate. Twenty to 25 percent of the people were cultivators, most living in the southern half of the country, on or between Somalia's two major rivers, the Jubba and the Shabeelle. The remainder were town dwellers, the vast majority of whom resided in Somalia's capital, Mogadishu.

With the fall of General Mahammad Siad Barre's regime on January 27, 1991, and the ensuing internal warfare that resulted in the disintegration of the Somali state, patterns of residency changed dramatically. For instance, the population of Mogadishu, estimated at 500,000 in the mid–1980s, witnessed the influx of thousands of refugees. As a result, Mogadishu reportedly had about 2 million inhabitants in early 1992.

Throughout the country the civil war, along with the lawlessness as Siad Barre's regime collapsed and the absence of functioning governmental and social institutions, produced a chaotic situation.

Although 95 percent of the population are ethnic Somalis, sharing a common culture, in traditional society they segmented themselves into a hierarchical system of patrilineal descent groups, each said to originate with a single male ancestor. The most comprehensive of these groups were the six clan–families (see Glossary).

Their constituent units were the clans (see Glossary), which in turn were made up of lineages (see Glossary), which themselves were further segmented. Among the sedentary interriverine Somalis, however, descent gave way in part to territoriality as a framework for social, political, and economic organization.

Membership in clans and lineages shaped the allocation of individual rights and obligations. The principle of descent, however, was modified (although rarely overridden) by Somali *heer*, or traditional jurisprudence.

Contracts or treaties bound specified descent groups and their individual members together for the making of war and peace and, above all, for the provision of compensation in cases of homicide and injury.

The Somali social order has been marked by competition and often by armed conflict between clans and lineages, even between units of the same clan–family or clan. Within each unit, Somali males considered better warriors, wiser arbiters, or abler speakers commanded greater respect in council. However, pastoral Somalis looked down on sedentary ones, and both looked down on non–Somali clients (see Glossary) of the sedentary Somalis and members of despised occupational groups such as hunters and smiths, who made up, however, only a very small proportion of the population.

The segmented social order, with relatively minor modifications, was carried into the independence period. In a very poor country, many Somalis were disaffected by the competition for power and wealth that often took the form of shifting alliances and conflicts between greater and lesser clans and lineage segments.

Simultaneously, new cleavages emerged between educated urban dwellers who had mastered a foreign language and the less–sophisticated rural Somalis.

Soon after the October 1969 military coup, Siad Barre's socialist government aimed an attack at the traditional system. In principle at least, his regime reduced the significance of clans and lineages, encouraged women to participate in government and attend school, and sanctioned the social equality of lowstatus groups. The gap that had opened between educated Englishor Italian–speaking Somalis and the rest of the population was reduced somewhat by the institution of a Somali script and the designation of Somali as the official language.

Siad Barre's government insisted that socialism was compatible with Islam, the religion of the overwhelming majority of Somalis. Although Somalis had not always conformed to the rigors of orthodox Islam, their identity was bound up with being Muslim. With few, if any, exceptions leaders of the socialist regime were Muslims and did not attack religion. However, they also did not hesitate to institute reforms that displeased conservative Muslim leaders.

Despite government encouragement of change, clan and lineage remained important throughout Siad Barre's rule, and Siad Barre remained in power by manipulating clans and clan leaders. In fact, soon after the revolution, kinship considerations and nepotism were evident at the highest levels of the regime.

The workings of the lineage system were predicated on the solidarity of the segments of the same order with one another and the relative equality of the members of each segment. The growth of the state and the development of different degrees of wealth and access to other private–sector resources caused an incipient stratification that had the potential to override lineage solidarity as it diminished equality.

PHYSICAL SETTING

Figure 3. Topography and Drainage Mountains near Merca, southwest of Mogadishu Courtesy Hiram A Ruiz Mountains west of Mogadishu, midway toward Luuq Courtesy Hiram A. Ruiz A rica's easternmost country, Somalia has a land area of 637,540 square kilometers, slightly less than that of the state of Texas. Somalia occupies the tip of a region commonly referred to as the Horn of Africa—because of its resemblance on the map to a rhinoceros's horn—that also includes Ethiopia and Djibouti.

Somalia's terrain consists mainly of plateaus, plains, and highlands. In the far north, however, the rugged east–west ranges of the Karkaar Mountains lie at varying distances from the Gulf of Aden coast (see fig. 3).

The weather is hot throughout the year, except at the higher elevations in the north. Rainfall is sparse, and most of Somalia has a semiarid–to– arid environment suitable only for the nomadic pastoralism practiced by well over half the population. Only in limited areas of moderate rainfall in the northwest, and particularly in the southwest, where the country's two perennial rivers are found, is agriculture practiced to any extent.

The local geology suggests the presence of valuable mineral deposits. As of 1992, however, only a few significant sites had been located, and mineral extraction played a very minor role in the economy (see Undeveloped Sectors , ch. 3).

Somalia's long coastline (3,025 kilometers) has been of importance chiefly in permitting trade with the Middle East and the rest of East Africa. The exploitation of the shore and the continental shelf for fishing and other purposes had barely begun by the early 1990s.

Sovereignty was claimed over territorial waters up to 200 nautical miles.

Climate

Climate is the primary factor in much of Somali life. For the large nomadic population, the timing and amount of rainfall are crucial determinants of the adequacy of grazing and the prospects of relative prosperity. During droughts such as occurred during 1974–75 and 1984–85, starvation can occur. There are some indications that the climate has become drier in the last century and that the increase in the number of people and animals has put a growing burden on water and vegetation.

Somalis recognize four seasons, two rainy *(gu* and *day*) and two dry *(jiilaal* and *hagaa*). The *gu* rains begin in April and last until June, producing a fresh supply of pasture and for a brief period turning the desert into a flowering garden. Lush vegetation covers most of the land, especially the central grazing plateau where grass grows tall. Milk and meat abound, water is plentiful, and animals do not require much care. The clans, reprieved from four months' drought, assemble to engage alternately in banter and poetic exchange or in a new cycle of hereditary feuds. They also offer sacrifices to Allah and to the founding clan ancestors, whose blessings they seek. Numerous social functions occur: marriages are contracted, outstanding disputes are settled or exacerbated, and a person's age is calculated in terms of the number of *gus* he or she has lived. The *gu* season is followed by the *hagaa* drought (July–September) and the *hagaa* by the *day* rains (October–November). Next is *jiilaal* (December–March), the harshest season for pastoralists and their herds.

Most of the country receives less than 500 millimeters of rain annually, and a large area encompassing the northeast and much of northern Somalia receives as little as 50 to 150 millimeters. Certain higher areas in the north, however, record more than 500 millimeters a year, as do some coastal sites. The southwest receives 330 to 500 millimeters. Generally, rainfall takes the form of showers or localized torrential rains and is extremely variable.

Mean daily maximum temperatures throughout the country range from 30° C to 40° C, except at higher elevations and along the Indian Ocean coast. Mean daily minimum temperatures vary from 20° C to more than 30° C. Northern Somalia experiences the greatest temperature extremes, with readings ranging from below freezing in the highlands in December to more than 45° C in July in the coastal plain skirting the Gulf of Aden. The north's relative humidity ranges from about 40 percent in midafternoon to 85 percent at night, varying somewhat with the season. During the colder months, December to February, visibility at higher elevations is often restricted by fog.

Temperatures in the south are less extreme, ranging from about 20° C to 40° C. The hottest months are February through April. Coastal readings are usually five to ten degrees cooler than those inland. The coastal zone's relative humidity usually remains about 70 percent even during the dry seasons.

Terrain, Vegetation, and Drainage

Physiographically, Somalia is a land of limited contrast. In the north, a maritime plain parallels the Gulf of Aden coast, varying in width from roughly twelve kilometers in the west to as little as two kilometers in the east. Scrub–covered, semiarid, and generally drab, this plain, known as the *guban* (scrub land), is crossed by broad, shallow watercourses that are beds of dry sand except in the rainy seasons. When the rains arrive, the vegetation, which is a combination of low bushes and grass clumps, is quickly renewed, and for a time the *guban* provides some grazing for nomad livestock.

Inland from the gulf coast, the plain rises to the precipitous northward–facing cliffs of the dissected highlands.

These form the rugged Karkaar mountain ranges that extend from the northwestern border with Ethiopia eastward to the tip of the Horn of Africa, where they end in sheer cliffs at Caseyr. The general elevation along the crest of these mountains averages about 1,800 meters above sea level south of the port town of Berbera, and eastward from that area it continues at 1,800 to 2,100 meters almost to Caseyr. The country's highest point, Shimber Berris, which rises to 2,407 meters, is located near the town of Erigavo.

Southward the mountains descend, often in scarped ledges, to an elevated plateau devoid of perennial rivers.

This region of broken mountain terrain, shallow plateau valleys, and usually dry watercourses is known to the Somalis as the Ogo.

In the Ogo's especially arid eastern part, the plateau— broken by several isolated mountain ranges—gradually slopes toward the Indian Ocean and in central Somalia constitutes the Mudug Plain. A major feature of this eastern section is the long and broad Nugaal Valley, with its extensive network of intermittent seasonal watercourses. The eastern area's population consists mainly of pastoral nomads. In a zone of low and erratic rainfall, this region was a major disaster area during the great drought of 1974 and early 1975.

The western part of the Ogo plateau region is crossed by numerous shallow valleys and dry watercourses.

Annual rainfall is greater than in the east, and there are flat areas of arable land that provide a home for dryland cultivators. Most important, the western area has permanent wells to which the predominantly nomadic population returns during the dry seasons. The western plateau slopes gently southward and merges imperceptibly into an area known as the Haud, a broad, undulating terrain that constitutes some of the best grazing lands for Somali nomads, despite the lack of appreciable rainfall more than half the year. Enhancing the value of the Haud are the natural depressions that during periods of rain become temporary lakes and ponds.

The Haud zone continues for more than sixty kilometers into Ethiopia, and the vast Somali Plateau, which lies between the northern Somali mountains and the highlands of southeast Ethiopia, extends south and eastward through Ethiopia into central and southwest Somalia. The portion of the Haud lying within Ethiopia was the subject of an agreement made during the colonial era permitting nomads from British Somaliland to pasture their herds there. After Somali independence in 1960, it became the subject of Somali claims and a source of considerable regional strife (see Pan–Somalism , ch. 1).

Southwestern Somalia is dominated by the country's only two permanent rivers, the Jubba and the Shabeelle.

With their sources in the Ethiopian highlands, these rivers flow in a generally southerly direction, cutting wide valleys in the Somali Plateau as it descends toward the sea; the plateau's elevation falls off rapidly in this area.

The adjacent coastal zone, which includes the lower reaches of the rivers and extends from the Mudug Plain to the Kenyan border, averages 180 meters above sea level.

The Jubba River enters the Indian Ocean at Chisimayu. Although the Shabeelle River at one time apparently also reached the sea near Merca, its course is thought to have changed in prehistoric times. The Shabeelle now turns southwestward near Balcad (about thirty kilometers north of Mogadishu) and parallels the coast for more than eighty–five kilometers. The river is perennial only to a point southwest of Mogadishu; thereafter it consists of swampy areas and dry reaches and is finally lost in the sand east of Jilib, not far from the Jubba River. During the flood seasons, the Shabeelle River may fill its bed to a point near Jilib and occasionally may even break through to the Jubba River farther south. Favorable rainfall and soil conditions make the entire riverine region a fertile agricultural area and the center of the country's largest sedentary population.

In most of northern, northeastern, and north–central Somalia, where rainfall is low, the vegetation consists of scattered low trees, including various acacias, and widely scattered patches of grass. This vegetation gives way to a combination of low bushes and grass clumps in the highly arid areas of the northeast and along the Gulf of Aden.

As elevations and rainfall increase in the maritime ranges of the north, the vegetation becomes denser. Aloes are common, and on the higher plateau areas of the Ogo are woodlands. At a few places above 1,500 meters, the remnants of juniper forests (protected by the state) and areas of *candelabra euphorbia* (a chandelier–type cactus) occur. In the more arid highlands of the northeast, boswellia and commiphora trees are sources, respectively, of the frankincense and myrrh for which Somalia has been known since ancient times.

A broad plateau encompassing the northern city of Hargeysa, which receives comparatively heavy rainfall, is covered naturally by woodland (much of which has been degraded by overgrazing) and in places by extensive grasslands. Parts of this area have been under cultivation since the 1930s, producing sorghum and corn; in the 1990s it constituted the only significant region of sedentary cultivation outside southwestern Somalia.

The Haud south of Hargeysa is covered mostly by a semiarid woodland of scattered trees, mainly acacias, underlain by grasses that include species especially favored by livestock as forage. As the Haud merges into the Mudug Plain in central Somalia, the aridity increases and the vegetation takes on a subdesert character.

Farther southward the terrain gradually changes to semiarid woodlands and grasslands as the annual precipitation increases.

The region encompassing the Shabeelle and Jubba rivers is relatively well watered and constitutes the country's most arable zone. The lowland between the rivers supports rich pasturage. It features arid to subarid savanna, open woodland, and thickets that include frequently abundant underlying grasses. There are areas of grassland, and in the far southwest, near the Kenyan border, some dry evergreen forests are found.

Along the Indian Ocean from Mereeg, about 150 kilometers northeast of Mogadishu, southwestward to near Chisimayu lies a stretch of coastal sand dunes. This area is covered with scattered scrub and grass clumps where rainfall is sufficient. Overgrazing, particularly in the area between Mogadishu and Chisimayu, has resulted in the destruction of the protective vegetation cover and the gradual movement of the once–stationary dunes inland. Beginning in the early 1970s, efforts were made to stabilize these dunes by replanting.

Other vegetation includes plants and grasses found in the swamps into which the Shabeelle River empties most of the year and in other large swamps in the course of the lower Jubba River. Mangrove forests are found at points along the coast, particularly from Chisimayu to near the Kenyan border. Uncontrolled exploitation appears to have caused some damage to forests in that area. Other mangrove forests are located near Mogadishu and at a number of places along the northeastern and northern coasts.

POPULATION AND SETTLEMENT PATTERNS

Mangrove swamp near Chisimayu; in rainy season dense roots protect coastal area from erosion Courtesy Hiram A. Ruiz S malia's first national census was taken in February 1975, and as of mid–1992 no further census had been conducted. In the absence of independent verification, the reliability of the 1975 count has been questioned because those conducting it may have overstated the size of their own clans and lineage groups to augment their allocations of political and economic resources. The census nonetheless included a complete enumeration in all urban and settled rural areas and a sample enumeration of the nomadic population. In the latter case, the sampling units were chiefly watering points. Preliminary results of that census were made public as part of the Three–Year Plan, 1979–81, issued by the Ministry of National Planning in existence at the time. (Because the Somali state had disintegrated and the government's physical infrastructure had been destroyed, no ministry of planning, or indeed any other government ministry, existed in mid–1992.) Somali officials suggested that the 1975 census undercounted the nomadic population substantially, in part because the count took place during one of the worst droughts in Somalia's recorded history, a time when many people were moving in search of food and water.

The total population according to the 1975 census was 3.3 million. The United Nations (UN) estimated Somalia's population in mid–1991 at nearly 7.7 million. Not included were numerous refugees who had fled from the Ogaden (Ogaadeen) in Ethiopia to Somalia beginning in the mid–1970s (see Refugees , this ch.).

The Ministry of National Planning's preliminary census data distinguished three main categories of residents:

nomads, settled farmers, and persons in nonagricultural occupations. Settled farmers lived in permanent settlements outside the national, regional, and district capitals, although some of these were in fact pastoralists, and others might have been craftsmen and small traders. Those living in urban centers were defined as nonagricultural regardless of their occupations. In 1975 nomads constituted nearly 59 percent of the population, settled persons nearly 22 percent, and nonagricultural persons more than 19 percent. Of the population categorized as nomads, about 30 percent were considered seminomadic because of their relatively permanent settlements and shorter range of seasonal migration.

Various segments of the population apparently increased at different rates. The nomadic population grew at less than 2 percent a year, and the seminomadic, fully settled rural and urban populations (in that order) at higher rates—well over 2.5 percent in the case of the urban population. These varied rates of growth coupled with increasing urbanization and the efforts, even if of limited success, to settle nomads as cultivators or fishermen were likely to diminish the proportion of nomads in the population.

The 1975 census did not indicate the composition of the population by age and sex. Estimates suggested, however, that more than 45 percent of the total was under fifteen years of age, only about 2 percent was over sixty–five years, and that there were more males than females among the nomadic population and proportionately fewer males in urban areas.

Population densities varied widely. The areas of greatest rural density were the settled zones adjacent to the Jubba and Shabeelle rivers, a few places between them, and several small areas in the northern highlands. The most lightly populated zones (fewer than six persons per square kilometer) were in northeastern and central Somalia, but there were some sparsely populated areas in the far southwest along the Kenyan border.

The nomadic and seminomadic segments of the population traditionally engage in cyclical migrations related to the seasons, particularly in northern and northeastern Somalia. During the dry season, the nomads of the Ogo highlands and plateau areas in the north and the Nugaal Valley in the northeast generally congregate in villages or large encampments at permanent wells or other reliable sources of water. When the rains come, the nomads scatter with their herds throughout the vast expanse of the Haud, where they live in dispersed small encampments during the wet season, or as long as animal forage and water last. When these resources are depleted, the area empties as the nomads return to their home areas. In most cases, adult men and women and their children remain with the sheep, goats, burden camels, and, occasionally, cattle. Grazing camels are herded at some distance by boys and young unmarried men.

A nomadic population also inhabits the southwest between the Jubba River and the Kenyan border. Little is known about the migratory patterns or dispersal of these peoples.

Somalia's best arable lands lie along the Jubba and Shabeelle rivers and in the interriverine area. Most of the sedentary rural population resides in the area in permanent agricultural villages and settlements. Nomads are also found in this area, but many pastoralists engage part–time in farming, and the range of seasonal migrations is more restricted. After the spring rains begin, herders move from the river edge into the interior.

They return to the rivers in the dry season *(hagaa)*, but move again to the interior in October and November if the second rainy season *(day)* permits. They then retreat to the rivers until the next spring rains. The sedentary population was augmented in the mid–1970s by the arrival of more than 100,000 nomads who came from the drought–stricken north and northeast to take up agricultural occupations in the southwest. However, the 1980s saw some Somalis return to nomadism; data on the extent of this reverse movement remain unavailable.

The locations of many towns appear to have been determined by trade factors. The present–day major ports, which range from Chisimayu and Mogadishu in the southwest to Berbera and Saylac in the far northwest, were founded from the eighth to the tenth centuries A.D. by Arab and Persian immigrants. They became centers of commerce with the interior, a function they continued to perform in the 1990s, although some towns, such as Saylac, had declined because of the diminution of the dhow trade and repeated Ethiopian raids.

Unlike in other areas of coastal Africa, important fishing ports failed to develop despite the substantial piscine resources of the Indian Ocean and the Gulf of Aden. This failure appears to reflect the centuries–old Somali aversion to eating fish and the absence of any sizable inland market. Some of the towns south of Mogadishu have long been sites of non–Somali fishing communities, however. The fisheries' potential and the need to expand food production, coupled with the problem of finding occupations for nomads ruined by the 1974–75 drought, resulted in government incentives to nomad families to settle permanently in fishing cooperatives; about 15,000 nomads were reported established in such cooperatives in late 1975.

Present–day inland trading centers in otherwise sparsely populated areas began their existence as caravan crossing points or as regular stopping places along caravan routes. In some cases, the ready availability of water throughout the year led to the growth of substantial settlements providing market and service facilities to nomadic populations. One such settlement is Galcaio, an oasis in the Mudug Plain that has permanent wells.

The distribution of town and villages in the agricultural areas of the Jubba and Shabeelle rivers is related in part to the development of market centers by the sedentary population. But the origin of a considerable number of such settlements derives from the founding of agricultural religious communities *(jamaat)* by various Islamic brotherhoods during the nineteenth century. An example is the large town of Baardheere, on the Jubba River in the Gedo Region, which evolved from a *jamaa* founded in 1819 (see Religious Orders and the Cult of the Saints , this ch.). Hargeysa, the largest town in northern Somalia, also started as a religious community in the second half of the nineteenth century. However, growth into the country's second biggest city was stimulated mainly by its selection in 1942 as the administrative center for British Somaliland. In 1988 Hargeysa was virtually destroyed by troops loyal to Siad Barre in the course of putting down the Isaaq insurrection.

After the establishment of a number of new regions (for a total of sixteen as of early 1992, including Mogadishu) and districts (second order administrative areas—sixty–nine as of 1989 plus fifteen in the capital region), the government defined towns to include all regional and district headquarters regardless of size.

(When the civil war broke out in 1991, the regional administrative system was nullified and replaced by one based on regional clan groups.) Also defined as towns were all other communities having populations of 2,000 or more. Some administrative headquarters were much smaller than that. Data on the number of communities specified as urban in the 1975 census were not available except for the region of Mogadishu. At that time, the capital had 380,000 residents, slightly more than 52 percent of all persons in the category of "nonagricultural"

(taken to be largely urban). Only three other regions—Woqooyi Galbeed, Shabeellaha Hoose, and the Bay—had urban populations constituting 7 to 9 percent of the total urban population in 1975. The sole town of importance in Woqooyi Galbeed Region at that time was Hargeysa. Berbera was much smaller, but as a port on the Gulf of Aden it had the potential to grow considerably. The chief town in Shabeellaha Hoose Region was Merca, which was of some importance as a port. There were several other port towns, such as Baraawe, and some inland communities that served as sites for light manufacturing or food processing. In the Bay Region the major towns, Baidoa and Buurhakaba, were located in relatively densely settled agricultural areas. There were a few important towns in other regions: the port of Chisimayu in Jubbada Hoose and Dujuuma in the agricultural area of Jubbada Dhexe.

THE SEGMENTARY SOCIAL ORDER

Figure 4. Major Clan—Families and Clans Design of village huts varies according to ethnic group.

Courtesy Hiram A. Ruiz Design of village huts varies according to ethnic group.

Courtesy Hiram A. Ruiz Baobab tree, a welcome source of shade, with village huts nearby,near Luuq Courtesy Hiram A. Ruiz E hnic Somalis are united by language, culture, devotion to Islam, and to a common ancestor, the Samaale, or Samaal. Genealogical ties have also provided the basis on which divisions among Somalis have occurred, division historically being more common than unity.

The overwhelming majority of Somalis trace their genealogical origin to the mythical founding father, Samaale or Samaal. Even those clan—families, such as the Digil and Rahanwayn in southern Somalia, whose members in many cases do not trace their lineage directly to Samaal, readily identify themselves as Somalis, thereby accepting the primacy of Samaal as the forebear of the Somali people. By language, traditions, and way of life, the Somalis share kinship with other members of the Eastern Cushitic groups of the Horn of Africa, including the Oromo, who constitute roughly 50 percent of the population of Ethiopia; the Afar (Danakil), who straddle the Great Rift Valley between Ethiopia and Djibouti; the Beja tribes of eastern Sudan; and the Reendille (Rendilli) and Boni (Aweera) peoples of northeastern Kenya (see The Somalis: Their Origins, Migrations, and Settlement , ch. 1).

Genealogy constitutes the heart of the Somali social system. It is the basis of the collective Somali inclination toward internal fission and internecine conflict, as well as of the Somalis' sense of being distinct—a consciousness of otherness that borders on xenophobia.

The major branches of the Somali lineage system are four overwhelmingly pastoral nomadic clan—families (the Dir, Daarood, Isaaq, and Hawiye, who are collectively denoted by the appellation of Samaal), and two agricultural ones (the Digil and Rahanwayn) (see fig. 4). As Israeli political scientist Saadia Touval noted in his brief study of Somali nationalism, these six clan–families correspond to the "Old Testament version of the tribal segmentation of the children of Israel." Like the children of Israel, the children of Samaale, with minor exceptions, are politically acephalous and prone to internal schism and factionalism. Although the modern Somali state, which is largely a creation of European colonialism, tried vainly to exercise a measure of centralized authority through the armed forces and the civilian bureaucracy, most Somalis continued to give greater political and emotional allegiance to their lineages. In 1992 the centralized state constructed on the Somali Peninsula had all but disintegrated into its constituent lineages and clans, whose internecine wars were drenching the country in bloodshed.

The Dir, Daarood, Isaaq, and Hawiye, which together make up the Samaal clans, constitute roughly 75 percent of the population. Most Samaal clans are widely distributed pastoralists, although a growing minority of them are settled cultivators. The Digil and Rahanwayn constitute about 20 percent of the population. They are settled in the riverine regions of southern Somalia and rely on a mixed economy of cattle and camel husbandry and cultivation.

Clan–families, too large and scattered for practical cooperation, in the past had no real political or economic functions. However, with the renewal and intensification of clan feuding in the wake of Siad Barre's fall from power in early 1991, the clan–families assumed crucial significance as nascent political parties pitted against one another along tribal lines in a disastrous civil war (see Lineage Segmentation and the Somali Civil War , this ch.). Membership in clan–families, primary lineages, and clans was traced through males from a common male ancestor.

Descent as the basis of group formation and loyalty was modified, but not overridden, by the principle of *heer*. Membership in the same clan or lineage did not automatically entail certain rights and obligations. These were explicitly the subject of treaties or contracts. Thus, some clans in a clanfamily might unite for political and military purposes, and some lineages within a clan might associate to pay and receive blood compensation in cases of homicide, injury, and other offenses. These alignments had a kinship base in that members often descended from a particular wife of a common ancestor, but units formed by contract or treaty could be dissolved and new ones formed.

The traditional social structure was characterized by competition and conflict between descent groups. Among the Samaal, the search for pasture and water drove clans and

114

lineages physically apart or pitted them against each other. The Digil and Rahanwayn (cultivators of the south) had a history of warfare over trade and religious matters and of fighting the encroachments of camel–herding nomads.

Whatever their common origin, the Samaal and the Digil and Rahanwayn evolved differently as they adapted to different physical environments. With some exceptions, the Samaal lived in areas that supported a pastoralism based mainly on camels, sheep, and goats. The Digil and Rahanwayn lived in the area between the rivers where they raised cattle and came to enslave the nonSomali cultivators who were there when they arrived. After the demise of slavery in the 1920s, the Digil and Rahanwayn themselves undertook cultivation.

The Samaal considered themselves superior to settled Somalis. Lineage remained the focal point of loyalty for pastoral nomads. The Digil and Rahanwayn developed a heterogeneous society that accorded status to different groups on the basis of origin and occupation. Group cohesion developed a territorial dimension among the settled agriculturists.

Relations between and within groups underwent changes during the colonial era and after independence.

Armed conflict between descent groups (or in the south, territorial units) became rare during the two decades (the 1960s and 1970s) following independence. However, in the 1980s and early 1990s, as President Siad Barre incited and inflamed clan rivalries to divert public attention from the problems of his increasingly unpopular regime, Somali society began to witness an unprecedented outbreak of inter– and intra–clan conflicts. The basic modes of social organization and relations persisted, however, particularly among the pastoral nomads. Moreover, national politics were often operated in terms of relationships between segments of various kinds.

Several thousand persons, including some ethnic Somalis, were integrated into traditional society but were not included in the six clan–families. Among them were Somali clans descended from ancestors predating or otherwise missing from the genealogies of the six clan–families. Others were lineages of relatively unmixed Arab or Persian descent, often much inbred; most members of these groups lived in the coastal towns. Such lineages or communities had varying relationships with local Somalis. Some were clients subordinate to Somali groups; others were independent entities in the larger towns. A second category consisted of the so–called *habash*, or *adoon*, cultivators or hunters of preSomali origin who lived among the Rahanwayn and Digil in the interriverine area. A third category consisted of occupationally specialized caste–like groups, members of which were attached to Somali lineages or clans. Finally, until the last were freed in the 1920s, there was a small number of slaves attached to both pastoral and sedentary Somali groups, but of greater economic importance among the latter.

Samaal

Among the Samaal clans were the largest political units, most of which had heads known as *soldaan* (sultan)

or *bokor* (concept derived from a belt binding people together). With few exceptions, a nomadic clan head's functions were honorary and ceremonial. The number and size of clans within a clan–family varied; the average clan in the twentieth century numbered about 100,000 people. Clans controlled a given territory, essentially defined by the circuit of nomadic migration but having unspecified boundaries, so that the territories of neighboring clans tended to overlap.

A Samaal clan kept count of the generations between living members of the group and the ancestor for whom it was named; the greater the number of generations (which often implied substantial internal segmentation into subclans or lineages) the greater the clan's prestige. Some ancient clans dwindled and found it necessary to attach themselves to other clans of the same or another clan–family. Similarly, lineages detached from the main body of their clan would ally with the clan in whose territory they were then living.

Clans living in contiguous territories sometimes joined in confederacies often marked by internal subgroupings. The Majeerteen clan, for example, was part of the Kombe–Harti confederacy, which was in turn part of the Kablalla. A confederacy consisted of related clans, but the decision to enter into a confederacy would be the consequence of history rather than genealogy. The purposes of the confederacy would be enumerated in a treaty or contract, often set down by a religious figure in an early Arabic script version of Somali.

Clans were segmented into primary lineages whose genealogical depth ranged from twelve to fourteen generations. These lineages were in turn segmented into secondary and sometimes tertiary lineages. The process of internal segmentation was continuous. The political (and sometimes the economic) relevance of a clan or lineage of a given genealogical depth varied with the context. Somali lacked specific terms for different levels of segmentation. According to anthropologist I M. Lewis, an authority on pastoral Somalis, there are three "points of unity and division at which political solidarity most frequently emerges . . . those of clan, primary lineage group, and *diya* –paying group."

The *diya*–paying (see Glossary) group was an alliance formed by related lineages within a clan by means of a contract, traditionally oral but filed in written form with district officials during the colonial era, at least in British Somaliland. The contract explicitly stated the rights and duties of members of the group with respect to the burdens of payment and the distribution of receipts of blood compensation, that is, distribution of the camels or money received, when the parties were members of the same or different *diya* –paying groups. In the case of a homicide, the lineages of the group shared in giving or receiving a specified portion of the compensation. A smaller but still substantial portion (the *jiffo*) was given or received by the relatively close kin of the killer or the deceased, that is, by an agnatic group descended from a common ancestor three or four generations back. In the case of offenses requiring the payment of a smaller compensation, sharing still occurred within the *diya* –paying group, but in minor cases the *jiffo*–paying group alone might be involved.

The lineages constituting a *diya*–paying group were often secondary; that is, the ancestors of each were fewer than the twelve to fourteen characteristic of a primary lineage. If a group with a remote ancestor lacked the numbers to constitute its own *diya*–paying group, it might join with another such group to form one, thus minimizing the financial burden. Moreover, the ultimate traditional sanction was armed conflict, and here again lack of manpower was clearly a liability.

Both *diya*–paying and *jiffo*–paying groups were important units of social and economic organization aside from their stated purpose. They functioned as mutual aid groups in times of economic hardship or other emergencies. They established and enforced regulations. In 1964 it was estimated that more than 1,000 such groups existed in the republic. Among the nomads, membership ranged from 300 to more than 5,000 men and among the sedentary Somalis from 5,000 to 100,000 men.

The political and economic business of any functioning segment in Samaal society was managed by a council call a *shir*, which included all adult males in the group. Each member might speak and take part in deliberation. Age and seniority of lineage took precedence in that an older man or one from an older lineage would customarily be asked to speak before others did, but the opinions of a persuasive speaker, whatever his seniority, would be given added weight. A wealthy herder might also have a greater say. The term *oday* (elder) could be applied to any adult male, but those with more prestige and experience might be asked to arbitrate disputes over a wide area and act as ad hoc leaders in political matters.

In traditional society, most Samaal men lived as warriors and herders; a warrior *(waranle—*see Glossary)

considered his vocation nobler than any other except the religious life. A religious person (*wadad*; pl., *wadaddo—*see Glossary) was considered the equal of a warrior, but few Samaal committed themselves to a religious life. Many who did so retained their ties to clan and lineage, although in principle they were supposed to avoid partisanship and armed conflict. This rule did not pertain to jihad or religious warfare. A few *wadaddo* settled in religious communities.

Cultivating groups of Samaal origin resided in various places. These groups, which also kept livestock, were accepted as fellow Samaal by the pastoralists but were considered to have lost prestige, even if they had gained economically. Some Samaal attached themselves as cultivating clients to stockraising Digil or Rahanwayn in the riverine region; the Samaal usually ended such relationships when they could resume their pastoral activities or when the economic advantages of cultivation diminished. The lineage pattern remained intact among Samaal cultivators.

Digil and Rahanwayn

Some texts refer to these two mainly agriculturist clans of Digil and Rahanwayn as *Sab*. However, members of the Digil and Rahanwayn and most Somalis consider the appellation *Sab* derogatory. Used as a common noun meaning "ignoble," the term *sab* was applied by the Samaal to groups that pursued certain disdained occupations. The

Samaal felt that the Sab had lowered themselves by their reliance on agriculture and their readiness to assimilate foreign elements into their clans. Traditionally, the Rahanwayn are considered a Digil offshoot that became larger than the parent group.

The social structure of the Sab resembled that of the Samaal in that it was based on descent groups. However, there were significant differences. Sab clans were confederations of lineages and included persons originating in all–Somali clanfamilies as well as assimilated peoples. They came into being through a pact between the original founding segments, one of which, of Sab origin, was dominant; the name of the Sab segment became the name of the clan. By the twentieth century, the descendants of that dominant lineage often constituted only a relatively small core of the clan. The constituent lineages of the clan tended to have much shallower genealogies than the Samaal. Another important difference between the nomadic Samaal societies and the sedentary Sab was in the significance accorded to territoriality. Sab clans lived within distinct borders. The entire clan (or large subclan) often constituted the *diya*– paying group in relation to other clans. The term *reer*, which the Samaal used in connection with descent, was used by the Sab with a place name, e g., *reer barawa* ("children of Baraawe").

Many clans were segmented into three subclans, called *gember*, although some, such as the Jiddu clans of the Digil clan–family, had only two subclans. Clans and subclans usually had single heads. In some cases, however, as among the Helai clans of the Rahanwayn, there were no clan heads. Clan affairs were handled by leading elders called *gobweyn*, who had assistants called *gobyar*.

Clans and subclans were subdivided into lineages that reckoned three to five generations from ancestor to youngest member. The lineage traditionally owned land and water rights, which the head men distributed to individual lineage members.

The manner in which Sab clans were formed led to recognized social inequalities, sometimes marked by differences in physical appearance owing to intermarriage within a stratum. Each stratum in a community consisted of one or more lineages. The basic distinction was between nobles (free clansmen) and *habash*, a group made up of pre–Somali cultivators and freed slaves (see Riverine and Coastal People of Non–Somali Origin , this ch.).

In some Rahanwayn and Digil communities, there was a further distinction between two sets of nobles.

Within the Geledi clan (located in Afgooye, just north of Mogadishu, and its environs) studied by anthropologist Virginia Luling, the nobles were divided into Darkskin and Lightskin categories, designations corresponding to the physical appearance of their members. The Darkskins were descendants of the core or founding group of the Geledi; the Lightskins had a separate line of descent, claimed partly Arab origin, and resembled the Arab populations of the old coastal towns. They had been completely Somalized, however. The wealth and position of the Lightskins were similar to that of the Darkskins, but the latter had precedence in certain traditional rites.

Each lineage (which consisted of perhaps 300 to 400 persons), or Darkskins, Lightskins, and *habash,* had its own set of elders and constituted a *diya*–paying group vis–à–vis the others, but was bound in a common contract concerning rates of compensation for injuries. In principle, *habash* lineages had equal rights under this system. Each lineage controlled specific segments of the land and allocated to an individual male as much as his family could cultivate. However, only the *habash* were subsistence cultivators in the nineteenth and the early twentieth centuries. The nobles, whether Darkskins or Lightskins, cultivated much larger areas by means of slave labor and exported surpluses via the coastal ports to Arab lands. In the case of the Geledi, wealth accrued to the nobles and to the sultan not only from market cultivation but also from involvement in the slave trade and other enterprises, such as commerce in ivory, cotton, and iron. The Geledi also raised cattle.

The sultan of the Geledi (a member of the Darkskin stratum) had a political and religious role. He also wielded somewhat greater authority than the sultans of the Samaal clans, but this authority was by no means absolute.

The sociopolitical organization and processes of the Geledi resembled those of many Digil and Rahanwayn communities. Not all such communities had a Lightskin component, and many were not located as auspiciously as the Geledi, for whom trade developed as a major economic factor. Most, however, had slaves who worked the land of the nobles.

The sedentary Somali communities in the coastal and interriverine areas, some of which were of Samaal origin, were more strongly affected by the advent of European colonization than the nomadic pastoralists were. Clans, and occasionally large lineages, came to have government chiefs appointed by colonial authorities, sometimes where there had been no chiefs of any kind. For the Geledi, the most important such chief was the sultan. Whatever his origin, the government–appointed chief was expected to be the intermediary between the colonial government and the people.

The abolition of the slave trade and the outlawing of slavery by 1920 changed not only the lives of the slaves but also the position of the nobles whose economic and political power depended on the slave economy. In Geledi areas and elsewhere, many slaves left to take up other land as subsistence cultivators. A few remained, and their descendants maintained a quasi–dependent relationship as clients of their former masters. By the second decade of the twentieth century, nobles were faced for the first time with having to cultivate their own land. None of the groups—nobles, *habash*, or ex–slaves—worked voluntarily for wages on the Italian plantations established at that time; colonial authorities usually made such labor mandatory.

Despite the radical social, political, and economic changes brought about by colonization, the nobles retained their superior position in Geledi (and probably in other Rahanwayn and Digil) communities. The nobles' status positioned them to profit from new income opportunities such as paid employment with the Italians or trade in the growing Afgooye market. They benefited from such business opportunities throughout the colonial period, as well as from educational and political opportunities, particularly during the trusteeship period (1950–60). Independence introduced still other changes to which the nobles responded (see Social Change , this ch.).

Riverine and Coastal People of Non–Somali Origin

Along the southern coast, in the valleys of the Jubba and Shabeelle rivers and in a few places between the rivers, live small groups—probably totaling less than 2 percent of the population—who differ culturally and physically from the Somalis. Some are descendants of pre–Somali inhabitants of the area who were able to resist absorption or enslavement by the Somalis. The ancestors of others were slaves who escaped to found their own communities or were freed in the course of European antislavery activity in the nineteenth century.

The Somali term for these people, particularly the riverine and interriverine cultivators, is *habash*.

The relations of the *habash* communities with neighboring Somali groups varied, but most have traditional attachments of some sort to a Somali lineage, and members of all but a few communities along the coast speak Somali as a first language. In earlier times, whereas some *habash* communities had considerable independence, in others *habash* were much like serfs cultivating land under the patronage of a Somali lineage.

In such cases, however, it was understood that *habash* could not be deprived of their land, and there was little reason for the pastoral Somalis to do so. Somalis and *habash* did not intermarry; nor would a Somali eat a meal prepared by *habash*. As these restrictions suggest, Somalis—whether Samaal or Sab—considered the *habash* their inferiors. Nevertheless, the political relationship of some *habash* groups to neighboring Somali groups was that of near–equals.

The attachment of *habash* groups to sections of Somali society usually entailed the participation of the *habash* c mmunity in the *diya*–paying group of Somali lineages or clans. Like the Somali, all but a few *habash* had been converted to Islam, and some of them had become leaders of religious communities in the interriverine area.

Most non–Somali peoples were primarily cultivators, but some, like the Eyle, also hunted, something the Somalis would not do. A few groups, including the Boni, remained primarily hunters into the twentieth century and were accordingly looked down on by the Somalis. By midcentury most of these peoples had turned to cultivation, and some had moved into the towns and become laborers.

Along the coast live the Bajuni and the Amarani. They are fishermen, sailors, and merchants, derived from a mixture of coastal populations. Their ancestors included Arab or Persian settlers and seafaring peoples of India and the East Indies. Both the Bajuni and the Amarani speak dialects of Swahili. The Amarani, who were estimated to number fewer than 1,000 in the early 1990s, inhabit small fishing communities in and near Baraawe, Mogadishu, Merca, and the inland town of Afgooye on the Shabeelle River.

The Bajuni inhabit the East African coast and Bajun Islands near Chisimayu in a continuous strip from Chisimayu southward into Kenya as far as Lamu, and maintain scattered communities as far away as Mozambique. Both the Amarani and the Bajuni have little contact with outsiders except in towns. Partial geographical isolation and an active ethnic consciousness distinguished by differences in languages separate them from the Somalis.

Specialized Occupational Groups

Certain occupational groups such as hunters, leatherdressers , and smiths are known as *sab* (ignoble) among the Samaal and as *bon* (low caste) among the Sab. They resemble Somalis, but their ethnic origin is uncertain.

Some authorities suggest—and group members believe—that they may be derived from the land's original population. They speak Somali, but also use local dialects.

In the late 1950s, when the Somali population was estimated at 2 million, the number of *sab* was estimated at more than 12,000, or less than 1 percent of the population. Of these, about three–quarters were of the *midgaan* (an appellation considered pejorative and ultimately legally forbidden) group whose men worked as barbers, circumcisers, and hunters. Less than a quarter of the total consisted of the Tumaal, who engaged chiefly in metalwork. The smallest group was the Yibir (Yahhar in the south), magicians called upon to make amulets for the newborn, bless Somali weddings, and act as soothsayers. In return for these services they would be given gifts.

Occupational groups had lineages, but these were not usually the foundation of *diya*–paying groups before Somalia's independence. Except perhaps for the Yibir, who moved from one group of Somalis to another, families of occupational specialists were attached to Somali lineages, which acted as their patrons and claimed compensation on their behalf. By the end of the colonial period, change had begun to take place in the political, legal, and social status of these groups.

Social Change

Colonial domination had various effects, such as the formal abolition of slavery in the years preceding World War II, particularly in the interriverine area. The effects of Western rule had a greater impact on the social and economic orders in urban than in rural areas. After World War II, the institution of the trusteeship in the Italian–administered south and greater attention to education in the British–run north gradually led to further change (see British Military Administration; Trusteeship and Protectorate , ch. 1).

The late colonial period and the first decade of independence saw the decline, in part legally enforced, of caste–like restrictions and impediments to the equality of *habash* and traditional occupational groups. In the south, although nobles were more likely to take advantage of educational opportunities, *habash* increasingly did so.

The growing importance of manual skills in the modern economy gave some occupational groups an economic, if not an immediate social, advantage. For example, many Tumaal blacksmiths became mechanics and settled in towns. In southern port towns, carpenters, weavers, and other artisans formed guilds to protect their common interests. As skilled manual work became more available and socially acceptable, tolerance of members of the traditional groups increased to the point where some intermarriage occurred in the towns. In the rural areas, members of these groups formed their own *diya*–paying units and in a few cases began to take part in the councils of the Somali lineages to which they remained attached.

Somali leaders tried to eliminate the traditional disabilities of low–status groups. In early 1960, just before independence, the legislative assembly of the Italian trust territory abolished the status of client, that is, of *habash* dependent on Somalis for land and water rights. The law stated that Somali citizens could live and farm where they chose, independent of hereditary affiliation. Patron lineages in the riverine area resisted the change and retaliated against *habash* assertions of independence. They withheld customary farming and watering rights, excluded *habash* from *diya*–paying arrangements, and, in some cases, sought to oust them from the land they had farmed for generations as clients. Some *habash* brought cases in court, seeking to affirm their new rights, but initially many continued to live under the old arrangements. Clientship appeared by the early 1990s to have diminished in fact as it had been abrogated in law.

Whereas some features of traditional stratification were eroded, new strata based on education and command of a foreign language—English or Italian—were forming in the late colonial period (see Education , this ch.).

With independence, a new elite arose as Somalis assumed the highest political and bureaucratic positions in national government. A subelite also emerged, consisting of persons with more modest educational qualifications who filled posts in local and regional government. In many cases, however, these government workers were the sons of men who had acquired a degree of wealth in nonprofessional activities such as landholding, trading, and herding, in part because the costs of secondary education in the colonial period could be met only by relatively affluent families.

Two somewhat contradictory forces affected educated urban Somalis in the 1950s and 1960s. On the one hand their income, education, and, above all, their literacy in a foreign language distanced them from most other Somalis. On the other hand, lineage and clan remained important to most of this new elite. Thus descent groups acquired a new importance in national politics.

Locally, particularly in the larger towns, a combination of outsiders and area residents provided middle–level administration. One administrative component would consist of members of the national subelite brought in by the Somali government. Typically, this group would include the district commissioner, the judge, the secretary to the municipality, the staff of some of these officials, teachers, and the national police. Locally elected councillors would constitute the other administrative component. Some councillors were lineage heads; others were businessmen or had some other basis for their local status. Some of the local notables had sons serving as district officials but, by regulation, not in their home communities. In Afgooye, a town in which the Geledi, the Wadaan (a group of the Hawiye clan–family), and others were represented, the local people and the subelite meshed well in the mid– and late 1960s, but Afgooye was not necessarily representative of local communities in the riverine areas or elsewhere.

Beginning in the nineteenth century, there was a growing distinction between the bulk of nomadic Somalis and their kinsmen in the towns acting as middlemen in the livestock trade with Aden. Some of these townsmen became relatively wealthy and appeared to have more influence in council than their pastoralist relatives.

By the 1960s, the demand for livestock in the Middle East had led to a great expansion of the livestock trade through the port of Berbera. Hargeysa and Burao became the points from which 150 to 200 major livestock dealers and their agents—all but a few of them Somalis—operated. The nomadic producers directed their activity toward the commercial market, but the traders controlled the terms of trade, the feedlots, and some of the better grazing land. The government did not interfere because the livestock trade was too important as a source of foreign exchange, and because the traders marketed the animals efficiently.

A new class of merchants thus emerged. They retained their connections with their lineages, but their interests differed from those of nomadic herders. If they were not educated, they tried to ensure that their children attended school.

After World War II and during the first decade of independence, the government stressed loyalty to the nation in place of loyalty to clan and lineage. The segmental system was seen as a divisive force, a source of nepotism and corruption; Somali politicians denounced it as "tribalism." A few Somalis rejected reference to clan and lineage. Nevertheless, persons meeting for the first time asked each other about their "ex–clans."

Clan–families, once functionally unimportant, became increasingly significant as political rallying points, particularly as Somalia approached independence, and they continued to be so in the 1990s. Clans and lineages remained the basic unit of society, serving many social, political, and economic functions regionally and locally. Although the Somali government opposed clans and lineages, it continued to appoint and pay lineage heads; lineages and clans were in fact voting blocs. Supreme Court decisions in 1962 and 1964 effected a major change in the role of the *diya*–paying group. The court's judgments forbade collective payment for premeditated homicide. Payments for unpremeditated homicide and injury, however, were defined as compensation for a tort and were permitted. In this era, too, the *diya*–paying group's responsibilities were extended to cover traffic fatalities.

The military leadership that took power in October 1969 introduced elements that constituted a radical break with the past. The new regime soon declared socialism as its frame of reference, in part as a means of obtaining Soviet aid (see Siad Barre and Scientific Socialism , ch. 1). The regime's basic ideas constituted a pragmatic version of Marxism adapted to local social and economic conditions. In this version, class struggle did not apply; the bourgeoisie was very small, composed of the new elite and subelite (chiefly employed in government), a few traders, and a few professionals. There was no significant proletariat, rural or urban, and no great Somali entrepreneurs or landholders.

In its initial zest for change, the new regime focused on the divisions in Somali society: the cleavages between clans and lineages, the settled and the nomadic, strong and weak pastoral lineages competing for grazing and water, patrons and clients in the cultivating regions, and urban and rural dwellers. Attention was also given to the continuing disdain shown to those of low status. Under the new regime, clan and lineage affiliations were irrelevant to social relations, and the use of pejorative labels to describe specific groups thought inferior to Somalis were forbidden. All Somalis were asked to call each other *jaalle* (comrade), regardless of hereditary affiliation.

Within limits the language of public discourse can be changed by fiat; much pejorative language was expurgated. Nevertheless, Somalis continued to learn each other's clan or lineage affiliation when it was useful to do so, and in private it was not uncommon for Somalis to refer to *habash* by the phrase "kinky hair."

The term *jaalle* was widely used in the media and in a range of public situations, but its use cannot be said to have reflected a change of perspective.

The government also sought to change the function of the clans and lineages by abolishing the title of *elder a* d replacing it with *peacekeeper*. Peacekeepers were the appointed spokesmen of what were officially regarded as local groups composed of either cultivators or pastoralists. In the early 1970s, collective responsibility *(diya* payment) in any guise was abolished.

Like most governments required to deal with a large nomadic population, the pre– and post–revolutionary regimes sought to find ways to settle the pastoralists, both to improve the pastoral economy and to facilitate control and services. Efforts to convert the nomads into ranchers made little progress, and in the early 1990s most herders were still nomadic or seminomadic. The 1974 drought, however, drove many nomads to seek government help; by 1975 about 105,000 had been resettled, 90,000 as cultivators and 15,000 as fishermen.

Clans were deliberately mixed within the settlements, and the settlers were expected to deal as individuals with local councils, committees, and courts, whose membership was also heterogeneous. Three years later, nearly 45 percent of the adult males had left the cultivating settlements, perhaps to resume herding. Most of those living in fishing communities remained. Neither the farmers nor the fishermen had been economically successful.

The dismantling of the *diya* system; the institution of several political and administrative offices intended to eliminate power vested in lineages and clans; and the establishment of committees, councils, and cooperatives were all part of a policy to replace the descent group system as the primary means of organizing political, economic, and social life. Another manifestation of this policy was the banning in 1972 of weddings, burials, and religious rites organized on a lineage or clan basis. Wedding ceremonies were henceforth to be held at orientation centers or other public places. Money could not be collected from lineage members for the burial of a dead member, and the law forbade religious rites tied to local traditions.

Most published observations refer to the continuing role of clan affiliation in national politics. The clan–family, which rose to considerable importance in Somali politics in the 1950s and 1960s, seemed in later years to lose its force as a rallying point. With the exception of northern Somalia's Isaaq people, the groups that exerted influence either for or against the regime were mostly of a single clan–family, the Daarood; President Mohammed Siad Barre's clan, Mareehaan; his mother's clan, Ogaden; his son–in–law's clan, Dulbahante; and the opposition clan, Majeerteen.

Among the revolutionary regime's concerns was the status of women. After World War II, all political parties had established women's committees. In the Italian–administered south, women voted for the first time in the 1958 municipal elections; in the formerly British north, women voted in the 1961 national referendum on the constitution. Women's role in public affairs remained minimal, however, and little was done to change their legal situation in the first decade of independence.

Under Somali customary law, a woman was under the legal protection of a male—her father or husband, or one of their kinsmen in the event of their deaths. In blood compensation, her life was usually valued at half that of a man. Islamic law permitted daughters to inherit half of what was inherited by sons, but in Somali practice daughters ordinarily did not share in the inheritance of valued property (camels or land). Few girls attended school and even fewer continued beyond the elementary level.

The revolutionary government quickly changed women's legal and political status. In principle, the question of *diya* payment for injuries to women became moot following the formal termination of the traditional system. Soon after the revolution, the government established committees to deal with women's affairs.

Women also began participating in government, committees, sports, and other social and cultural activities. In early 1975, Siad Barre announced a decision by the Supreme Revolutionary Council (SRC) and the Council of Ministers to give equal rights to women in several respects, including equal inheritance rights, a move that led to protests by some Islamic leaders (see Challenges to the Regime , ch. 1). Perhaps more important was the government's insistence that girls attend school, particularly beyond the elementary level.

There were women in visible public posts in Somalia in 1990. Until the 1991 collapse of the state, 6 of the 171 elected members of the People's Assembly were women. Increasing numbers of females were attending secondary school and university. Further progress for women was interrupted by the civil war and would have to await reconstruction of the country.

The Siad Barre government also acted in the economic sphere, fostering various government agencies at the national, regional, and local levels. The regime initiated some enterprises and placed others under state control. Much productive and distributive enterprise remained in private hands, however.

In the rural areas, the government (beginning with colonial administrations) and large–scale private farmers had acquired much of the irrigated land. In the late 1970s, small–scale farmers had worked some of the irrigated land and much of the flood land, but by the mid–1980s much of the latter had been converted to controlled irrigation and had come under state control. For the most part, rain–fed land cultivation remained in the hands of traditional smallholders engaged in subsistence farming, some of whom earned the cash they needed by working on state farms. Most extensions of the irrigation system facilitated development of large state farms, rather than small farms. Some rural Somalis held no land and relied on wage labor on state farms and large private holdings (chiefly banana plantations) for their livelihood.

Under Siad Barre's regime, animal husbandry remained primarily in the hands of individual pastoral Somalis.

The chief change lay in the readiness of these pastoralists to sell their livestock in response to overseas demand. Marketing was in the hands of private traders who had accumulated enough capital to construct water storage units and invest in a transport fleet. In addition, a number of traders had enclosed rangeland to produce hay, thereby excluding herders who formerly had used the land. These traders benefited not only from the government construction of roads and other facilities but also from arrangements whereby their overseas earnings might be used in part to buy imports for domestic sale.

Although income distinctions existed among Somalis in the private sphere, until 1991 those who combined comparatively large incomes with reasonable security were government employees such as administrators, technical personnel, and managers of state– owned enterprises. As under the first independence regime, administrators did not serve in their home territories and were therefore not linked by kinship to the more affluent Somalis in the local private sector.

Despite the otherwise fluid character of the system, the apex of the local hierarchy in a rural settled area consisted of the high–level (and to some extent the middle–level) representatives of the state. These included regional and local administrators, managers of state farms and agro–industries such as the sugar refinery at Giohar, technicians, and highly skilled workers. Members of this group had relatively high incomes and could be reasonably sure of seeing that their children finished school, an important prerequisite to finding a good position. Because they often determined the flow of resources to the private sector, this elite group exercised economic power greater than that of wealthy merchants or large landholders whose income might be the same as, or larger than, theirs.

At the bottom of the economic hierarchy were most rural Somalis, whether sedentary or nomadic. Living primarily by subsistence cropping or herding, they sold what they could. They had little contact with government and had been relatively untouched by development projects because of their isolation or insufficient government efforts to reach them. The farmers among them cultivated the poorest land and barely earned survival incomes with wage work. The pastoralists were most affected by the demands of a difficult environment. Beginning in the late 1970s, limits on migration resulting from hostile relations between Somalia and Ethiopia caused them additional hardship.

As of the early 1990s, two other significant categories of rural residents were workers whose wages derived from state–owned or state–sponsored activities, and landholders or herders who operated on a smaller scale than the plantation owners. Neither of these categories was homogeneous. Wage workers ranged from landless and relatively unskilled agricultural workers whose income might be intermittent, to low–level workers in government agencies whose income was likely to be steadier and who might be heads of or members of families with subsistence farms or herds. Plots or herds owned by farmers or herders varied considerably in size and quality, as did the income derived from them. Nevertheless farmers and herders fared better than subsistence farmers. They joined cooperatives, took advantage of adult education, and participated in government programs that promised to enhance their incomes and the status of the next generation.

Members of this category sent their children to school and arranged for some of them to seek more lucrative or prestigious employment in Mogadishu or other large towns.

Rural petty traders did not clearly belong to any one economic category. Their incomes were not large, but equaled those of many lower–level wage workers and small–scale market– oriented farmers.

Particularly in Mogadishu, the national capital and the largest town, another social pattern developed prior to the fall of the Siad Barre regime. Because of their incomes and the power they wielded, the highest party and government officials became the new apex of Somali society. In the early 1990s, the salaries and allowances of cabinet ministers were twice that of the next highest officials, the directors general of ministries, and nearly twenty–five times that of the lowest levels of the civil service. Below the ministers and directors general but well above the clerks of the bureaucracy were other high–level administrators, executives, and skilled personnel. For instance, the manager of a large state–owned factory earned somewhat less than a minister but more than a director general. An unskilled laborer in a state farm earned less than the poorest–paid civil servant, but an unskilled worker in a factory earned a little more. Unskilled farm and factory workers and bottom–level government employees earned only 5 to 10 percent of a manager's salary.

As in the rural areas, in the towns there were many people involved in the private sector. In some respects, merchants and traders had the deepest urban roots. Most of them were petty traders and shopkeepers whose income and status were closer to those of craftsmen than to those of the wealthier merchants.

In the mid–1970s, a manufacturing census indicated that about 6,000 enterprises in Somalia employed five or fewer persons, most of them probably family members. Unlike the larger, often foreign–owned industrial concerns, these had not been nationalized.

Most urban dwellers were wage workers, but they had various skills, sources of employment, and incomes.

For example, low– and middle–level clerks in the government bureaucracy and in state enterprises earned no more (and sometimes less) than skilled artisans in state firms, and both earned perhaps twice as much as unskilled factory laborers.

The situation of the urban population had changed radically by early 1992. Following the fall of Siad Barre, urban areas consisted largely of refugees or war victims who had migrated from the countryside after the civil war began.

LINEAGE SEGMENTATION AND THE SOMALI CIVIL WAR

From the early 1980s to the early 1990s, Somali society underwent a profound crisis—of identity, purpose, and direction—that threatened its very existence. As a result of its humiliating 1977–78 defeat in the Ogaden War with Ethiopia, the revolutionary regime began to founder (see The Ogaden War: Performance and Implications of Defeat , ch. 5). Confronted by armed opposition at home and diplomatic isolation abroad, the regime turned inward. President Siad Barre, an expert in the art of dividing and ruling since his early days as an intelligence officer under the Italian fascists, skillfully harnessed the limited resources of the state. His aim was to pit clan against clan and to inflame clan passions in order to divert public attention from his increasingly vulnerable regime.

A civil war began in the early 1980s with an armed uprising against the regime by Majeerteen clans (Daarood) in southern Somalia under the banner of the Somali Salvation Democratic Front (SSDF). Armed resistance spread to the Isaaq clans in the north. The regime's efforts to suppress Isaaq resistance resulted in May 1988 in the virtual destruction of the urban centers of the north, most notably Hargeysa, until then the second largest city in the country, and Burao, a provincial capital. This action was followed in mid–1989 by a massive uprising by the Hawiye clans in Mogadishu and adjacent regions under the leadership of the clanbased United Somali Congress (USC). In the escalating waves of government repression and resulting popular resistance that followed, Somali society exploded into violence and anarchy, and Siad Barre and his remaining supporters were forced to flee in early 1991.

Instead of peace, Somalia experienced a power struggle among various clan– and region–based organizations:

the Somali National Movement (SNM, Isaaq–affiliated); the SSDF (Majeerteen); the Somali Patriotic Movement (SPM, Ogaden); Somali Democratic Alliance (SDA, Gadabursi); and the Somali Democratic Movement (SDM, Rahanwayn). Lineages and sublineages, fighting over the spoils of state, turned on one another in an orgy of internecine killings (see Somalia's Difficult Decade, 1980–90 , ch. 1). The state collapsed and Somali society splintered into its component clans.

The collapse resulted from certain features of Somali lineage segmentation. Somali clan organization is an unstable, fragile system, characterized at all levels by shifting allegiances. This segmentation goes down to the household level with the children of a man's two wives sometimes turning on one another on the basis of maternal lines. Power is exercised through temporary coalitions and ephemeral alliances between lineages. A given alliance fragments into competitive units as soon as the situation that necessitated it ceases to exist. In urban settings, for example, where relatively large economic and political stakes are contested, the whole population may be polarized into two opposing camps of clan alliances. To varying degrees, the poles of power in the politics of independent Somalia generally have tended to form around the Daarood clanfamily and a confederacy of the Hawiye and the Isaaq clanfamilies .

Two features of lineage segmentation require further comment. First, the system lacks a concept of individual culpability. When a man commits a homicide, for example, the guilt does not remain with him solely as an individual murderer as in most Western societies; the crime is attributed to all of the murderer's kin, who become guilty in the eyes of the aggrieved party by reason of their blood connection with the perpetrator.

Members of the aggrieved group then seek revenge, not just on the perpetrator, but on any member of his lineage they might chance upon. In the Somali lineage system, one literally may get away with murder because the actual killer may escape while an innocent kinsman of his may be killed. Second, the system is vulnerable to external manipulation by, for example, a head of state such as Siad Barre, who used the resources of the state to reward and punish entire clans collectively. This was the fate of the Isaaq and Majeerteen clans, which suffered grievous persecutions under Siad Barre's regime.

The meaning of segmentation is captured in an Arab beduin saying: My full brother and I against my half–brother, my brother and I against my father, my father's household against my uncle's household, our two households (my uncle's and mine) against the rest of the immediate kin, the immediate kin against nonimmediate members of my clan, my clan against other clans, and, finally, my nation and I against the world. In a system of lineage segmentation, one does not have a permanent enemy or a permanent friend—only a permanent context. Depending on the context, a man, a group of men, or even a state may be one's friends or foes. This fact partially explains why opposition Somalis did not hesitate to cross over to Ethiopia, the supposed quintessential foe of Somalis. Ethiopia was being treated by the Somali opposition as another clan for purposes of temporary alliance in the interminable shifting coalitions of Somali pastoral clan politics.

Lineage segmentation of the Somali variety thus inherently militates against the evolution and endurance of a stable, centralized state. Although exacerbated by Siad Barre's exploitation of interclan rivalries, institutional instability is actually woven into the fabric of Somali society. The collapse of the Siad Barre regime in early 1991 led to interclan civil war that was continuing in 1992.

RELIGIOUS LIFE

Modern mosque in Mogadishu Courtesy R W S. Hudson Italian–built Roman Catholic cathedral in Mogadishu, subsequently gutted by bombs in the civil war Courtesy R W S. Hudson M st Somalis are Sunni Muslims. (Less than 1 percent of ethnic Somalis are Christians.) Loyalty to Islam reinforces distinctions that set Somalis apart from their immediate African neighbors, most of whom are either Christians (particularly the Amhara and others of Ethiopia) or adherents of indigenous African faiths.

The Islamic ideal is a society organized to implement Muslim precepts in which no distinction exists between the secular and the religious spheres. Among Somalis this ideal had been approximated less fully in the north than among some groups in the settled regions of the south where religious leaders were at one time an integral part of the social and political structure. Among nomads, the exigencies of pastoral life gave greater weight to the warrior's role, and religious leaders were expected to remain aloof from political matters.

The role of religious functionaries began to shrink in the 1950s and 1960s as some of their legal and educational powers and responsibilities were transferred to secular authorities. The position of religious leaders changed substantially after the 1969 revolution and the introduction of scientific socialism. Siad Barre insisted that his version of socialism was compatible with Quranic principles, and he condemned atheism.

Religious leaders, however, were warned not to meddle in politics.

The new government instituted legal changes that some religious figures saw as contrary to Islamic precepts.

The regime reacted sharply to criticism, executing some of the protesters (see Islam in the Colonial Era and After , this ch.). Subsequently, religious leaders seemed to accommodate themselves to the government.

The Tenets of Islam

Founded in A.D. 622 when the Prophet Muhammad migrated with his followers from Mecca to Medina, Islam was probably brought to Somalia by early followers of the Prophet who sought refuge from persecution in Mecca. It is also possible that Islam came to Somalia through contacts with Persian and Arab merchants and seamen who founded settlements along the Somali coast 1,000 or more years ago (see Coastal Towns , ch. 1).

Somalia, a country study

Before Islam reached the Somalis, quarrels over the succession to leadership had led to a split of the Islamic community into the Sunni (orthodox) and the Shia (from Shiat Ali, or partisans of Ali as the legitimate successor to Muhammad). The overwhelming majority of Somalis are Sunni Muslims.

The word *islam* means "submission to God," and a Muslim is one who has submitted. The religion's basic tenet is stated in its creed: "There is no god but God (Allah) and Muhammad is His prophet." Recitation of the creed, daily prayers performed according to prescribed rules, fasting during the lunar month of Ramadan (when Muhammad received his initial revelations), almsgiving, and the pilgrimage to Mecca constitute the five pillars of the faith. Four of these duties may be modified by the situation in which believers find themselves. If they are ill, they may pray without prostrations and reduce the number of times they pray from the obligatory five to three. Muslims may be excused from fasting (going without food, drink, tobacco, and sexual relations from dawn until sunset) during a journey, but should compensate at a later time. Participation in almsgiving and the pilgrimage depend upon one's ability to afford them.

The basic teaching of Islam is embodied in the Quran, believed to have been given to Muhammad by God through the angel Gabriel. After Muhammad's death, his followers sought to regulate their lives by his divinely inspired works; if the Quran did not cover a specific situation, they turned to the hadith (tradition, remembered actions, and sayings of the Prophet). Together, the Quran and the hadith form the sunna (custom or usage), a comprehensive guide to the spiritual, ethical, and social life of Muslims.

Islamic sharia or religious law derives from the Quran, the hadith, and from a large body of interpretive commentary that developed in the early Islamic period. Several schools of legal thought arose, among them the Shafii school (named for Muhammad ibn Idris ash Shafii, 767–820), which is represented in Somalia. The sharia covers several categories of behavior: obligatory actions, desirable or recommended actions, indifferent actions, objectionable but not forbidden actions, and prohibited actions. The five pillars of the faith fall in the first category; nightlong prayer in the second, and many ordinary secular activities in the third. Divorce is in the objectionable but permitted category, whereas adultery and other sinful acts are prohibited.

Settled and nomadic Somalis conformed to Muslim requirements for ritual purity, such as washing after contact with unclean things. Some settled Somalis, particularly in communities founded by religious orders, are more likely to observe Islamic requirements than are nomads. By the 1960s, ordinary settled Somalis were likely to pay less attention to religious observance. Devout Somalis, and others who valued the title of *hajj* (pilgrim) for its prestige, might make the pilgrimage to Mecca, but many more would visit the tombs of the local saints (see Religious Orders and the Cult of the Saints , this ch.).

Religious Roles in Somali Islam

In Islam, no priests mediate between the believer and God, but there are religious teachers, preachers, and mosque officials. Until the civil war in Somalia, religious training was most readily available in urban centers or wherever mosques existed. There boys learned to memorize parts of the Quran. Some teachers traveled on foot from place to place with their novices, depending on the generosity of others for their living. The teachers served the community by preaching, leading prayers, blessing the people and their livestock, counseling, arbitrating disputes, and performing marriages. Few teachers were deeply versed in Islam, and they rarely stayed with one lineage long enough to teach more than rudimentary religious principles.

In the absence of a wandering teacher, nomads depended on a person associated with religious devotion, study, or leadership, called a *wadad* (pl., *wadaddo*). The *wadaddo* constituted the oldest stratum of literate people in Somalia. They functioned as basic teachers and local notaries as well as judges and authorities in religious law. They were rarely theologians; some belonged to a religious brotherhood, or to a lineage with a strong religious tradition. In the latter case, they were not necessarily trained, but were entitled to lead prayers and to perform ritual sacrifices at weddings, on special holidays, and during festivals held at the tombs of saints.

Religious Orders and the Cult of the Saints

Religious orders have played a significant role in Somali Islam. The rise of these orders (*turuq*; sing., *tariqa*, "way" or "path") was connected with the development of Sufism, a mystical current in Islam that began during the ninth and tenth centuries and reached its

137

height during the twelfth and thirteenth. In Somalia Sufi orders appeared in towns during the fifteenth century and rapidly became a revitalizing force. Followers of Sufism seek a closer personal relationship to God through special spiritual disciplines. Escape from self is facilitated by poverty, seclusion, and other forms of self–denial. Members of Sufi orders are commonly called dervishes (from the Persian plural, *daraawish*; sing., *darwish*, one who gave up worldly concerns to dedicate himself to the service of God and community). Leaders of branches or congregations of these orders are given the Arabic title *shaykh*, a term usually reserved for these learned in Islam and rarely applied to ordinary *wadaddo*.

Dervishes wandered from place to place, teaching and begging. They are best known for their ceremonies, called *dhikr* (see Glossary), in which states of visionary ecstasy are induced by group–chanting of religious texts and by rhythmic gestures, dancing, and deep breathing. The object is to free oneself from the body and to be lifted into the presence of God. Dervishes have been important as founders of agricultural religious communities called *jamaat* (sing., *jamaa*). A few of these were home to celibate men only, but usually the *jamaat* were inhabited by families. Most Somalis were nominal members of Sufi orders but few underwent the rigors of devotion to the religious life, even for a short time.

Three Sufi orders were prominent in Somalia. In order of their introduction into the country, they were the Qadiriyah, the Ahmadiyah–Idrisiyah, and the Salihiyah. The Rifaiyah, an offshoot of the Qadiriyah, was represented mainly among Arabs resident in Mogadishu.

The Qadiriyah, the oldest order in Islam, was founded in Baghdad by Abd al Qadir al Jilani in 1166 and introduced into Harer (Ethiopia) in the fifteenth century. During the eighteenth century, it was spread among the Oromo and Somalis of Ethiopia, often under the leadership of Somali shaykhs. Its earliest known advocate in northern Somalia was Shaykh Abd ar Rahman az Zeilawi, who died in 1883. At that time, Qadiriyah adherents were merchants in the ports and elsewhere. In a separate development, the Qadiriyah order also spread into the southern Somali port cities of Baraawe and Mogadishu at an uncertain date. In 1819 Shaykh Ibrahim Hassan Jebro acquired land on the Jubba River and established a religious center in the form of a farming community, the first Somali *jamaa*.

Outstanding figures of the Qadiriyah in Somalia included Shaykh Awes Mahammad Baraawi (d. 1909), who spread the teaching of the order in the southern interior. He wrote much devotional poetry in Arabic and attempted to translate traditional hymns from Arabic into Somali, working out his own phonetic system.

Another was Shaykh Abdirrahman Abdullah of Mogadishu, who stressed deep mysticism. Because of his reputation for sanctity, his tomb at Mogadishu became a pilgrimage center for the Shabeelle area and his writings continued to be circulated by his followers in the early 1990s.

The Ahmadiyah–Idrisiyah order was founded by Ahmad ibn Idris al Fasi (1760–1837) of Mecca. It was brought to Somalia by Shaykh Ali Maye Durogba of Merca, a distinguished poet who joined the order during a pilgrimage to Mecca. His visions and the miracles attributed to him gained him a reputation for sanctity, and his tomb became a popular objective among pilgrims. The AhmadiyahIdrisiyah , the smallest of the three orders, has few ritual requirements beyond some simple prayers and hymns. During its ceremonies, however, participants often go into trances.

A conflict over the leadership of the Ahmadiyah–Idrisiyah among its Arab founders led to the establishment of the Salihiyah in 1887 by Muhammad ibn Salih. The order spread first among the Somalis of the Ogaden area of Ethiopia, who entered Somalia about 1880. The Salihiyah's most active proselytizer was Shaykh Mahammad Guled ar Rashidi, who became a regional leader. He settled among the Shidle people (Bantu–speakers occupying the middle reaches of the Shabeelle River), where he obtained land and established a *jamaa*. Later he founded another *jamaa* among the Ajuran (a section of the Hawiye clanfamily)

and then returned to establish still another community among the Shidle before his death in 1918. Perhaps the best known Somali Salihiyah figure was Mahammad Abdille Hasan, leader of a lengthy resistance to the British until 1920 (see Mahammad Abdille Hasau's Dervish Resistance to Colonial Occupation, ch. 1).

Generally, the Salihiyah and the Ahmadiyah–Idrisiyah leaders were more interested in the establishment of *jamaat* along the Shabeelle and Jubba rivers and the fertile land between them than in teaching because few were learned in Islam. Their early efforts to establish farming communities resulted in cooperative cultivation and harvesting and some effective agricultural methods. In Somalia's riverine region, for example, only *jamaat* members thought of stripping the brush from areas around their fields to reduce the breeding places of tsetse flies.

Local leaders of brotherhoods customarily asked lineage heads in the areas where they wished to settle for permission to build their mosques and communities. A piece of land was usually freely given; often it was an area between two clans or one in which nomads had access to a river. The presence of a *jamaa* not only provided a buffer zone between two hostile groups, but also caused the giver to acquire a blessing since the land was considered given to God. Tenure was a matter of charity only, however, and sometimes became precarious in case of disagreements. No statistics were available in 1990 on the number of such settlements, but in the 1950s there were more than ninety in the south, with a total of about 35,000 members. Most were in the Bakool, Gedo, and Bay regions or along the middle and lower Shabeelle River. There were few *jamaat* in other regions because the climate and soil did not encourage agricultural settlements.

Membership in a brotherhood is theoretically a voluntary matter unrelated to kinship. However, lineages are often affiliated with a specific brotherhood and a man usually joins his father's order. Initiation is followed by a ceremony during which the order's *dhikr* is celebrated. Novices swear to accept the branch head as their spiritual guide.

Each order has its own hierarchy that is supposedly a substitute for the kin group from which the members have separated themselves. Veneration is given to previous heads of the order, known as the Chain of Blessing, rather than to ancestors. This practice is especially followed in the south, where place of residence tends to have more significance than lineage.

Leaders of orders and their branches and of specific congregations are said to have baraka, a state of blessedness implying an inner spiritual power that is inherent in the religious office and may cling to the tomb of a revered leader, who, upon death, is considered a saint. However, some saints are venerated because of their religious reputations whether or not they were associated with an order or one of its communities.

Sainthood also has been ascribed to others because of their status as founders of clans or large lineages.

Northern pastoral nomads are likely to honor lineage founders as saints; sedentary Somalis revere saints for their piety and baraka.

Because of the saint's spiritual presence at his tomb, pilgrims journey there to seek aid (such as a cure for illness or infertility). Members of the saint's order also visit the tomb, particularly on the anniversaries of his birth and death.

Folk Islam and Indigenous Ritual

Somalis have modified Islam, for example with reference to the social significance of baraka. Baraka is considered a gift from God to the founders and heads of Sufi orders. It is likewise associated with secular leaders and their clan genealogies.

A leader has power to bless, but his baraka may have potentially dangerous side effects. His curse is greatly feared, and his power may harm others. When a clan leader visits the leader of another clan, the host's relative receives him first to draw off some of the visitor's power so that his own chief may not be injured.

The traditional learning of a *wadad* includes a form of folk astronomy based on stellar movements and related to seasonal changes. Its primary objective is to signal the times for migration, but it may also be used to set the dates of rituals that are specifically Somali. This folk knowledge is also used in ritual methods of healing and averting misfortune, as well as for divination.

Wadaddo help avert misfortune by making protective amulets and charms that transmit some of their baraka to others, or by adding the Quran's baraka to the amulet through a written passage. The baraka of a saint may be obtained in the form of an object that has touched or been placed near his tomb.

Although *wadaddo* may use their power to curse as a sanction, misfortune generally is not attributed to curses or witchcraft. Somalis have accepted the orthodox Muslim view that a man's conduct will be judged in an afterlife. However, a person who commits an antisocial act, such as patricide, is thought possessed of supernatural evil powers.

Despite formal Islam's uncompromising monotheism, Muslims everywhere believe in the existence of mortal spirits (jinn), said to be descended from Iblis, a spirit fallen from heaven. Most Somalis consider all spirits to be evil but some believe there are benevolent spirits.

Certain kinds of illness, including tuberculosis and pneumonia, or symptoms such as sneezing, coughing, vomiting, and loss of consciousness, are believed to result from spirit possession, namely, the *wadaddo* of the spirit world. The condition is treated by a human *wadad*, preferably one who has himself recovered from the sickness. He reads portions of the Quran over the patient and bathes him with perfume, which in Somalia is associated with religious celebrations.

In the case of possession by the *zar*, a spirit, the ceremony of exorcism used to treat it is sometimes referred to as the *"zar* cult." The victims are women with grievances against their husbands. The symptoms are extreme forms of hysteria and fainting fits. The *zar* exorcism ritual is conducted by a woman who has had the affliction and thus supposedly has some authority over the spirit. The ritual consists of a special dance in which the victim tends to reproduce the symptoms and fall into a trance. The "illness" enables a disgruntled wife to express her hostility without actually quarreling with her husband.

A third kind of spirit possession is known as *gelid* (entering), in which the spirit of an injured person troubles the offender. A jilted girl, for example, cannot openly complain if a promise of marriage arranged by the respective families has been broken. Her spirit, however, entering the young man who was supposed to marry her and stating the grievance, causes him to fall ill. The exorcism consists of readings from the Quran and commands from a *wadad* that the spirit leave the afflicted person.

Gelid is also thought to be caused by the curse or evil power of a helpless person who has been injured. The underlying notion is that those who are weak in worldly matters are mystically endowed. Such persons are supposed to be under the special protection of God, and kind acts toward them bring religious merit, whereas unkind acts bring punishment. The evil eye, too, is associated with unfortunates, especially women. Thus, members of the Yibir, the numerically smallest and weakest of the special occupation groups and traditionally the lowliest socially, are the most feared for their supernatural powers.

Somalis also engage in rituals that derive from pre–Islamic practices and in some cases resemble those of other Eastern Cushitic–speaking peoples. Perhaps the most important of these rituals are the annual celebrations of the clan ancestor among northern Somalis—an expression of their solidarity—and the collective rainmaking ritual (*roobdoon*) performed by sedentary groups in the south.

Islam in the Colonial Era and After

Because Muslims believe that their faith was revealed in its complete form to the Prophet Muhammad, it has been difficult to adapt Islam to the social, economic, and political changes that began with the expansion of colonial rule in the late nineteenth century. Some modifications have occurred, however. One response was to stress a return to orthodox Muslim traditions and to oppose Westernization totally. The Sufi brotherhoods were at the forefront of this movement, personified in Somalia by Mahammad Abdille Hasan in the early 1900s. Generally, the leaders of Islamic orders opposed the spread of Western education.

Another response was to reform Islam by reinterpreting it. From this perspective, early Islam was seen as a protest against abuse, corruption, and inequality; reformers therefore attempted to prove that Muslim scriptures contained all elements needed to deal with modernization. To this school of thought belongs Islamic socialism, identified particularly with Egyptian nationalist Gamal Abdul Nasser (1918–70). His ideas appealed to a number of Somalis, especially those who had studied in Cairo in the 1950s and 1960s.

The 1961 constitution guaranteed freedom of religion but also declared the newly independent republic an Islamic state. The first two postindependence governments paid lip service to the principles of Islamic socialism but made relatively few changes. The coup of October 21, 1969, installed a radical regime committed to profound change. Shortly afterward, *Stella d'Ottobre*, the official newspaper of the SRC, published an editorial about relations between Islam and socialism and the differences between scientific and Islamic socialism. Islamic socialism was said to have become a servant of capitalism and neocolonialism and a tool manipulated by a privileged, rich, and powerful class. In contrast, scientific socialism was based on the altruistic values that inspired

143

genuine Islam. Religious leaders should therefore leave secular affairs to the new leaders who were striving for goals that conformed with Islamic principles. Soon after, the government arrested several protesting religious leaders and accused them of counterrevolutionary propaganda and of conniving with reactionary elements in the Arabian Peninsula. The authorities also dismissed several members of religious tribunals for corruption and incompetence.

When the Three–Year Plan, 1971–73, was launched in January 1971, SRC leaders felt compelled to win the support of religious leaders so as to transform the existing social structure (see Scientific Socialism, 1970–75 , ch. 3). On September 4, 1971, Siad Barre exhorted more than 100 religious teachers to participate in building a new socialist society. He criticized their method of teaching in Quranic schools and charged some with using religion for personal profit.

The campaign for scientific socialism intensified in 1972. On the occasion of Id al Adha, the major Muslim festival associated with the pilgrimage, the president defined scientific socialism as half practical work and half ideological belief. He declared that work and belief were compatible with Islam because the Quran condemned exploitation and moneylending and urged compassion, unity, and cooperation among Muslims.

But he stressed the distinction between religion as an ideological instrument for the manipulation of power and as a moral force. He condemned the antireligious attitude of Marxists. Religion, Siad Barre said, was an integral part of the Somali worldview, but it belonged in the private sphere, whereas scientific socialism dealt with material concerns such as poverty. Religious leaders should exercise their moral influence but refrain from interfering in political or economic matters.

In early January 1975, evoking the message of equality, justice, and social progress contained in the Quran, Siad Barre announced a new family law that gave women the right to inheritance on an equal basis with men.

Some Somalis believe the law was proof that the SRC wanted to undermine the basic structure of Islamic society. In Mogadishu twenty–three religious leaders protested inside their mosques. They were arrested and charged with acting at the instigation of a foreign power and with violating state security; ten were executed.

Most religious leaders, however, kept silent. The government continued to organize training courses for shaykhs in scientific socialism.

Rising Islamism

Somali Islam rendered the world intelligible to Somalis and made their lives more bearable in a harsh land.

Amidst the interclan violence that characterized life in the early 1990s, Somalis naturally sought comfort in their faith to make sense of their national disaster. The traditional response of practicing Muslims to social trauma is to explain it in terms of a perceived sin that has caused society to stray from the "straight path of truth" and consequently to receive God's punishment. The way to regain God's favor is to repent collectively and rededicate society in accordance with Allah's divine precepts.

On the basis of these beliefs, a Somali brand of messianic Islamism (sometimes seen as fundamentalism)

sprang up to fill the vacuum created by the collapse of the state. In the disintegrated Somali world of early 1992, Islamism appeared to be largely confined to Bender Cassim, a coastal town in Majeerteen country. For instance, a Yugoslav doctor who was a member of a United Nations team sent to aid the wounded was gunned down by masked assailants there in November 1991. Reportedly, the assassins belonged to an underground Islamist movement whose adherents wished to purify the country of "infidel" influence.

LANGUAGE AND EDUCATION

Rural Quran school, with students using wooden slates to learn Arabic Courtesy Hiram A. Ruiz **Language**
Except for a few communities along the southern Somali coast where Swahili (a Bantu language) and Arabic dialects are spoken, Somali nationals (including persons of non–Somali origin) speak one of several Somali dialects. Somali belongs to a set of languages called lowland Eastern Cushitic spoken by peoples living in

Ethiopia, Somalia, Djibouti, and Kenya. Eastern Cushitic is one section of the Cushitic language family, which in turn is part of the great Afro–Asiatic stock.

Of the Somali dialects, the most widely used is Common Somali, a term applied to several subdialects, the speakers of which can understand each other easily. Common Somali is spoken in most of Somalia and in adjacent territories (Ethiopia, Kenya, and Djibouti), and is used by broadcasting stations in Somalia and in Somali–language broadcasts originating outside the country. Coastal Somali is spoken on the Banaadir Coast (from Cadale to south of Baraawe) and its immediate hinterland. Central Somali is spoken in the interriverine area, chiefly by members of the Rahanwayn clan–family. Speakers of Common and Coastal Somali can understand each other after a few weeks of close contact, speakers of Common and Central Somali only after a few months.

Facility with language is highly valued in Somali society; the capability of a suitor, a warrior, or a political or religious leader is judged in part by his verbal adroitness. In such a society, oral poetry becomes an art, and one's ability to compose verse in one or more of its several forms enhances one's status.

Speakers in political or religious assemblies and litigants in courts traditionally were expected to use poetry or poetic proverbs. Even everyday talk tended to have a terse, vivid, poetic style, characterized by carefully chosen words, condensed meaning, and alliteration.

Until the establishment of the Somali script in January 1973, there were two languages of government—English and Italian. In the prerevolutionary era, English became dominant in the school system and in government, which caused some conflict between elites from northern and southern Somalia. However, the overarching issue was the development of a socioeconomic stratum based on mastery of a foreign language. The relatively small proportion of Somalis (less than 10 percent) with a grasp of such a language—preferably English—had access to government positions and the few managerial or technical jobs in modern private enterprises. Such persons became increasingly isolated from their nonliterate Somali–speaking brethren, but because the secondary schools and most government posts were in urban areas the socioeconomic and linguistic distinction was in large part a rural–urban one. To some extent, it was also a north–south distinction because those educated in the Italian system and even in Italian universities found it increasingly difficult to reach senior government levels.

Even before the 1969 revolution, Somalis had become aware of social stratification and the growing distance, based on language and literacy differences, between ordinary Somalis and those in government. The 1972 decision to designate an official Somali script and require its use in government demolished the language barrier and an important obstacle to rapid literacy growth.

In the years following the institution of the Somali script, Somali officials were required to learn the script and attempts were made to inculcate mass literacy—in 1973 among urban and rural sedentary Somalis, and in 1974–75 among nomads. Although a few texts existed in the new script before 1973, in most cases new books were prepared presenting the government's perspective on Somali history and development. Somali scholars also succeeded in developing a vocabulary to deal with a range of subjects from mathematics and physics to administration and ideology.

By the late 1970s, sufficient Somali materials were available to permit the language to be the medium of instruction at all school levels below the university. Arabic was taught to all students, beginning at the elementary level and continuing into the secondary phase. Because Italians dominated the senior faculty at the national university in the late 1970s, Italian remained in wide use. By the late 1980s, Somali was the language of instruction at the university as well.

Education

In the colonial period, Italian Somaliland and British Somaliland pursued different educational policies. The Italians sought to train pupils to become farmers or unskilled workers so as to minimize the number of Italians needed for these purposes. The British established an elementary education system during the military administration to train Somali males for administrative posts and for positions not previously open to them.

They set up a training school for the police and one for medical orderlies.

During the trusteeship period, education was supposedly governed by the Trusteeship Agreement, which declared that independence could only be based on "education in the broadest sense." Despite Italian opposition, the UN had passed the Trusteeship

Agreement calling for a system of public education:

elementary, secondary, and vocational, in which at least elementary education was free. The authorities were also to establish teacher training institutions and to facilitate higher and professional education by sending an adequate number of students for university study abroad.

The result of these provisions was that to obtain an education, a Somali had the choice of attending a traditional Quranic school or the Roman Catholic mission−run government schools. The language of instruction in all these schools was Arabic, not Somali. The fifteen pre−World War I schools (ten government schools and five orphanage schools) in Italian Somaliland had an enrollment of less than one−tenth of 1 percent of the population. Education for Somalis ended with the elementary level; only Italians attended intermediate schools. Of all Italian colonies, Somalia received the least financial aid for education.

In British Somaliland, the military administration appointed a British officer as superintendent of education in 1944. Britain later seconded six Zanzibari instructors from the East Africa Army Education Corps for duty with the Somali Education Department. In 1947 there were seventeen government elementary schools for the Somali and Arab population, two private schools, and a teachers' training school with fifty Somali and Arab students.

Until well after World War II, there was little demand for Western−style education. Moreover, the existence of two official languages (English and Italian) and a third (Arabic, widely revered as the language of the Quran if not widely used and understood) posed problems for a uniform educational system and for literacy training at the elementary school level.

The relative lack of direction in education policy in the prerevolutionary period under the SRC gave way to the enunciation in the early 1970s of several goals reflecting the philosophy of the revolutionary regime.

Among these goals were expansion of the school system to accommodate the largest possible student population; introduction of courses geared to the country's social and economic requirements; expansion of technical education; and provision of higher education within Somalia so that most students who pursued advanced studies would acquire their knowledge in a Somali context. The government also announced its intention to eliminate illiteracy. Considerable progress toward these goals had been achieved by the early 1980s.

In the societal chaos following the fall of Siad Barre in early 1991, schools ceased to exist for all practical purposes. In 1990, however, the system had four basic levels—preprimary, primary, secondary, and higher.

The government controlled all schools, private schools having been nationalized in 1972 and Quranic education having been made an integral part of schooling in the late 1970s.

The preprimary training given by Quranic schools lasted until the late 1970s. Quranic teachers traveled with nomadic groups, and many children received only the education offered by such teachers. There were a number of stationary religious schools in urban areas as well. The decision in the late 1970s to bring Islamic education into the national system reflected a concern that most Quranic learning was rudimentary at best, as well as a desire for tighter government control over an autonomous area.

Until the mid–1970s, primary education consisted of four years of elementary schooling followed by four grades designated as intermediate. In 1972 promotion to the intermediate grades was made automatic (a competitive examination had been required until that year). The two cycles subsequently were treated as a single continuous program. In 1975 the government established universal primary education, and primary education was reduced to six years. By the end of the 1978–79 school year, however, the government reintroduced the eight–year primary school system because the six–year program had proved unsatisfactory.

The number of students enrolled in the primary level increased each year, beginning in 1969–70, but particularly after 1975–76. Primary schooling theoretically began at age six, but many children started later.

Many, especially girls, did not attend school, and some dropped out, usually after completing four years.

In 1981 Somalia informed the UN Conference on the Least Developed Countries that the nomadic population was "omitted from the formal education program for the purposes of forecasting primary education enrollment." In the late 1970s and early 1980s, the government provided a three–year education program for nomadic children. For six months of each year, when the seasons permitted numbers of nomads to aggregate, the children attended school; the rest of the year the children accompanied their families. Nomadic families who wanted their children to attend school throughout the year had to board them in a permanent settlement.

In addition to training in reading, writing, and arithmetic, the primary curriculum provided social studies courses using new textbooks that focused on Somali issues. Arabic was to be taught as a second language beginning in primary school, but it was doubtful that there were enough qualified Somalis able to teach it beyond the rudimentary level. Another goal, announced in the mid–1970s, was to give students some modern knowledge of agriculture and animal husbandry. Primary school graduates, however, lacked sufficient knowledge to earn a living at a skilled trade.

In the late 1980s, the number of students enrolled in secondary school was less than 10 percent of the total in primary schools, a result of the dearth of teachers, schools, and materials. Most secondary schools were still in urban areas; given the rural and largely nomadic nature of the population, these were necessarily boarding schools. Further, the use of Somali at the secondary level required Somali teachers, which entailed a training period. Beginning in the 1980–81 school year, the government created a formula for allocating postprimary students. It assumed that 80 percent of primary school graduates would go on to further education. Of these, 30 percent would attend four–year general secondary education, 17.5 percent either three– or four–year courses in technical education, and 52.5 percent vocational courses of one to two years' duration.

The principal institution of higher education was Somali National University in Mogadishu, founded in 1970.

The nine early faculties were agriculture, economics, education, engineering, geology, law, medicine, sciences, and veterinary science. Added in the late 1970s were the faculty of languages and a combination of journalism and Islamic studies. The College of Education, which prepared secondary–school teachers in a two–year program, was part of the university. About 700 students were admitted to the university each year in the late

1970s; roughly 15 percent of those completed the general secondary course and the four-year technical course. Despite a high dropout rate, the authorities projected an eventual intake of roughly 25 percent of general and technical secondary school graduates.

In 1990 several other institutes also admitted secondaryschool graduates. Among these were schools of nursing, telecommunications, and veterinary science, and a polytechnic institute. The numbers enrolled and the duration of the courses were not known.

In addition, several programs were directed at adults. The government had claimed 60 percent literacy after the mass literacy campaign of the mid–1970s, but by early 1977 there were signs of relapse, particularly among nomads. The government then established the National Adult Education Center to coordinate the work of several ministries and many voluntary and part–time paid workers in an extensive literacy program, largely in rural areas for persons sixteen to forty–five years of age. Despite these efforts, the UN estimate of Somali literacy in 1990 was only 24 percent.

HEALTH

Woman feeding her baby in a maternal and child feeding center, Mogadishu, 1991 Courtesy Hiram A. Ruiz The collapse of the government in January 1991 with the fall of Siad Barre led to further deterioration of Somalia's health situation. The high incidence of disease that persisted into the early 1990s reflected a difficult environment, inadequate nutrition, and insufficient medical care. In the years since the revolutionary regime had come to power, drought, flood, warfare (and the refugee problem resulting from the latter) had, if anything, left diets more inadequate than before. Massive changes that would make the environment less hostile, such as the elimination of disease–transmitting organisms, had yet to take place. The numbers of medical personnel and health facilities had increased, but they did not meet Somali needs in the early 1990s and seemed unlikely to do so for some time.

The major maladies prevalent in Somalia included pulmonary tuberculosis, malaria, and infectious and parasitic diseases. In addition, schistosomiasis (bilharzia), tetanus, venereal disease (especially in the port towns), leprosy, and a variety of skin and eye ailments severely impaired health and productivity. As elsewhere, smallpox had been virtually wiped out, but occasional epidemics of measles could have devastating effects. In early 1992, Somalia had a human immunovirus (HIV) incidence of less than 1 percent of its population.

Environmental, economic, and social conditions were conducive to a high incidence of tuberculosis among young males who grazed camels under severe conditions and transmitted the disease in their nomadic wanderings. Efforts to deal with tuberculosis had some success in urban centers, but control measures were difficult to apply to the nomadic and seminomadic population.

Malaria was prevalent in the southern regions, particularly those traversed by the country's two major rivers.

By the mid1970s , a malaria eradication program had been extended from Mogadishu to other regions; good results were then reported, but there were no useful statistics for the early 1990s.

Approximately 75 percent of the population was affected by one or more kinds of intestinal parasites; this problem would persist as long as contaminated water sources were used and the way of life of most rural Somalis remained unchanged. Schistosomiasis was particularly prevalent in the marshy and irrigated areas along the rivers in the south. Parasites contributed to general debilitation and made the population susceptible to other diseases.

Underlying Somali susceptibility to disease was widespread malnutrition, exacerbated from time to time by drought and since the late 1970s by the refugee burden (see Refugees , this ch.). Although reliable statistics were not available, the high child mortality rate was attributed to inadequate nutrition.

Until the collapse of the national government in 1991, the organization and administration of health services were the responsibility of the Ministry of Health, although regional medical officers had some authority. The Siad Barre regime had ended private medical practice in 1972, but in the late 1980s private practice returned as Somalis became dissatisfied with the quality of government health care.

From 1973 to 1978, there was a substantial increase in the number of physicians, and a far greater proportion of them were Somalis. Of 198 physicians in 1978, a total of 118 were Somalis, whereas only 37 of 96 had been Somalis in 1973.

In the 1970s, an effort was made to increase the number of other health personnel and to foster the construction of health facilities. To that end, two nursing schools opened and several other health–related educational programs were instituted. Of equal importance was the countrywide distribution of medical personnel and facilities. In the early 1970s, most personnel and facilities were concentrated in Mogadishu and a few other towns. The situation had improved somewhat by the late 1970s, but the distribution of health care remained unsatisfactory.

REFUGEES

Figure 5. Refugee Camps in Somalia, 1990 The 1977–78 Ogaden War caused a massive influx of Somalis who had been living in eastern Ethiopia (and to a lesser extent from other areas) into Somalia. Most refugees were ethnic Somalis, but there were also many Oromo, an ethnic group that resided primarily in Ethiopia. The Somali government appealed for help to the United Nations High Commissioner for Refugees (UNHCR) in September 1979, but UNHCR did not initiate requests for international aid until March 1980.

In its first public appeal to the UN, the Somali government estimated 310,000 in the camps in September 1979. By mid–1980 estimates had risen to 750,000 persons in camps and at least half that number outside them. In early 1981, Mogadishu estimated that there were more than 1.3 million refugees in the camps and an additional 700,000 to 800,000 refugees at large, either attempting to carry on their nomadic way of life or quartered in towns and cities.

In 1980 representatives of international agencies and other aid donors expressed skepticism at the numbers Somalia claimed, and in 1981 these agencies asked UN demographers to conduct a survey. The survey estimated 450,000 to 620,000 refugees in the camps; no estimate was made of the number of refugees outside the camps. The Somali government rejected the survey's results; international agencies subsequently based their budgeting on a figure of 650,000.

Conflicting figures concerning the composition of the refugee population by age and sex led a team of epidemiologists from the Centers for Disease Control of the United States Public Health Service to determine the demographic characteristics of a sample of refugee camps in mid–1980. They found the very young (under five years of age) to range from 15 to 18 percent of the camp population; those from five to fifteen years of age ranged from 45 to 47 percent; from 29 to 33 percent were between fifteen years of age and forty–four; 6 to 8 percent were forty–five years or older. The epidemiologists did not find the male–female ratio unusually distorted.

In 1990 there were refugee camps in four of Somalia's sixteen regions, or administrative districts (see fig. 5).

The number of persons in these camps ranged from under 3,000 to more than 70,000, but most held 35,000 to 45,000 refugees. According to a government document, the camps in Gedo held a total of more than 450,000 persons, in Hiiraan more than 375,000, in Woqooyi Galbeed well over 400,000, and in Shabeellaha Hoose nearly 70,000.

The burden of the refugee influx on Somalia was heavy. Somalia was one of the world's poorest countries, an importer of food in ordinary circumstances and lacking crucial elements of physical and social infrastructure such as transportation and health facilities. The general poverty of the indigenous population and the ad hoc character of the National Refugee Commission established under the Ministry of Local Government and Rural Development and other government agencies dealing with the refugee problem contributed to the misuse and even the outright theft of food and medical supplies intended for refugees.

In a country with limited arable land and fuels and visited fairly often by drought or flash floods, refugees were hard put to contribute to their own support. Some refugee camps were so located that transportation of food and medical supplies was fairly easy, but that was not true for many other camps. Some were in or near areas where, in a year of good rain, crops could be grown, but others were not. In almost all cases, easily accessible firewood had been rapidly depleted by early 1981, and the refugees had to go long distances for what little could be found.

Despite the responses of a number of countries—including the United States—to the nutritional and medical requirements of the refugees, their situation in mid–1981 remained difficult. Epidemiologists from the Centers for Disease Control reported in early 1980 that the "major problem affecting the refugee children was protein energy malnutrition." Child mortality was high, particularly among newly arrived refugees. A 1980 epidemic of measles was responsible for many deaths in camps in Gedo and Woqooyi Galbeed. Another leading cause of children's deaths was diarrhea, a consequence in part of the severe lack of adequate sanitation, particularly with respect to water sources.

To sustain the refugee population even at a low level required regular contributions from other countries, an adequate and competently managed distribution system and, if possible, some contribution by the refugees themselves to their own subsistence. In April 1981, Somalia's Ministry of National Planning and Jubba Valley Development issued its *Short– and Long–Term Programme for Refugees* detailing projected needs and proposals, all of which required international support in various forms—money, food, medical supplies, and foreign staff, among others. When the program was published, overall responsibility for refugees lay with the Ministry of Local Government and Rural Development and its National Refugee Commission. Other ministries, including those of health and education, had responsibility for specific projects. By 1990 many ministries had special divisions or sections devoted to refugee matters. However, as noted earlier, by mid–1991 government ministries had ceased functioning.

Age and sex composition, camp conditions, and refugee needs remained roughly constant until 1988, when the civil war, particularly in the north, produced a new and massive wave of refugees. This time the refugees went from Somalia to Ethiopia, where a large number of displaced northerners, mainly members of the Isaaq clan–family fleeing the violence and persecution from the Somali Army's "pacification" campaigns, sought sanctuary in Ethiopia's eastern province, Harerge Kifle Hager. The new wave of asylum–seekers almost doubled the number of displaced persons in the region. According to the UNHCR, Ethiopia and Somalia between them hosted in 1989 a refugee population of about 1.3 million. Nearly 960,000 of the total were ethnic Somalis. Somalia hosted 600,000 refugees, of whom nearly 80 percent were ethnic Somalis from Harerge, Ogaden, Bale, and Borena regions. The remaining 20 percent were Oromo, the largest ethnic group in the Horn of Africa, from Harerge, Bale, and Borena regions.

In southern Somalia, refugees lived in camps in the Gedo and Shabeellaha Hoose regions. In the northwest, camps were distributed in the corridor between Hargeysa and Boorama, northwest of Hargeysa. Because of the nomadic tendency of the Somali and Oromo refugees, major population shifts occurred frequently.

According to UNHCR statistical data for 1990, the camps in southern and central Somalia housed about 460,000 displaced persons. No reliable statistical data existed on the gender and age composition of the refugee population in Somalia. Informed conjecture put the sex ratio at 60 percent female and 40 percent male—the differential resulting from the migration of some of the men to the oil-rich Middle East countries, where they sought employment.

A significant number of Somali refugees emigrated to European countries, in particular Britain, the Netherlands, Sweden, Finland (where Somalis constituted the largest number of refugees), and Canada.

Britain had a particularly generous asylum policy toward Isaaq refugees.

In providing assistance and relief programs, the UNHCR had collaborated in the past with an assortment of nongovernmental organizations and voluntary agencies. Their assistance fell into two general categories: care and maintenance programs, and what was described as a "durable solution." The former were assistance programs alleviating immediate needs for food, water, sanitation, health, shelter, community services, legal assistance, and related requirements. Durable solutions were voluntary repatriation based on prior clearance given by the Ethiopian government, local integration in Somalia with limited assistance, and facilitation of integration of refugees who demonstrated a well-founded fear for their safety should they repatriate. For most refugee assistance programs, local difficulties caused problems that led to charges of mismanagement, insensitivity, and corruption.

In 1990 there were approximately 360,000 Somali refugees in eastern Ethiopia, almost all of whom belonged to the Isaaq clan from northern Somalia. These refugees had sought asylum as a result of the May 1988 attack in which Somali National Movement guerrillas seized the city of Burao for three days and almost occupied Hargeysa. In the counteroffensive, government troops indiscriminately shelled cities, causing practically the entire Isaaq urban population to flee in panic into Ethiopia. Six refugee camps contained the displaced Isaaq:

140,000 in the Aware camps of Camabokar, Rabasso, and Daror; 10,000 in Aysha; and 210,000 in two camps at Hartishek.

According to the UNHCR, in the camps for Somali refugees the refugees generally lived in family units.

Although the 1988 influx contained mainly urban dwellers from Hargeysa and Burao, by the end of 1989 the camp population included many pastoralists and nomads. Their tendency to remain in one location for only short periods presented major problems for public health monitoring.

With the flight of Siad Barre and consequent fall of his government in late January 1991, significant population shifts occurred. According to sketchy UNHCR reports, there were more than 50,000 Somali refugees in various camps in Mombasa, Kenya. These were mainly Daarood who had fled as a result of Hawiye clan–family assaults on them when the state disintegrated and the Daarood residents of Mogadishu became the objects of revenge killings. Another 150,000 were scattered in the North Eastern Province of Kenya, especially in and around the border town of Liboi and slightly farther inland. Other thousands had fled to eastern Ethiopia, where the UNHCR stated it was feeding more than 400,000 ethnic Somalis. Many others were dispersed throughout the border areas.

BREAKDOWN OF THE INFRASTRUCTURE

The Somali environment—both human and ecological—has deteriorated since the collapse of the state in early 1991. The consequent outbreak of intra- and interclan conflicts engulfed the peninsula in a catastrophic civil war that had claimed, by a conservative estimate, more than 200,000 Somali lives by early 1992. The cities of Mogadishu and Hargeysa had been reduced to rubble, with government buildings and homes looted or razed by gangs armed with assault rifles. Even telephone wires had been dug up, stolen, and exported for sale to the United Arab Emirates.

In the fields of education and health, a sharp decline occurred and only minimal services continued to exist.

Because of the destruction of schools and supporting services, a whole generation of Somalis faced the prospect of a return to illiteracy. Many people who had fled to the cities initially because of the civil war sought refuge in camps elsewhere, often refugee camps outside Somalia. More than one year of civil war had wiped out most of the intellectual and material progress of the preceding thirty years. In short, Somali society had retrogressed to a collection of warring clans reminiscent of preindustrial times.

* * * Enrico Cerulli's three–volume work, *Somalia: Scritti Vari Editi ed Inediti*, remains the most comprehensive study of Somali society: pastoral institutions, history, politics, literature, and language. The classic work on the social and political system of pastoral nomadic Somalis of northern Somalia (based on research done in the 1950s) is I M. Lewis's *A Pastoral Democracy. Peoples of the Horn of Africa: Somalia, Afar, and Saho a* so by Lewis is a major source on Somali ethnic groups. The dean of Somali studies, Lewis has written numerous articles, several of which deal with Somali Islam and indigenous religion. His "From Nomadism to Cultivation" provides an introduction to the traditional social and political orders of the interriverine sedentary Somalis. Virginia Luling has published some of her findings on one group of sedentary Somalis (the Geledi clan and its neighbors) in "Colonial and Postcolonial Influences on a South Somali Community." David Laitin's *Politics, Language, and Thought: The Somali Experience* concerns the political aspects of deciding on a written form for the Somali language.

Lee Cassanelli's *The Shaping of Somali Society* sheds valuable light on the evolution and structure of southern Somali tribes, such as the Geledi and Biyamaal, as well as on Islamic institutions such as the cult of saints.

Said S. Samatar's *Oral Poetry and Somali Nationalism* provides a comprehensive treatment of the intimate interplay between pastoralism and oral poetry and that literary form's uses as a tool in mobilizing public opinion, in mass communication, and in related areas of oratory and rhetoric. (For further information and complete citations, see Bibliography.)

Chapter 3. The Economy

Bananas, one of Somalia's principal commercial crops A READY SERIOUSLY WEAKENED by a devastating civil war, the Somali economy was further undermined by the fall of President Mahammad Siad Barre's government in late January 1991 and the subsequent absence of political consensus. Economic statistics from the early post–Siad Barre period were not available in early 1992; however, one can gain some understanding of Somalia's economic situation during that period by looking at the country's prior economic history.

Generally, interventions in the Somali economy, whether by Italian fascists, Somali Marxists, or International Monetary Fund (IMF—see Glossary) economists, have had minimal impact on economic development. Yet the shrewd Somalis have been able to survive and even prosper in their harsh desert homeland.

PASTORALISM AND COMMERCE IN HISTORICAL PERSPECTIVE

The Somalis raise cattle, sheep, and goats, but the camel plays the central role as an indicator of wealth and success. Camels can survive in an environment where water and grazing areas are scarce and widely scattered.

They provide meat, milk, and transportation for Somali pastoralists, and serve as their principal medium of exchange. Camels are provided as compensation for homicides and are a standard component of the dowry package.

For centuries, nomads have relied on their livestock for subsistence and luxuries. They have sold cows, goats, and older camels to international traders and butchers in the coastal cities, and in the urban markets have bought tea, coffee beans, and salt. In the nineteenth century, northern Somalis were quick to take advantage of the market for goats with middlemen representing the British, who needed meat for their enclave in Aden, a coaling station for ships traveling through the Suez Canal. By the turn of the century, about 1,000 cattle and 80,000 sheep and goats were being exported annually

159

from Berbera to Aden.

Starting in the fifteenth century, the ports of Saylac and Berbera were well integrated into the international Arab economy, with weapons, slaves, hides, skins, gums, ghee (a type of butter), ostrich feathers, and ivory being traded. On the Banaadir coast, especially in Mogadishu but also in Merca and Baraawe, a lively trade with China, India, and Arabia existed as early as the fourteenth century. Finally, starting with the Somalis who for centuries have joined the crews of oceangoing ships, the exportation of labor has long been a crucial element in Somalia's ability to sustain itself.

The temporary file will be purged from our system in a few hours.

THE COLONIAL ECONOMY

The colonial era did not spark foreign economic investment despite the competition of three major European powers in the area of present–day Somalia. Italy controlled southern Somalia; Britain northern Somalia, especially the coastal region; and France the area that became Djibouti (see Imperial Partition , ch. 1). Italian parliamentary opposition restricted any government activity in Somalia for years after European treaties recognized Italian claims. In the early twentieth century, projects aimed at using Somalia as a settlement for Italian citizens from the crowded homeland failed miserably. Although in the early 1930s Benito Mussolini drew up ambitious plans for economic development, actual investment was modest.

There was still less investment in British Somaliland, which India had administered. During the prime mininstership of William Gladstone in the 1880s, it was decided that the Indian government should be responsible for administering the Somaliland protectorate because the Somali coast's strategic location on the Gulf of Aden was important to India. Customs taxes helped pay for India's patrol of Somalia's Red Sea Coast.

The biggest investment by the British colonial government in its three–quarters of a century of rule was in putting down the rebellion of the dervishes. In 1947, long after the dervish war of the early 1900s (see Mahammad Abdille Hasau's Dervish Resistance to

Colonial Occupation, ch. 1), the entire budget for the administration of the British protectorate was only £213,139. If Italy's rhetoric concerning Somalia outpaced performance, Britain had no illusions about its protectorate in Somaliland. At best, the Somali protectorate had some strategic value to Britain's eastern trading empire in protecting the trade route to Aden and India and helping assure a steady supply of food for Aden.

The two major economic developments of the colonial era were the establishment of plantations in the interriverine area and the creation of a salaried official class. In the south, the Italians laid the basis for profitable export–oriented agriculture, primarily in bananas, through the creation of plantations and irrigation systems. In both the north and the south, a stable petty bourgeois class emerged. Somalis became civil servants, teachers, and soldiers, petty traders in coastal cities, and small–business proprietors.

The plantation system began in 1919, with the arrival in Somalia of Prince Luigi Amedeo of Savoy, duke of Abruzzi, and with the technical support of the fascist administration of Governor Cesare Maria de Vecchi de Val Cismon. The Shabeelle Valley was chosen as the site of these plantations because for most of the year the Shabeelle River had sufficient water for irrigation. The plantations produced cotton (the first Somali export crop), sugar, and bananas. Banana exports to Italy began in 1927, and gained primary importance in the colony after 1929, when the world cotton market collapsed. Somali bananas could not compete in price with those from the Canary Islands, but in 1927 and 1930 Italy passed laws imposing tariffs on all non–Somali bananas. These laws facilitated Somali agricultural development so that between 1929 and 1936 the area under banana cultivation increased seventeenfold to 3,975 hectares. By 1935 the Italian government had constituted a Royal Banana Plantation Monopoly (Regia Azienda Monopolio Banane—RAMB) to organize banana exports under state authority. Seven Italian ships were put at RAMB's disposal to encourage the Somali banana trade. After World War II, when the United Nations (UN) granted republican Italy jurisdiction over Somalia as a trust territory, RAMB was reconstituted as the Banana Plantation Monopoly (Azienda Monopolio Banane—AMB) to encourage the revival of a sector that had been nearly demolished by the war.

Plantation agriculture under Italian tutelage had short–term success, but Somali products never became internationally competitive. In 1955 a total of 235 concessions embraced more than 45,300 hectares (with only 7,400 hectares devoted to bananas), and produced

94,000 tons of bananas. Under fixed contracts, the three banana trade associations sold their output to the AMB, which exacted an indirect tax on the Italian consumer by keeping out cheaper bananas from other sources. The protected Italian market was a mixed blessing for the Somali banana sector. Whereas it made possible the initial penetration by Somali bananas of the Italian marketplace, it also eliminated incentives for Somali producers to become internationally competitive or to seek markets beyond Italy.

The investment in cotton showed fewer long–term results than the investment in bananas. Cotton showed some promise in 1929, but its price fell following the collapse in the world market. Nearly 1,400 tons in 1929 exports shrank to about 400 tons by 1937. During the trust period, there were years of modest success; in 1952, for example, about 1,000 tons of cotton were exported. There was however, no consistent growth. In 1953 exports dropped by two–thirds. Two reasons are given for cotton's failure as an export crop: an unstable world market and the lack of Somali wage labor for cotton harvesting. Because of the labor scarcity, Italian concessionaires worked out coparticipation contracts with Somali farmers; the Italians received sole purchasing rights to the crop in return for providing seed, cash advances, and technical support.

Another plantation crop, sugarcane, was more successful. The sugar economy differed from the banana and cotton economies in two respects: sugar was raised for domestic consumption, and a single firm, the Italo–Somali Agricultural Society (Societa Agricola Italo–Somala—SAIS), headquartered in Genoa, controlled the sector. Organized in 1920, the SAIS estate near Giohar had, by the time of the trust period, a little less than 2,000 hectares under cultivation. In 1950 the sugar factory's output reached 4,000 tons, enough to meet about 80 percent of domestic demand; by 1957 production had reached 11,000 tons, and Italian Somaliland no longer imported sugar.

Labor shortages beset Italian concessionaires and administrators in all plantation industries. Most Somalis refused to work on farms for wage labor. The Italians at first conscripted the Bantu people who lived in the agricultural region. Later, Italian companies paid wages to agricultural families to plant and harvest export crops, and permitted them to keep private gardens on some of the irrigated land. This strategy met with some success, and a relatively permanent work force developed. Somali plantation agriculture was of only marginal significance to the world economy, however. Banana exports reached US$6.4 million in 1957; those of cotton, US$200,000. But in 1957 plantation exports constituted 59 percent of total exports, representing a major

162

contribution to the Somali economy.

The colonial period also involved government employment of salaried officials and the concomitant growth of a small urban petty bourgeoisie. In the north, the British administration originally had concentrated on the coastal area for trading purposes but soon discovered that livestock to be traded came from the interior.

Therefore, it was necessary to safeguard caravan routes and keep peace in port areas, requiring the development of police forces and other civil services. In British Somaliland, many of the nomads scorned European education and opposed the establishment of Christian missions. Consequently, only a small pool of literate Somalis was available to work for the British administration. Kenyans therefore were hired. In the south, however, Somalis sent children to colonial and mission schools, and the graduates found civil service positions in the police force and as customs agents, bookkeepers, medical personnel, and teachers. These civil servants became a natural market for new retail businesses, restaurants, and coffee shops. Hargeysa in the precolonial period had almost no permanent commercial establishments; by 1945, nearly 500 businesses were registered in the district. The new salaried class filled the ranks of the Somali nationalist movement after World War II. Literate in Italian or English, these urban Somalis challenged colonial rule.

ECONOMIC DEVELOPMENT, 1960–69

At independence the Somali economy was at a near subsistence level, and the new state lacked the administrative capacity to collect taxes from subsistence herders and farmers. The state could rely on the customs taxes from international trade, which were easier to collect, but tariffs failed to meet the needs of a government with ambitious development goals. Somalia therefore relied on Italian and British subsidies, which funded about 31 percent of the new nation's current budget in the first three years of independence.

Somalia also received grants and loans from countries in the East and the West, which made possible the articulation of an ambitious development plan by 1963. A five–year plan with a budget of more than US$100 million in grants and loans, it focused on investment in infrastructure. The plan's thesis was that plantation crops and livestock exports would increase if there were better roads, transportation facilities, ports, and irrigation works. Another large investment was made in the creation of model farms to attract farmers from around the country, who would learn improved techniques to apply on their own farms. Model farms in Baidoa in the Bay Region, Afgooye near Mogadishu, and Tog Wajaale, west of Hargeysa, were established during this period.

In the pastoral sector, the Livestock Development Agency, formed in 1965–66, emphasized veterinary services, the provision of water and of holding grounds for cattle while they were undergoing inoculation, and transportation. Somali pastoralists responded with enthusiasm to the prospects for wealth by entering the international market for livestock. In the early 1960s, the value and number of exported livestock approximately doubled, and livestock soon surpassed bananas as Somalia's leading export.

There were therefore some notable successes among Somalia's early development projects. The nation became nearly selfsufficient in sugar, and banana exports grew, albeit haltingly. Livestock exports increased, and investments in roads and irrigation facilities resulted in some genuine improvements.

But the 1960s also yielded great disillusionment. The country could not overcome its dependence on foreign assistance, even to meet its current budget. Moreover, imports of foreign grains increased rapidly, indicating that the agricultural sector was not meeting the needs of the growing urban population. The modern agricultural techniques of state farms had little influence on traditional farming practices. Because of a boom in livestock export from Hargeysa, cows, goats, and camels were becoming concentrated in northern Somalia, much to the detriment of rangelands. The UN Food and Agriculture Organization (FAO) foresaw the dire effects of the 1974 drought in a 1967 report that noted the severe range deterioration. Finally, and perhaps most important, many Somalis were enervated by the feeling that political incumbents, through electoral manipulations, were squandering the nation's economic resources for their private benefit (see The Igaal Government , ch. 1).

SCIENTIFIC SOCIALISM, 1970–75

Herd of cattle and flock of goats at watering hole north of Chisimayu; such animals represent a major Somali export Courtesy Hiram A. Ruiz M hammad Siad Barre legitimated his 1969 coup d'état in terms of the national economic malaise. On October 20, 1970, the first anniversary of the coup, he announced:

In our Revolution we believe that we have broken the chain of a consumer economy based on imports, and we are free to decide our destiny. And in order to realize the interests of the Somali people, their achievement of a better life, the full development of their potentialities and the fulfillment of their aspirations, we solemnly declare Somalia to be a Socialist State.

Relying on Soviet advisers and a committed group of Italianeducated Somali "leftist" intellectuals, Siad Barre announced the 1971–73 Three–Year Plan (see Siad Barre and Scientific Socialism , ch. 1). The plan emphasized a higher standard of living for every Somali, jobs for all who sought work, and the eradication of capitalist exploitation. Agricultural "crash programs" and creation of new manufacturing plants were the immediate results.

Siad Barre quickly brought a substantial proportion of the modern economy under state control. The government nationalized banks, insurance companies, petroleum distribution firms, and the sugar–refining plant and created national agencies for construction materials and foodstuffs. Although the Somali neologism for socialism, *hantiwadaag*, could be translated as the "sharing of livestock," camel herds were not nationalized, and Siad Barre reassured pastoralists that *hantiwadaag* would not affect their animals. To mollify international business, in 1972 Siad Barre announced a liberal investment code. Because the modern economy was so small, nationalization was more showmanship than a radical change in the economy.

The creation of cooperatives soon became a cornerstone in building a socialist economy. In 1973 the government decreed the Law on Cooperative Development, with most funds going into the agricultural sector.

In the precoup years, agricultural programs had received less than 10 percent of total spending. By 1974 the figure was 29.1 percent. The investment in cooperatives had limited long–term results, however. In Galole near Hargeysa, for example, a government team established a cooperative in 1973, and government funds helped purchase a tractor, a cooperative center, and a grain storage tank. Members received token salaries as well. But in July 1977, with the beginning of the Ogaden War, state involvement in Galole ended; by 1991 the cooperative was no longer in operation.

Cooperatives also aimed at the nomad, although on a smaller scale. The 1974–78 Development Plan allocated only 4.2 percent of the budgeted funds to livestock. Government officials argued that the scientific management of rangeland—the regeneration of grazing lands and the drilling of new water holes—would be possible only under socialist cooperation. In the fourteen government–established cooperatives, each family received an exclusive area of 200 to 300 hectares of grazing land; in times of drought, common land under reserve was to become available. The government committed itself to providing educational and health services as well as serving as a marketing outlet for excess stock. Neither agricultural nor fishing cooperatives, however, proved economically profitable.

Integrated agricultural development projects were somewhat more successful than the cooperatives. The Northwest Region Agricultural Development Project, for example, survived the 1980s. Building upon the bunding (creation of embankments to control the flow of water) done by the British in the 1950s and by the United States Agency for International Development (AID) in the 1960s, the World Bank (see Glossary)

picked up the program in the 1970s and 1980s. Yields from bunded farms increased between 2.40 and 13.74 quintals per hectare over the yields from unbunded farms. However, overall improvement in agricultural production was hardly noticeable at a macroeconomic level (see table 2, Appendix).

Somalia's rural–based socialist programs attracted international development agencies. The Kuwait Fund for Arab Economic Development (KFAED), AID, and the FAO participated first in the Northern Rangelands Development Project in 1977 and in the Central Rangelands Project in 1979. These projects called for rotating grazing areas, using reserves, and creating new boreholes, but the drought of 1974 and political events undid most efforts.

During 1974–75 a drought devastated the pastoral economy. Major General Husseen Kulmiye headed the National Drought Relief Committee, which sought relief aid from abroad, among other programs. By January 1975, China, the United States, the European

Economic Community, the Soviet Union, Italy, Sweden, Switzerland, Sudan, Algeria, Yugoslavia, Yemen, and others had pledged 66,229 tons of grain, 1,155 tons of milk powder, and tons of other food products. Later that year, with aid from the Soviet Union, the government transported about 90,000 nomads from their hamlets to agricultural and fishing cooperatives in the south. The regime established new agricultural cooperatives at Dujuuma on the Jubba River (about 18,000 hectares), Kurtun Waareycnear the Shabelle River (about 6,000 hectares), and Sablaale northwest of Chisimayu (about 6,000 hectares). The KFAED and the World Bank supported irrigation projects in these cooperatives, in which corn, beans, peanuts, and rice were planted. Because the government provided seeds, water, management, health facilities, and schools, as well as workers' salaries, the farms were really state–owned farms rather than cooperatives. Essentially, they became havens for women and children because after the drought the men went off inland with whatever money they had accumulated to buy livestock to replenish their stock of animals.

The government also established fishing cooperatives. Despite a long coastline and an estimated potential yield of 150,000 tons per year of all species of fish, in the early 1970s fishing accounted for less than 1 percent of Somalia's gross domestic product (GDP—see Glossary). In 1975 cooperatives were established at Eyl, a post in the Nugaal region; Cadale, a port 1200 kilometers northeast of Mogadishu; and Baraawe. The Soviet Union supplied modern trawlers; when Soviet personnel left Somalia in 1978, Australia and Italy supported these fishing projects. Despite their potential and broad–based international support, these cooperatives failed to become profitable.

Siad Barre emphasized the great economic successes of the socialist experiment, a claim that had some truth in the first five years of the revolution. In this period, the government reorganized the sole milk–processing plant to make it more productive; established tomato–canning, wheat flour, pasta, cigarette, and match factories; opened a plant that manufactured cardboard boxes and polyethylene bags; and established several grain mills and a petroleum refinery. In addition, the state put into operation a meat–processing plant in Chisimayu, as well as a fish–processing factory in Laas Qoray northeast of Erigavo. The state worked to expand sugar operations in Giohar and to build a new sugar–processing facility in Afgooye. In three of the four leading light industries—canned meats, milk, and textiles—there were increases in output between 1969 and 1975.

Progress in the early socialist period was not uniform, however. The government heralded various programs in the transport, packaging, irrigation, drainage, fertilization, and spraying of the banana crop. Yet, despite the boom year of 1972, banana exports declined.

The temporary file will be purged from our system in a few hours.

THE SOCIALIST REVOLUTION after 1975

Camels at watering hole near Luuq on the Jubba River; camels remain a mainstay of tribal herders Courtesy Hiram A. Ruiz Water pump directing water into a trough for communal use Courtesy Hiram A. Ruiz P pular enthusiasm for the revolution began to dissipate by the mid–1970s. Many officials had become corrupt, using their positions for personal gain, and a number of ideologues had been purged from the administration as potential threats to their military superiors. Perhaps most important, Siad Barre's regime was focusing its attention on the political goal of "liberating" the Ogaden (Ogaadeen) rather than on the economic goal of socialist transformation. The Somali economy was hurt as much by these factors and by the economic cost of creating a large modern army as it was by the concurrent drought. Two economic trends from this period were noteworthy: increasing debt and the collapse of the small industrial sector.

During the 1970s, foreign debt increased faster than export earnings. By the end of the decade, Somalia's debt of 4 billion shillings (for value of the shilling—see Glossary) equaled the earnings from seventy–five years' worth of banana exports (based on 1978 data). About one–third was owed to centrally planned economies (mainly the Soviet Union, US$110 million; China, US$87.2 million; with small sums to Bulgaria and the German Democratic Republic East Germany). Another one–third of the debt was owed to countries in the Organisation for Economic Cooperation and Development (OECD). Finally, one–third was owed to members of the Organization of the Petroleum Exporting Countries (OPEC) (principally Saudi Arabia, US$81.9 million; Abu Dhabi, US$67.0 million; the Arab Fund for Economic and Social Development, US$34.7 million; Kuwait, US$27.1 million; and smaller amounts to Iraq, Qatar, the OPEC special account, Libya, and Algeria, in that order). Many loans, especially from the Soviet Union, were, in effect, written off. Later, many loan repayments to OECD states were rescheduled. But thanks to the accumulated debt burden, by the 1980s the economy could not attract foreign capital, and virtually all international funds made available to Somalia in rescheduling agreements came with the provision that international civil servants would monitor all expenditures. As a result of its international debt, therefore, Somalia lost control over its macroeconomic structure.

A second ominous trend in the 1975–81 period was the decline of the manufacturing sector. Exports of manufactured goods were negligible when the 1969 coup occurred; by the mid–1970s, manufactured goods constituted 20 percent of total exports. By 1978, as a consequence of the Ogaden War, such exports were almost nonexistent. Production likewise suffered. In 1969 Somalia refined 47,000 tons of sugar; by 1980 the figure was 29,100 tons (all figures are for fiscal year (FY)—see Glossary). In 1975 the country produced 14.4 million cans of meat and 2,220 tons of canned fish. In 1979 it produced 1.5 million cans of meat and a negligible amount of canned fish. Textile output rose over the period. The only material produced, however, was a coarse fabric sold to rural people (and worn by the president) at less than cost. In milk, pasta, packaging materials, cigarettes, and matches, the trend was downward in the second half of the 1970s.

FROM SCIENTIFIC SOCIALISM TO "IMF–ISM," 1981–90

Two stages of hut building: men construct the pole framework and women do the thatching Courtesy Hiram A. Ruiz I s socialist program in disarray and its alliance with the Soviet Union lost in the wake of the 1977–78 Ogaden War, Somalia once again turned to the West (see Relations with the United States; Other Foreign Relations , ch. 4; Foreign Military Assistance , ch. 5). Like most countries devastated by debt in the late 1970s, Somalia could rely only on the nostrums of the IMF and its program of structural adjustment.

In February 1980, a standby macroeconomic policy agreement with the IMF was signed, but not implemented.

The standby agreements of July 1981 and July 1982 were completed in July 1982 and January 1984, respectively. To meet IMF standards, the government terminated its policy of acting as the last–resort employer of all secondary school graduates and abolished its monopoly on grain marketing. The government then prepared a medium–term recovery program consisting of a public investment program for 1984–86 and a phased program of policy reforms. Because the International Development Association (IDA) (see World Bank—Glossary) considered this program too ambitious, the government scaled down its projects, most notably the construction of the Baardheere Dam, which AID had advised against. The government abandoned its first reform program in 1984. In March 1984, the government signed a letter of intent accepting the terms of a new US$183 million IMF extended credit facility to run for three years. In a Somali Council of Ministers meeting in April, however, this agreement was canceled by one vote, as the soldier–ministers chafed at the proposed 60 percent cut in the military budget. The agreement also called for a further devaluation of the shilling and reductions in government personnel.

A new crisis hit Somalia in June 1983. The Saudi Arabian government decided to stop importing Somali cattle, and this ban soon was expanded to include sheep and goats. Saudi officials claimed that rinderpest had been detected in Somali livestock, making them unsafe. Cynics pointed out that Saudi businessmen recently had invested in Australian ranches and were seeking to carve out an export market for their product. In any event, the ban created a large budget deficit, and arrears on debt service started to accumulate. A major obstacle to expanding livestock and other exports was Somalia's lack of communications infrastructure: good roads and shipping facilities as well as effective telecommunications and postal services. Lack of banking facilities also posed a problem. Somalia could not easily avoid the medicine of structural adjustment.

In March 1985, in negotiations with the Paris Club (the informal name for a consortium of eighteen Western creditor countries), Somalia's debt service schedule was restructured, and the government adopted a reform program that included a devaluation and the establishment of a free market for foreign exchange for most private transactions (see table 3, Appendix). In November 1985, in conjunction with the Consultative Group of Aid Donors, a technical body of the Paris Club, the government presented its National Development Strategy and Programme with a revised three–year investment program. Western aid officials criticized this program as too ambitious. In June 1986, the government negotiated an agricultural sector adjustment program with IDA. In September 1986, a foreign exchange auction system was initiated, but its operation encountered severe difficulties because to its complete dependence on external aid. Many exchange rates applicable to different types of transactions consequently came into existence.

AID prepared a second−stage project report in 1986 that renewed the call for privatization. It praised the government for permitting the free importation of petroleum products, but chided the Somalis for not yet allowing the free marketing of hides and skins. AID put great pressure on the government, especially by means of lobbyists, to take action on legislation to permit private banking. To encourage the private sector further, AID was prepared to fund the Somali Chamber of Commerce if the Somali government would allow it to become an independent body. The 1986 report went beyond privatization by calling for means of improving the government's revenue collection and budgetary control systems. Building a government capable of collecting taxes, making policy reforms, and addressing fiscal problems became the new focus.

Along these lines, AID encouraged the elimination of civil service jobs. As of in 1985, although 5,000 civil servants had been dismissed AID felt that 80 percent of the civil service was still redundant. AID officials, however, urged pay raises for those in useful jobs.

Somalia's Five−Year Plan for 1987–91 largely reflected the international pressures and incentives of the IMF and AID. Privatization was written into the plan, as were development projects that were smaller in scale and more easily implemented. By 1988 the government had announced implementation of many IMFand AID−encouraged structural adjustment policies. In regard to foreign exchange, the government had taken many intermediate steps that would lead to the merger of the pegged and market rates. As for banking, legislation had been enacted allowing private banks to operate. In public finance, the government had reduced its deficit from 10 to 7 percent of GDP, as had been advised, but acknowledged that the increased taxes on fuel, rent, and sales had been only partially implemented. A value−added tax on fuel imports remained under consideration, but the tax on rental income had been increased and the sales tax raised from 5 to 10 percent.

The government continued to procrastinate concerning public enterprises, holding only informal discussion of plans to liquidate unprofitable enterprises.

The IMF corrected some of the worst abuses of the socialist experiment. With the devaluation of the shilling, the real cost of foreign grain became apparent to consumers, and the relative price of domestic grain rose.

Rectifying prices induced a 13.5 percent increase in agricultural output between 1983 and 1985. Inflation was tamed as well, falling from an annual rate of 59 percent in 1980 to 36 percent in 1986. World Bank officials used these data to publicize the Somali success in structural adjustment.

The overall picture was not that encouraging, however. Manufacturing output declined, registering a drop of 0.5 percent per annum from 1980 to 1987. Exports decreased by 16.3 percent per annum from 1979 to 1986.

Moreover, the 0.8 percent rise in GDP per annum from 1979 to 1986 did not keep up with population growth.

World Bank estimates put Somalia's 1989 (gross national product GNP—see Glossary) at US$1,035 million, or US$170 per person, and further estimated that between 1980 and 1989 real GNP per person had declined at 1.7 percent per year.

In the period from 1987 to 1989, the economic results of agricultural production were mixed. Although corn, sorghum, and sugarcane were principal crops, livestock and bananas remained major exports (see table 4, Appendix; Foreign Trade, this ch.). The value of livestock and banana exports in 1989 (the latest year for which data were available in May 1992) was US$26 million and US$25 million, respectively. Livestock, consisting primarily of camels, cattle, goats, and sheep, served several purposes. The animals provided milk and meat for domestic consumption, and livestock, hides, and skins for export (see table 5; table 6; Appendix).

As a result of the civil war in many areas, the economy deteriorated rapidly in 1989 and 1990. Previously, livestock exports from northern Somalia represented nearly 80 percent of foreign currency earned, but these exports came to a virtual halt in 1989. Shortages of most commodities, including food, fuel, medicines, and water, occurred virtually countrywide. Following the fall of the Siad Barre regime in late January 1991, the situation failed to improve because clan warfare intensified. Statistical data were minimal, however, for the period from 1990 onward.

NATURAL RESOURCES AND ECONOMIC INFRASTRUCTURE

Figure 6. Transportation System, 1992 S malia is not well–endowed with natural resources that can be profitably marketed internationally, and at independence the economic infrastructure was poorly developed. Throughout all three eras in postindependence Somalia, officials had sought, with mixed results, to develop the economic infrastructure.

Land

Estimates vary, but from 46 to 56 percent of Somalia's land area can be considered permanent pasture. About 14 percent is classified as forest. Approximately 13 percent is suitable for cultivation, but most of that area would require additional investments in wells and roads for it to be usable. The remaining land is not economically exploitable. In the highlands around Hargeysa, relatively high rainfall has raised the organic content in the sandy calcareous soils characteristic of the northern plains, and this soil has supported some dry farming. South of Hargeysa begins the Haud, whose red calcareous soils continue into the Ethiopian Ogaden.

This soil supports vegetation ideal for camel grazing. To the east of the Haud is the Mudug Plain, leading to the Indian Ocean coast; this region, too, supports a pastoral economy. The area between the Jubba and Shabeelle rivers has soils varying from reddish to dark clays, with some alluvial deposits and fine black soil.

This is the area of plantation agriculture and subsistence agropastoralism.

Practices concerning land rights varied from rural to urban areas. In precolonial times, traditional claims and interclan bargaining were used to establish land rights. A small market for land, especially in the plantation areas of the south, developed in the colonial period and into the first decade of independence. The socialist regime sought to block land sales and tried to lease all privately owned land to cooperatives as concessions.

Despite the government's efforts, a de facto land market developed in urban areas; in the bush, the traditional rights of clans were maintained.

173

The Siad Barre regime also took action regarding the water system. In northern Somalia from 1988 to 1991, the government destroyed almost all pumping systems in municipal areas controlled by the Somali National Movement (SNM) or failing that, stole the equipment. In rural areas, the government poisoned the wells by either inserting animal carcasses or engine blocks that leaked battery acid. As a result, northern Somalis had to rely on older gravity water systems, use poor quality water, or buy expensive water. Following the declaration of the independent Republic of Somaliland in the north in May 1991, the government of the republic began ongoing efforts to reconstruct the water system.

In the south, in the late 1980s onward, as a result of war damage and anarchy, the water situation in the towns tended to resemble that in the north. Few pumping systems were operational in early 1992. Conditions in rural areas varied. Many villages had at least one borehole from which poor quality water could be obtained in buckets; pumps generally were nonfunctioning. Somalis who lived near the Jubba or Shabeelle rivers could obtain their water directly from the river.

Energy

Somalia relied principally on domestic wood and charcoal and on imported petroleum to meet its energy needs. Attempts to harness the power of the Jubba River at the proposed Baardheere Dam had not come to fruition as of early 1992. Electrical utilities had been state owned since 1970, when foreign-owned enterprises were nationalized. Throughout the country, about eighty different oil-fired thermal and diesel power plants relied on imported petroleum. With aid from Finland, new plants were constructed in the Chisimayu and Baidoa areas in the mid-1980s.

Somalia relied on foreign donors (first the Soviet Union and then Saudi Arabia) to meet its petroleum needs.

In the late 1970s, Iraq helped Somalia build a refinery at Jasiira, northeast of Baraawe, that had a capacity of 10,000 barrels a day. But when the Iran-Iraq War broke out in 1980, deliveries were suspended, and Somalia again required refined oil imports. As of mid-1989, Somalia's domestic requirements were again being met by this refinery, but deliveries of Iraqi crude oil were erratic. In May 1989, Somalia signed an agreement with the Industrial Export, Import, and Foreign Trade Company of Romania by which the company was to construct an oil refinery on the outskirts of Mogadishu. The project was to cost US$500 million and result in a refining capacity of 200,000 barrels per day. Because of events in Romania and Somalia, the refinery project had not materialized as of early 1992.

Throughout the 1980s, various international oil companies explored for oil and natural gas deposits in Somalia. In October 1991, the World Bank and the UN Development Programme announced the results of its hydrocarbon study in the countries bordering the Red Sea and the Gulf of Aden. The study indicated the potential for oil and gas in northern Somalia was good. In view of the civil war in Somalia following the fall of Siad Barre, however, various foreign oil exploration plans were canceled.

A successful innovation was the completion of a wind energy utilization project. Four wind turbines, each rated at 50 kilowatts, were embedded in the Mogadishu electrical grid. In 1988 these turbines produced 699,420 kilowatt hours of energy. Total electric energy produced in 1988, the latest year for which figures were available in early 1992, was 257 million kilowatt hours. Five self–contained wind energy conversion systems in rural centers also were planned, but as of May 1992 there was no information that these had been built.

Transportation

In 1988 the total expenditure for transportation and communications was US$57.8 million. Nearly 55 percent of this amount was for new infrastructure; 28 percent was for rehabilitation and maintenance of existing infrastructure. This activity must be understood in the context of the ongoing civil war in Somalia; much of the infrastructure particularly bridges in the north, either had deteriorated or been destroyed, as a result of the fighting. As of early 1992, no systematic study existed of the infrastructural costs of the civil war.

At independence, Somalia inherited a poorly developed transportation system consisting of a few paved roads in the more populated areas in the south and northwest, four undeveloped ports equipped only with lighterage facilities, and a handful of usable airstrips (see fig. 6). During the next three decades, some improvement was made with the help of substantial foreign aid. By 1990 all–weather roads connected most of the important towns and linked the northern and southern parts of the country. Three ports had been substantially improved, eight airports had paved runways, and regular domestic air service also was available. But in early 1992, the country still lacked the necessary highway infrastructure to open up undeveloped areas or to link isolated regions, and shipping had come to a virtual halt because of the security situation.

In 1990 Somalia had more than 21,000 kilometers of roads, of which about 2,600 kilometers were paved, 2,900 kilometers were gravel, and the remainder were improved earth. The country's principal highway was a 1,200–kilometer two–lane paved road that ran from Chisimayu in the south through Mogadishu to Hargeysa in the north. North of Mogadishu, this route ran inland, roughly paralleling the border with Ethiopia; a 100–kilometer spur ran to the Gulf of Aden at Berbera. By early 1992 much of this road, especially the northern part between Hargeysa and Berbera, was relatively unsafe because of land mines. Somalia's 1988 plan provided for another connection from this main route to Boosaaso on the Gulf of Aden. Somalia had only one paved road that extended from north of Mogadishu to Ethopia; all other links to neighboring countries were dirt trails impassable in rainy weather.

Four ports handled almost all of Somalia's foreign trade. Berbera, Mogadishu, and Chisimayu were deepwater ports protected by breakwaters. Merca, just south of Mogadishu, was a lighterage port that required ships to anchor offshore in open roadsteads while loading and unloading. Mogadishu was the principal port of entry for most general cargo. Berbera received general cargo for the northern part of the country and handled much of the nation's livestock exports. United States aid enabled the doubling of the berths at the port of Barkera and the deepening of the harbor, completed in 1985 at a cost of US$37.5 million. Maydh, northwest of Erigaro, was the only other and much smaller northern port. Chisimayu's main function was the export of bananas and meat; the meat was processed and packed at the port. The United States also financed the US$42 million development of Chisimayu port in the latter half of the 1980s. Merca was an export point for bananas.

In 1986 the Somali Ports Authority launched a modernization project for all ports, with concentration on Mogadishu. The cost was estimated at US$24.4 million, of which the

IDA provided US$22.6 million as a credit.

Mogadishu International Airport was the nation's principal airfield; in the 1980s, was a runway extended to 4,500 meters one of the runway was Africa's longest with United States financial aid. The airport was further expanded in 1989 by Italy's contribution from its emergency aid fund for Africa. Only Mogadishu offered international flights. Somali Airlines, the nation's flag carrier, was partially owned by Alitalia, the Italian national airline. Somali Airlines in 1989 replaced its fleet of five aging 707 airplanes with one Airbus 310, making it a one–plane international airline. In 1990 domestic service linked Mogadishu with Berbera and six other Somali cities; flights were scheduled at least once a week. As of April 1992, Somali Airlines had no scheduled flights, domestic or international, and no other regular flights existed.

Communications

Somalia's telecommunications system was rudimentary. In 1991 a ground satellite station linked with the International Telecommunications Satellite Organization's (Intelsat) Indian Ocean satellite provided television, telephone, and data links with the rest of the world. A second ground satellite station, part of the satellite system for Arab nations (Arabsat), was under construction. It was not known in May 1992 whether any of these systems were operative. To improve the telecommunications system between Somalia and European and Persian Gulf countries, the European Development Fund in 1988 provided 5 million European currency units (ECU). Japan contributed a further US$83 million in 1988 for a telecommunications project to be completed in 1991; implementation was delayed, however, by the anarchy prevailing after the fall of Siad Barre.

Domestic communications were poor. The civil war in 1988 destroyed the Hargeysa radio station but the SNM in early 1992 continued to broadcast daily on a frequency modulation (FM) station near Hargeysa renamed the Voice of the Republic of Somaliland. Two factions of the United Somali Congress (USC) in early 1992 reportedly had radio transmitters in the south with regular transmissions. The entire country in 1990 had only 17,000 telephones, of which 14,000 were in the capital. In early 1992, however, the telephone system was virtually inoperative.

THE "REAL" SOMALI ECONOMY IN THE 1980s

Camel caravan transporting goods in northern Somalia between Hargeysa and Berbera Courtesy Hiram A. Ruiz Truck loaded with passengers and household goods Courtesy Hiram A. Ruiz The Somali economy in the 1980s, when viewed in standard economic terms, was characterized by minimal economic reform and declining GDP per capita. But the macroeconomic perspectives, which were based on questionable data, presented an unreliable picture of the actual Somali economy. In fact, the macroeconomic figures used by the IMF and the World Bank would lead one to wonder how any Somalis could have physically survived the recent years of economic crisis. Yet visitors to Somalia, although distressed by the civil war and the wanton killing, observed a relatively well—fed population up until the 1991—92 drought.

Clearly a Somali economy existed outside the realm of international data collection. Examination of what has been called Somalia's "unconventional" economy allows a better appreciation of how the Somali economy actually worked.

Export of Labor

Somalia was an exporter of labor to other members of the League of Arab States (Arab League), and Somali citizens received remittances from these workers. These remittances constituted the largest source of foreign exchange in the economy. Based on an assumption of 165,000 Somali overseas workers, with an average annual wage of US$6,150, one—third of which was being remitted, one economist has calculated that more than US$330 million was being remitted annually. This figure represented fifteen times the sum of Somalia—based yearly wages and nearly 40 percent of total GNP, including remittances. The official remittance figure was US$30 million, the amount channeled through banks. Most unofficial remittances—in the form of foreign exchange and household goods and appliances sent home from abroad—went to urban traders. This fact explains the apparent abundance of supplies in Somali cities, which, based on the foreign exchange estimates from official sources, would not have been possible. A large portion of the remittances went to supply arms to the rural guerrillas who toppled the government in January 1991 (see Sources of Opposition , ch. 5).

178

Export of Livestock

As the macroeconomic data made clear, Somalia was primarily an exporter of livestock to the Arab states.

The macroeconomic data did not make clear the proportions in which the foreign exchange earnings from livestock exports went to the government, based on the official exchange rate of those recorded sales, and to the traders and herders themselves, based on the difference between the official and informal exchange rates plus all revenues from unofficially recorded sales. A system known as *franco valuta* (see Glossary) enabled livestock middlemen to hoard a considerable foreign exchange surplus. In the livestock export sector, traders had to give the government only 40 percent of their foreign exchange earnings; the traders could import anything they wished with the remaining foreign exchange. Thus, imports were substantial amid data of collapse. One needed only to be connected to a trading family to enjoy massive increases in consumption during the 1980s. In the livestock export system, *franco valuta* was officially discontinued as a result of the IMF structural adjustment program, but in practice *franco valuta* continued to be observed.

In the 1970s, northern trading families used their profits to buy real estate, much of it in Mogadishu. In the 1980s, they helped subsidize the rebels fighting the government of Siad Barre.

Rural Subsistence Sector

Somalia's rural subsistence sector produced sufficient grain and animal products (mostly milk) to sustain the country's growing population, including its massive refugee population. According to economist Vali Jamal, data on the subsistence sector underestimated the amount of milk and grain produced. The official 1978 estimate of milk production was 451.4 million liters; by using alternate data (for example, statistics on lactating animals from an anthropology study, consumption surveys, and interviews with nomads), Jamal estimated 2.92 billion liters of production, 6.5 times the official estimate. Taking into account only this change in milk production would raise GDP by 68 percent, making Somalia the forty–first rather than the eighth poorest country in the world, with an average annual per capita income of US$406.

Jamal's data showed a 58 percent increase in grain production between 1972–74 and 1984. Production of sorghum and corn reached a high of an estimated 260,000 tons and 382,000 tons respectively in 1985, before declining in the period 1987–89. Grain imports increased sixfold, however, between the early 1970s and 1985; the increase was largely caused by the refugee influx and the added imports needed to fill the food gap.

After 1980 food production increased but imports continued, primarily as a result of food aid. Governments did not cut off food aid although the need for it steadily receded. Despite donor objectives, most of the imports went to urban shops rather than rural refugee camps.

Often missed by macroeconomic analyses was the vibrant agropastoralist sector of the southern interriverine area. Families mixed pastoralism—the raising of goats and sheep, and sometimes camels—with grain production. The family unit was highly versatile, and the division of labor within it changed depending on the season and the amount of rainfall. During a drought when women were obliged to trek for days in search of water, men tended the household and crops. When water was abundant, women maintained the household, and enabling the men to concentrate on the livestock.

Trade between the pastoralist and agropastoralist sectors has been greater than standard models of the Somali GNP have assumed. Agropastoralists accumulated small grain surpluses in the 1980s, and bartered this grain to pastoralists in exchange for milk. The agropastoralists received more value from this trade than by selling their grain directly to the government because government prices for grain were lower than the growers' costs.

IMF agreements with the government repealed price limits on the sale of grain; the consequences of this agreement for trade between pastoralists and agropastoralists had not been reported as of early 1992.

One of the great agricultural success stories of privatization caused great embarrassment to the IMF. Qat (also spelled "kat," *catha edulis*) is a mild stimulant narcotic; many Somalis chew the qat leaf during leisure time.

Qat is grown in the Ethiopian highlands and in Kenya and is transported through Somalia. In the late 1960s, farmers near Hargeysa began growing it. During the drought of the 1970s, the qat plants survived and their cultivators made handsome profits. Investment in qat plants soared in the 1980s. Sales of qat enabled farmers to stay ahead of inflation during a time when prices for other crops fell. Many farmers used their profits to rent tractors and to hire day laborers; doing so enabled them to increase food production while continuing to grow qat. The large surplus income going to qat farmers created a free market in land, despite national laws prohibiting land sales. The IMF never mentioned this economic success as part of the positive results of its program. The government wrongly believed that the production of qat was cutting into grain production; the data of political scientist Abdi Ismail Samatar indicates that farmers producing qat grew more grain than those who did not produce qat. The government also believed that qat was harmful because it was making the general population drug–dependent. The Siad Barre regime hence banned qat production, and in 1984 qat fields were destroyed by government teams. Nevertheless, the qat story of the 1980s demonstrated the vibrancy of the Somali economy outside the regulatory regimes of the government and the IMF.

Urban Subsistence and Government Employment

The Somali government and its officials collected grants and bribes from foreign governments and taxes on internal trade that provided substantial wealth to the ruling elite. As of July 1991, domestic trade in the south for the most part had been disrupted. Only small quantities of goods such as fruit, sugarcane, and charcoal moved from the villages to the towns, in return for cornmeal and, since 1988, guns and ammunition. At a national level, armed trucks traveled from Jilib, on the Jubba River, or Chisimayu, to Mogadishu, carrying from the Jubba River area agricultural products such as mangoes and sesame and returning with corn, wheat, refined sugar, and diesel fuel. International trade by sea was at a virtual standstill, but goods were smuggled across the border with Kenya in return for qat primarily. In the north at the same period, the anarchic situation since 1988 had severely curtailed agricultural trade, particularly livestock exports. In addition, those farmers in areas where planting was potentially feasible in 1991, such as around Erigabo and Boorama, northwest of Horgeysa, lacked sorghum, corn, and vegetable seeds, as well as tools, and were hindered by the presence of minefields in many locations. Internationally, goods were smuggled across the Ethiopian border, largely in exchange for qat.

The funds collected in the past on internal trade also provided below–subsistence wages to a number of urban Somalis because for much of the 1980s the government served as the employer of last resort of all secondary–school graduates. Using these revenues, the government also sustained an army that was in continual warfare beginning in 1977, first against Ethiopia, and then against an internal guerrilla movement.

Largely as a result of structural adjustment in the latter half of the 1980s, government employment was not lucrative at face value. A family of six needed an estimated 6,990 shillings monthly for food, clothing, rent, fuel, light, and water. The highest civil service salary was 2,000 shillings per month, of which 525 shillings was deducted for taxes and other charges. The highest take–home pay, including allowances, in government was about 2,875 shillings.

Urban wages that were inadequate to address basic human needs might lead an analyst to expect near–starvation in urban Somalia. However, a 1984–85 household survey in Mogadishu reported that only 17 percent of the city's families lived below the poverty threshold. A November 1986 study in the Waaberi district of Mogadishu found only 7 percent had incomes below the poverty line. Informal observations of urban life in Somalia reported in the 1980s concurred that the population appeared well–fed.

The puzzle of low government wages coupled with a reasonable urban standard of living can be solved by examining the survival strategies of urban families. In the potential urban labor force of 300,000 to 360,000 people, there were only 90,282 wage earners, which suggested that government employment was only one part of a family survival strategy. Many families had one member working for the government, not so much for the salary, but for the access to other officials that enabled the family to engage in quasi–legal trading activities. Remittances from overseas prevented starvation for some families. Many urban families had members who were livestock traders and through *franco valuta* had access to foreign exchange. Many government workers prospered on bribery from the profiteers in the so–called gray economy. Other government workers could obtain "letters of credit" (the right to draw funds from government–held foreign exchange accounts) allowing them to import goods for sale and for family use. Still other civil servants moonlighted for international agencies, receiving valuable foreign currency for their efforts. These strategies were excluded from most macroeconomic assessments.

Undeveloped Sectors

In the early 1990s, the plantation economy remained undeveloped, even for bananas, which remained Somalia's principal cash crop and second most important export, after livestock. Because of government taxation of exports, this sector had been in decline in the early 1980s. In 1983 the government National Banana Board formed a joint venture with an Italian company to create Somalfruit. The higher producer prices, increased input availability, and improved marketing and shipping facilities resulted in a 180–percent increase in banana production from 60,000 tons in 1980 to 108,000 tons in 1987. By 1986 banana exports accounted for 13 percent of total exports, up from just over 1 percent in 1982 (see Foreign Trade , this ch.).

Mining

Somalia's mineral sector was of minuscule value in the overall Somali economy (in 1988 it represented only .3 percent of GDP; see; table 7, Appendix). There was some production of salt with solar evaporation methods, mining of meerschaum (sepiolite) in the Galguduud Region, mining of limestone for cement in the Berbera and Baardheere areas, and some exploitation of some of the world's largest deposits of gypsum–anhydrite near Berbera, and of quartz and piezoquartz (useful for electronics). Somalia also has some large uranium deposits in the Galguduud and Bay regions, and in 1984 work began to develop them. In the Bay Region, there are also large iron ore deposits. The development plan in 1986 reported that results of natural gas exploration in Afgooye near Mogadishu were negative, but indications of favorable oil and gas resources in the country persisted (see Energy , this ch.). Results of testing for gold in the Ceelbuur area in Galguduud Region and Arabsiyo area near Hargeysa had not been published as of early 1992.

Forestry

Nearly 14 percent of Somalia's land area was covered by forest in 1991. Frankincense and myrrh, both forest products, generated some foreign exchange; for example, in 1988 myrrh exports were valued at almost 253 million shillings. A government parastatal in 1991 no longer had monopoly rights on the sale of frankincense and myrrh, but data on sales since privatization were not available. Savanna trees had been Somalia's principal source of fuel, but desertification had rapidly eroded this fuel source, especially because refugees from the Ogaden War had foraged the bush in the vicinity of refugee camps for fuel. The government's 1988 development report stated that its sand dune stabilization project on the southern coast remained active: 265 hectares of a planned 336 hectares had been treated. Furthermore, thirty–nine range reserve sites and thirty–six forestry plantation sites had been established. Forestry amounted to about 6 percent of the GDP.

Fishing

In part because Somalia has 3,025 kilometers of coastline, fishing was a sector with excellent economic potential. Considerable attention had been paid to this sector, especially since the 1974 drought, when 15,000 nomads were resettled in fishing cooperatives. Data in the latter half of the 1980s showed improvement in the fishing industry. Food and Agriculture Organization estimates of total tons of fish caught and processed rose from 16,900 in 1986 to 18,200 in 1988, an increase that resulted from the development of a national fishing fleet. Yet fishing remained a largely unexploited sector, contributing less than 1 percent of GDP in 1990.

Manufacturing

Manufacturing achieved some success in the early 1970s, and was primarily based on processing of agricultural product. In 1986 the government planned to bring its sugar– and milkprocessing plants up to full production, to add a new cement factory in Berbera, and to contract with an Italian firm to operate its urea factory, which was producing at less than 30 percent of capacity. In 1989 a hides– and skins–processing plant in

Mogadishu was completed with Italian government financing. Despite this activity, manufacturing did not respond to IMF incentives as well as agriculture had. In 1988 there was a decline of 4.9 percent in production.

The decline followed a 5 percent increase in 1987. The government blamed the decline on shortages of inputs and spare parts and on poor management. By 1990 manufacturing had all but ceased to play a significant role in the economy, contributing only about 5 percent of GDP.

Foreign Trade

Somalia's major exports consisted of agricultural raw materials and food products. Livestock was the principal export, with sheep and goats representing the leading categories, followed by cattle and camels. Banana exports rose sharply in the 1980s and by 1986 occupied second place, followed in descending order by hides and skins, fish and fish products, and myrrh (see table 8, Appendix).

The largest single import was food, with 1986 food imports reflecting the effects of the drought being experienced in the area (see table 9, Appendix). Transportation equipment was in second place among imports, followed by nonelectrical machinery, mineral fuels, cement and building materials, and iron and steel.

In 1990 Italy was the leading importer of Somali goods, having narrowly replaced Saudi Arabia. Other Arab states, such as Yemen and the United Arab Emirates, were also important customers for Somali products. In 1990 Italy was the primary country of origin for goods imported into Somalia, with other nations such as Norway, Bahrain, and Britain distant sources of imports. Somalia consistently experienced an overall negative trade balance, which contributed to its balance of payments deficit (see table 10, Appendix).

In summary, with the 1991 overthrow of Siad Barre's government, Somalia faced a new era. Past economic experience had taught valuable lessons. First, the Somali people have for millennia been able to survive and even prosper in a harsh environment, whether it be natural or political. Second, grand economic strategies, whether from Benito Mussolini, Karl Marx, or the IMF, have not provided Somalia with a means to live beyond the subsistence level. Third, the handful of successful projects in the colonial, postindependence, socialist, and IMF–led economies suggest that a nondoctrinaire combination of approaches could promote a richer economy.

* * * Sources on the Somali economy remain scarce. The most perceptive study of the economy is a journal article by Vali Jamal, "Somalia: Understanding an Unconventional Economy." Jamal has worked in Somalia as part of an International Labour Organisation team that published *Economic Transformation in a Socialist Framework*. Two books written in the 1980s provide excellent background information and interpretation.

Abdi Ismail Samatar's *The State and Rural Transformation in Northern Somalia, 1884–1986* focuses on government economic policy, largely as it has affected the northern region. Garth Massey's *Subsistence and Change: Lessons of Agropastoralism in Somalia* provides an insightful and carefully researched examination of the agropastoral economy in the interriverine area. David Laitin and Said Samatar have written a chapter on the economy in their text, *Somalia: Nation in Search of a State*, which forms the basis of the analysis in this chapter. Statistical data are available in various publications of the Ministry of National Planning and Jubba Valley Development: *Somalia in Figures*; *Annual Development Plan, 198* 6; *National Accounts Aggregates, 1977–1988*; and *Performance of the Somali Economy, 1988*. Further data for this chapter have been culled from Ravi Gulhati's *The Making of Economic Policy in Africa* and the World Bank's *World Development Report*. (For further information and complete citations, see Bibliography.)

Chapter 4. Government and Politics

Statue of Sayyid Mahammad Abdille Hasan, the national hero of Somalia, in Mogadishu I JANUARY 1991, a bloody rebellion that had begun in 1988 finally succeeded in ending the twenty–one–year authoritarian regime of President Mahammad Siad Barre. The civil war had taken more than 50,000 civilian lives and had left the capital, Mogadishu, in shambles. Many other cities and towns also were in ruins, and hundreds of thousands of Somalis had fled to neighboring countries as refugees.

Although the major clans had been united in their opposition to Siad Barre, their leaders had no common political vision of Somalia's future. Consequently, civil strife continued at a reduced level after Siad Barre was deposed. The dominant faction in the north, the Somali National Movement (SNM), refused to accept the legitimacy of the provisional government established by the United Somali Congress (USC). Responding to widespread popular resentment of the central government, in June 1991 the SNM declared an independent Republic of Somaliland in the region that had constituted the British Somaliland before independence and unification with the former colony of Italian Somaliland in 1960.

The legacy Siad Barre left of a country devastated by civil war and riven by intense clan rivalries contrasted starkly with the future he had envisaged for Somalia when he took power in a military coup d'état in October 1969. Siad Barre, at the time a major general and commander of the army, and his fellow officers overthrew an elected civilian government that had become widely perceived as corrupt and incompetent. Siad Barre was determined to implement policies to benefit the country economically and socially and to diminish the political influence of the clans. During his regime's early years, Somalia experienced considerable economic development and efforts were made to replace clan loyalty with national pride.

However, Siad Barre proved susceptible to a cult of personality and over the years grew increasingly intolerant of criticism. Following his army's disastrous 1978 defeat in Ethiopia, Siad Barre's rule became more authoritarian and arbitrary, which only caused opposition to his regime to increase. Forsaking appeals to nationalism, Siad Barre tried to maintain control by exploiting historical clan animosities and by relying more and more on the loyalty of his own family and clan. By the mid-1980s, the opposition to Siad Barre had developed into several organized movements determined to overthrow his regime by force. Angered by what he perceived as local support of the opposition, particularly in the north, Siad Barre ordered the machine-gunning of livestock herds and the poisoning of wells in disaffected rural areas, as well as the indiscriminate bombing of cities. In the most notorious of these air attacks, the north's administrative center and largest city, Hargeysa, was virtually leveled in 1988.

Siad Barre's tactics inflamed popular anger and greatly strengthened the appeal of the various guerrilla groups.

Nevertheless, the opposition's ultimate triumph caught the rebels themselves by surprise. Their only common goal, to be rid of Siad Barre, was achieved by USC forces essentially without assistance from the other rebel groups. USC fighters had entered Mogadishu clandestinely at the end of December 1990 to assist clan members who had formed popular committees of self–defense to protect themselves from attacks by a rival clan that supported Siad Barre. The presence of the USC guerrillas prompted the intervention of the Red Berets (Duub Cas), an elite military unit whose members acted as bodyguards for Siad Barre, and which was commanded by Siad Barre's eldest son. The fighting quickly escalated, forcing the USC to send more of its forces into the city. The USC guerrillas and the Red Berets battled in the streets of the capital for four weeks.

After the USC defeated Siad Barre's forces, the other rebel movements declined to cooperate with it. Each of the several opposition groups drew its primary support from a particular clan–family (see Glossary), and Siad Barre's sudden removal from the political scene opened the way for traditional clan suspicions to reassert themselves. The reemergence of clan politics cast doubt on the prospects for Somalia's stability and unity.

By September 1991, intense rivalry among leaders of the USCdominated interim government had degenerated into street fighting within the Mogadishu area. Because the different clans resorted to the use of armed force to buttress their claims for political power, government and civil society disintegrated, and essential services such as food distribution collapsed. Nature compounded the political disaster with a prolonged drought. In 1992 severe famine affected much of southern Somalia. International relief agencies mounted a food and medical aid campaign, but an estimated 80 percent of food shipments were looted by armed groups affiliated with various clans. The worsening situation prompted the United Nations (UN) to intervene. On April 22, 1992, the UN proposed to send a 550–man mission to Somalia; and on April 24, in UN Resolution 751, the Security Council voted to send fifty UN observers to monitor the cease–fire in Mogadishu.

GOVERNMENT STRUCTURE

Poster in Mogadishu of Mahammad Siad Barre, a revolutionary leader of Somalia, deposed in 1991 Courtesy Hiram A. Ruiz F llowing its defeat of Siad Barre, the

Executive Committee of the USC announced the formation of an interim provisional government, even though it did not exercise effective authority over the entire country.

The USC chose one of its own members, Ali Mahdi Mahammad (b. 1939), as provisional president. The president served as head of state, but the duties and responsibilities of the office were not defined. For the most part, the provisional president retained the same powers that had been stipulated in the constitution of 1979. This included the authority to appoint a prime minister, and subsequently Mahammad named Umar Arteh Ghalib to that position on interim basis. Ghalib's cabinet, called the Provisional Government of National Unity, initially consisted of twenty–seven full ministers and eight deputy ministers. The ministerial portfolios included agriculture, commerce, culture and higher education, defense, exports, finance, fisheries, health, industry, information, interior, justice, labor and social affairs, livestock and forestry, petroleum and minerals, post and telecommunications, public works and housing, reconstruction and settlement, transportation, tourism, and youth.

Although the president announced that elections for a permanent government would be held as soon as security had been reestablished, rivalries within the USC, as well as opposition to the interim government in other parts of the country, made the questions of elections a moot point. Mahammad's most serious challenger was General Mahammad Faarah Aidid, leader of a USC faction that supported cooperation with the SNM.

Initially, Aidid contested the authority of the Mogadishu–based USC Executive Committee to form an interim government without consultation with other political groups that had opposed the Siad Barre regime.

Relations between the Mahammad and Aidid wings of the USC continued to deteriorate throughout the spring and summer of 1991. By September, Aidid had established his own rival government in the southern part of the capital. A series of clashes between forces loyal to Aidid and those loyal to Mahammad compelled the latter to retreat to northern Mogadishu.

Mahammad was a member of the Abgaal clan of the Hawiye clanfamily , whereas Aidid was a member of that same clan–family's Habar Gidir clan. The Abgaal clan comprised nine subclans, several of which traditionally have been dominant in the Mogadishu area. Because Abgaal leaders had not become involved in the struggle against Siad Barre until

1989, other clans tended to view them as upstarts trying to usurp control of the opposition movement. This perception was especially strong among the Habar Gidir clan, whose five subclans lived predominantly in central Somalia. Some Habar Gidir leaders had joined the SNM as early as 1984, and they had resisted efforts to create a separate Hawiye force—the USC—between 1987 and 1989. Once the USC was established, Aidid emerged as leader of the mainly Habar Gidir faction that maintained an affiliation with the SNM. The Abgaal and Habar Gidir wings of the USC were clearly distinct by November 1990 when Aidid, on behalf of this group, signed an agreement with the SNM and the Somali Patriotic Movement (SPM)

to unify military operations.

Despite their political differences, both Mahammad and Aidid had long histories of opposition to Siad Barre.

A former teacher and civil servant, Mahdi Mahammad had been elected to the 123–member National Assembly of the Republic in the March 1969 parliamentary elections. Following the military coup in October 1969, Mahdi Mahammad was arrested along with several other civilian politicians. He was released after several years in prison and subsequently became a successful Mogadishu entrepreneur. During the 1980s, he served as director of a local UN office. Eventually Mahammad used his wealth to provide crucial financial support to the USC guerrillas. In May 1990, he was one of 114 prominent citizens who signed a public manifesto calling on the government to resign and requesting that Siad Barre introduce democratic reforms.

When Siad Barre began arresting signatories to the manifesto, Mahammad fled to exile in Italy, where he worked in the USC's Rome office.

The appointment of Ghalib as provisional prime minister demonstrated the sensitivity of Mahammad and other USC leaders to the role of clans in the country's politics. Ghalib belonged to the important Isaaq clan–family of northern Somalia. Although the main opposition group in the north, the SNM, was closely identified with the Isaaqs, Ghalib was not an SNM member. Rather, his political career had associated him with national government. From 1969 to 1976, Ghalib had served as Siad Barre's first foreign minister. He was dismissed after disagreeing with Siad Barre's increasingly overt policy of supporting the ethnic Somali insurrection in Ethiopia's Ogaden (Ogaadeen) region.

Ghalib was subsequently arrested, and in 1989, after spending seven years in prison without charges, he was tried for treason and sentenced to death. Following protests from various foreign governments, Siad Barre commuted Ghalib's sentence but kept him under house arrest. In late January 1991, as his regime was collapsing, Siad Barre asked Ghalib to form a new government that would negotiate with the rebels, but the USC military successes forced Siad Barre's flight from the capital before any transfer of power could be completed.

Constitution

The provisional government called for a new constitution to replace the 1979 document that had been the law of the land at the time of Siad Barre's overthrow. The provisional government created a Ministry of Constitutional Affairs, which was charged with planning for a constitutional convention and revising an October 1990 draft constitution that Siad Barre had proposed in an unsuccessful effort to stem opposition to his rule. As of May 1992, however, the lack of consensus among the USC–dominated government and the various guerrilla groups that controlled more than half of the nation had prevented completion of a final version of the new constitution. Consequently, those provisions of the constitution of 1979 that had not been specifically voided by the interim government remained in force.

Like its 1984 amendments, the constitution of 1979 had been approved in a popular referendum. Somalia had universal suffrage for persons over eighteen years of age, but women did not play a significant role in politics (see From Independence to Revolution , ch. 1). The constitution of 1979 resembled the constitution of 1961, also approved in a nationwide referendum after the former Italian and British colonies had been unified as independent Somalia. The main difference between the two documents concerned executive power. The constitution of 1961 had provided for a parliamentary democracy, with the prime minister and Council of Ministers (cabinet) being drawn from the membership of the legislature. The legislature also elected the head of state, or president of the republic. The constitution of 1979 provided for a presidential system under which the president served as both head of state and head of government. As head of government, the president selected the members of the Council of Ministers, which he chaired. The constitution of 1979 initially called for the president to be elected to a six–year, renewable term of office by a two–thirds majority vote of the legislature. Constitutional amendments enacted in 1984 provided for direct popular election of the president to a seven–year term. The first presidential election was held in 1986. Siad Barre, the sole candidate, received 99.9 percent of the votes.

Both the 1961 and 1979 constitutions granted broad powers to the president. The constitution of 1979 authorized the president to conduct foreign affairs, declare war, invoke emergency powers, serve as commander in chief of the armed forces, and appoint one or more vice presidents, the president of the Supreme Court, up to six members of the national legislature, and the members of the Council of Ministers.

Both constitutions also provided for a unicameral legislature subject to stand for election at least once every five years; the president could dissolve the legislature earlier.

Legislature

Although the Siad Barre government suspended the National Assembly following the 1969 coup, a decade later it created a new single–chamber legislature, the People's Assembly. The constitution of 1979 stipulated that the People's Assembly have 177 members, including 6 members appointed by the president and 171 chosen by popular election. By contrast, the precoup National Assembly had only 123 members. Members of the People's Assembly served a five–year term. Two such assemblies were elected, one in 1979 and another in 1984. The elections scheduled for 1989 were postponed as a result of the civil strife that by then had engulfed most of the country.

Critics and opponents of the regime were not permitted to run in either the 1979 or the 1984 election. Instead, the government drew up lists of candidates, all of whom were members of the only legally permitted party (the Somali Revolutionary Socialist Party—SRSP), and submitted the entire lists for voter approval. In both instances, the government announced that more than 99 percent of the electorate had approved the official lists. The People's Assembly also did not truly debate any legislation. It met for several days each year and ratified whatever laws the executive had decided to submit for its "approval."

The People's Assembly was not in session when the Siad Barre government was toppled. The provisional government announced its intention to hold elections for a new legislature, but as of the spring of 1992 the continuing political disturbances in the country had prevented the formulation of definite plans for such elections.

Local Government

One of the consequences of the civil strife that began in 1988 was the alienation of many local governments from the effective authority of Mogadishu. Whereas the domestic situation as of May 1992 remained unstable, the trend appeared to be toward a decentralized system of local government similar to that existing prior to the 1969 coup. The constitution of 1961 had provided for the decentralization of administrative functions wherever feasible, and throughout the country elected councils had been responsible for municipal and district government. However, direct supervision of local government affairs by central authorities also was part of Somalia's recent history, and a return to a centralized system could not be ruled out. Indeed, the local government structures that existed in 1992 were the same ones that had been established during Siad Barre's dictatorship.

One of Siad Barre's first decrees following the 1969 military coup dissolved all the elected municipal and district councils. This edict was followed by acts that eventually reorganized local government into sixteen regions, each containing three to six districts, with the exception of the capital region (Banaadir), which was segmented into fifteen districts. Of the total eightyfour districts, some were totally urban, while others included both urban and rural communities. Local government authority was vested in regional and district councils, the members of which were appointed by the central government. A 1979 law authorized district council elections, but reserved to the government the right to approve candidates before their names were submitted to voters. Permanent settlements in rural areas had elected village councils, although all candidates had to be approved by government officials at the district level.

The Ministry of Local Government and Rural Development exercised authority over the structure of local government. Throughout Siad Barre's twenty–one–year rule, a high–ranking military officer usually headed this ministry. Military officers also were appointed as chairmen of the regional councils. Most members of the regional and district councils were drawn from the army, the police, and security personnel. Such practices ensured that those in charge of carrying out administrative functions at the local level were directly responsible to Mogadishu.

All levels of local government were staffed by personnel of the national civil service who had been assigned to their posts by the central authorities. Local councils were permitted to plan local projects, impose local taxes, and borrow funds (with prior ministerial approval), for demonstrably productive development projects.

Legal System

At independence, Somalia had four distinct legal traditions: English common law, Italian law, Islamic sharia or religious law, and Somali customary law (traditional rulers and sanctions). The challenge after 1960 was to meld this diverse legal inheritance into one system. During the 1960s, a uniform penal code, a code of criminal court procedures, and a standardized judicial organization were introduced. The Italian system of basing judicial decisions on the application and interpretation of the legal code was retained. The courts were enjoined, however, to apply English common law and doctrines of equity in matters not governed by legislation.

In Italian Somaliland, observance of the sharia had been more common than in British Somaliland, where the application of Islamic law had been limited to cases pertaining to marriage, divorce, family disputes, and inheritance. Qadis (Muslim judges) in British Somaliland also adjudicated customary law in cases such as land tenure disputes and disagreements over the payment of *diya* (see Glossary) or blood compensation. In Italian Somaliland, however, the sharia courts had also settled civil and minor penal matters, and Muslim plaintiffs had a choice of appearing before a secular judge or a qadi. After independence the differences between the two regions were resolved by making the sharia applicable in all civil matters if the dispute arose under that law. Somali customary law was retained for optional application in such matters as land tenure, water and grazing rights, and the payment of *diya*.

The military junta suspended the constitution of 1961 when it took power in 1969, but it initially respected other sources of law. In 1973 the Siad Barre regime introduced a unified civil code. Its provisions pertaining to inheritance, personal contracts, and water and grazing rights sharply curtailed both the sharia and Somali customary law. Siad Barre's determination to limit the influence of the country's clans was reflected in sections of the code that abolished traditional clan and lineage rights over land, water resources, and grazing.

In addition, the new civil code restricted the payment of *diya* as compensation for death or injury to the victim or close relatives rather than to an entire *diya*–paying group. A subsequent amendment prohibited the payment of *diya* entirely.

The attorney general, who was appointed by the minister of justice, was responsible for the observance of the law and prosecution of criminal matters. The attorney general had ten deputies in the capital and several other deputies in the rest of the country. Outside of Mogadishu, the deputies of the attorney general had their offices at the regional and district courts.

Courts

The constitution of 1961 had provided for a unified judiciary independent of the executive and the legislature.

A 1962 law integrated the courts of northern and southern Somalia into a four–tiered system: the Supreme Court, courts of appeal, regional courts, and district courts. Sharia courts were discontinued although judges were expected to take the sharia into consideration when making decisions. The Siad Barre government did not fundamentally alter this structure; nor had the provisional government made any significant changes as of May 1992.

At the lowest level of the Somali judicial system were the eighty–four district courts, each of which consisted of civil and criminal divisions. The civil division of the district court had jurisdiction over matters requiring the application of the sharia, or customary law, and suits involving claims of up to 3,000 Somali shillings (for value of the shilling, see Glossary). The criminal division of the district court had jurisdiction over offenses punishable by fines or prison sentences of less than three years.

There were eight regional courts, each consisting of three divisions. The ordinary division had jurisdiction over penal and civil cases considered too serious to be heard by the district courts. The assize division considered only major criminal cases, that is, those concerning crimes punishable by more than ten years' imprisonment. A third division handled cases pertaining to labor legislation. In both the district and regional courts, a single magistrate, assisted by two laymen, heard cases, decided questions of fact, and voted on the guilt or innocence of the accused.

Somalia's next-highest tier of courts consisted of the two courts of appeal. The court of appeals for the southern region sat at Mogadishu, and the northern region's court of appeals sat at Hargeysa. Each court of appeal had two divisions. The ordinary division heard appeals of district court decisions and of decisions of the ordinary division of the regional courts, whereas the assize division was only for appeals from the regional assize courts. A single judge presided over cases in both divisions. Two laymen assisted the judge in the ordinary division, and four laymen assisted the judge in the assize division. The senior judges of the courts of appeal, who were called presidents, administered all the courts in their respective regions.

The Supreme Court, which sat at Mogadishu, had ultimate authority for the uniform interpretation of the law.

It heard appeals of decisions and judgments of the lower courts and of actions taken by public attorneys, and settled questions of court jurisdiction. The Supreme Court was composed of a chief justice, who was referred to as the president, a vice president, nine surrogate justices, and four laymen. The president, two other judges, and four laymen constituted a full panel for plenary sessions of the Supreme Court. In ordinary sessions, one judge presided with the assistance of two other judges and two laymen. The president of the Supreme Court decided whether a case was to be handled in plenary or ordinary session, on the basis of the importance of the matter being considered.

Although the military government did not change the basic structure of the court system, it did introduce a major new institution, the National Security Courts (NSCs), which operated outside the ordinary legal system and under the direct control of the executive. These courts, which sat at Mogadishu and the regional capitals, had jurisdiction over serious offenses defined by the government as affecting the security of the state, including offenses against public order and crimes by government officials. The NSC heard a broad range of cases, passing sentences for embezzlement by public officials, murder, political activities against the state, and thefts of government food stocks. A senior military officer was president of each NSC. He was assisted by two other judges, usually also military officers. A special military attorney general prosecuted cases brought before the NSC. No other court, not even the Supreme Court, could review NSC sentences. Appeals of NSC verdicts could be taken only to the president of the republic. Opponents of the Siad Barre regime accused the NSC of sentencing hundreds of people to death for political reasons. In October 1990, Siad Barre announced the abolition of the widely feared and detested courts; as of May 1992, the NSCs had not been reinstituted by the provisional government.

Before the 1969 coup, the Higher Judicial Council had responsibility for the selection, promotion, and discipline of members of the judiciary. The council was chaired by the president of the Supreme Court and included justices of the court, the attorney general, and three members elected by the National Assembly. In 1970 military officers assumed all positions on the Higher Judicial Council. The effect of this change was to make the judiciary accountable to the executive. One of the announced aims of the provisional government after the defeat of Siad Barre was the restoration of judicial independence.

POLITICAL DYNAMICS

Mogadishu seafront, with city in background Courtesy R W S. Hudson Chisimayu, one of Somalia's leading ports Courtesy R W S. Hudson The most significant political consequence of Siad Barre's twenty–one–year rule was an intensified identification with parochial clans. By 1992 the multiplicity of political rivalries among the country's numerous clans seriously jeopardized Somalia's continued existence as a unified state. There was considerable irony in this situation because Siad Barre, following the 1969 military coup that had brought him to power, had proclaimed his opposition to clan politics and had justified the banning of political parties on the grounds that they were merely partisan organizations that impeded national integration. Nevertheless, from the beginning of his rule Siad Barre favored the lineages and clans of his own clan–family, the Daarood (see The Segmentary Social Order , ch. 2). In particular, he distributed political offices and the powers and rewards concomitant with these positions disproportionately to three clans of the Daarood: his own clan, the Mareehaan; the clan of his son-in-law, the Dulbahante; and the clan of his mother, the Ogaden. The exclusion of other clans from important government posts was a gradual process, but by the late 1970s there was a growing perception, at least among the political elite, that Siad Barre was unduly partial toward the three Daarood clans to which he had family ties.

The forced dissolution of political parties in 1969 and the continuing prohibition of political activity tended to enhance the importance of clans because family gatherings remained virtually the only regular venue where politics could be discussed freely. The creation in 1976 of the governmentsponsored Somali Revolutionary Socialist Party (SRSP) failed to fill the political vacuum created by the absence of legitimate parties. Siad Barre and his closest military advisers had formed the SRSP as the country's sole political organization, anticipating that it would transcend clan loyalties and mobilize popular support for government policies. The SRSP's five-member politburo, which Siad Barre chaired, decided the party's position on issues. The members of the SRSP, who never numbered more than 20,000, implemented directives from the politburo (via the central committee) or the government; they did not debate policy. Because most of the top SRSP leaders by 1980 were of the Mareehaan, Dulbahante, or Ogaden clans, the party became another example to disaffected clans of their exclusion from any meaningful political role.

Opposition Movements

The first clan to feel politically deprived by the military regime was the Majeerteen, which, like Siad Barre's own Mareehaan clan, belonged to the Daarood clan-family. The Majeerteen clan, along with certain clans of the Hawiye and Isaaq clan-families, had played a significant role in national politics before the 1969 military coup, and individual Majeerteen held important positions in the bureaucracy and the military. Siad Barre apparently resented the clan's prominence, and as early as 1970 was singling out the Majeerteen lineages for alleged opposition to his reform efforts. As a clan, the Majeerteen probably did not oppose Siad Barre at the outset. However, his insensitive rhetoric and discriminatory appointment and promotion policies had the effect, by the mid–1970s, of alienating the heads of the leading Majeerteen lineages, the very persons whose attitudes were decisive in determining the clan's political orientation.

Majeerteen officers were the primary organizers of an unsuccessful coup in April 1978, following the army's humiliating defeat in the Ogaden War (see Persecution of the Majeerteen , ch. 1). An estimated 500 rebel soldiers were killed in fighting with forces loyal to Siad Barre, and subsequently seventeen officers, all but one of them Majeerteen, were executed. Several colonels suspected of plotting the coup escaped capture, however, and fled abroad;one of then, Yusuf Ahmad, played a major role in forming the Somali Salvation Front (SSF), the first opposition movement dedicated to the overthrow of the Siad Barre regime by force (The SSF became the Somali Salvation Democratic Front (SSDF) in October 1981—see Sources of Opposition , ch. 5). In 1982 SSDF guerrillas with Ethiopian army units, occupied areas along the border, including two district towns, but it was not until 1988 that they began to extend their control over the western districts of Mudug Region and the southern areas of Nugaal and Bari regions.

The Isaaq clans of northwestern Somalia also resented what they perceived as their inadequate representation in Siad Barre's government. This disaffection crystallized in 1981 when Isaaq dissidents living in London formed the Somali National Movement (SNM) with the aim of toppling the Siad Barre regime. The following year, the SNM transferred its headquarters to Dire Dawa, Ethiopia, from where it launched guerrilla raids into the Woqooyi Galbeed and Togdheer regions of Somalia. Like the SSDF, the SNM had both military and political wings, proclaimed itself as a nationwide opposition movement, and tried to enlist the support of non–Isaaq clans. Initially, the SNM was more successful than the SSDF in appealing to other clans, and some Hawiye clan leaders worked with the SNM in the early and mid1980s . Prior to establishing itself within Somalia in 1988, the SNM used its Ethiopian sanctuary to carry out a number of sensational activities against the Siad Barre regime, most notably the 1983 attack on Mandera Prison near Berbera, which resulted in the freeing of several northern dissidents.

Siad Barre's response to the guerrilla movements included increased repression of suspected political dissent nationwide and brutal collective punishments in the Majeerteen and Isaaq regions. These measures only intensified opposition to his regime (see Oppression of the Isaaq , ch. 1). Nevertheless, the opposition failed to unite because Siad Barre's strategy of using one clan to carry out government reprisals against a disfavored clan had the effect of intensifying both inter– and intra–clan antagonisms. For example, Hawiye leaders who had previously cooperated with the SNM decided in 1989 to form their own clanbased opposition movement, the United Somali Congress (USC) (see Harrying of the Hawiye , ch. 1). Also, the Gadabursi and Iise clans of the Dir clan–family in northwestern Somalia and the Dulbahante and Warsangali clans of the Daarood clan–family in the Sanaag and Bari regions grew increasingly resentful of Isaaq domination of districts "liberated" from government control. In 1990 the north's largest non–Isaaq clan, the Gadabursi, created its own movement, the Somali Democratic Alliance (SDA).

The divisions within the opposition, however, did not work to Siad Barre's long–term advantage because he was gradually alienating an increasing number of the country's clans, including the very lineages of the Dulbahante and Ogaden clans that had provided his most loyal support. In particular, the Ogaden clan, living in both Somalia and Ethiopia and strongly interested in pan–Somali issues, tended to blame Siad Barre for Somalia's defeat in the 1977–78 Ogaden War. This suppressed resentment turned to defiant opposition after Siad Barre decided in 1988 to conclude a peace agreement with Ethiopia. The deteriorating relations between Siad Barre and former Ogaden supporters climaxed in 1990 with a mass desertion of Ogaden officers from the army. These officers allied with the Somali Patriotic Movement (SPM), a group that had formed in 1985 as a result of a split within the SSDF. The greatly enhanced military strength of the SPM enabled it to capture and hold several government garrisons in the south.

Politics of Reconciliation

During the final three years of Siad Barre's rule, there was relatively intense fighting throughout the country as the opposition groups gradually wrested control of extensive areas: the SNM in the northwest, the SSDF in the northeast, the USC in central Somalia, and the SPM in the south. Demonstrations against Siad Barre's rule spread even to the capital, where the military was used to suppress protests. A July 1989 mass demonstration in Mogadishu was dispersed only after government troops shot and killed a number of persons variously estimated to be between 200 and 300. The deteriorating situation alarmed those civilian politicians, businessmen, intellectuals, and religious leaders who were critical of the regime's repressive policies and supportive of introducing democratic reforms peacefully. A group of these prominent leaders, who included representatives of all the country's major clans, eventually formed the Council for National Reconciliation and Salvation (CNRS) to press demands for political change. In addition to their commitment to democratization, those involved with the CNRS also wished to create a political organization that would transcend clan loyalties. The CNRS issued its first open manifesto in May 1990. This document, signed by 114 leading citizens of Mogadishu, called for Siad Barre's resignation, the establishment of an interim government consisting of representatives of the opposition movements, and a timetable for multiparty elections.

The CNRS's manifesto aroused interest both in and outside Somalia, although it was not welcomed by Siad Barre. Nevertheless, the president was reluctant to take immediate action against the signatories because of the risks involved in antagonizing so many different clans and further straining diplomatic relations with donor countries that had become critical of his regime's human rights policies (see Foreign Relations , this ch.). Siad Barre eventually did order the arrest of the signers, although security forces were able to round up only forty–five of them. Their detention prompted strenuous protests from Egypt, Italy, and other countries, and after a few weeks the regime released them. The experience emboldened the CNRS to push more assertively for peaceful resolution of the country's political crisis. With the support of Egypt and Italy, the CNRS called in September 1990 for a national reconciliation roundtable. The CNRS invited the Siad Barre regime and five guerrilla groups to send representatives to Cairo to discuss how to end the dictatorship and return the country to democratic government. Neither Siad Barre nor the armed opposition, however, were willing to attend such a roundtable unless each party agreed to the other's conditions.

In 1990 guerrilla leaders generally were disinclined to negotiate with the Siad Barre regime because they had become convinced of their eventual success. The prospect of defeating Siad Barre inevitably compelled them to focus on relations among their various organizations. A series of informal talks concluded in August 1990 with an announcement from the SNM, the Aidid faction of the USC, and the SPM that they had agreed to coordinate strategy toward the government. In September leaders of the three groups met in Ethiopia, where they signed an agreement to form a military alliance. Although cooperation among the major opposition forces was essential to a smooth transition to a post–Siad Barre era, the pace of events after September did not provide adequate time for mutual trust and cooperative relations to develop. The SNM, USC, and SPM fighters, who for the most part operated in clan–based enclaves, never participated in any joint actions. During the final assault on Siad Barre's forces, in December 1990 and January 1991, guerrillas of the Abgaal faction of the USC infiltrated Mogadishu, whose population was approximately 80 percent Hawiye, and successfully fought without the assistance of either the SNM, the SPM, or the Habar Gidir faction of the USC.

Politics of Succession

The USC's announcement of a provisional government in February 1991 angered its allies, who maintained that they had not been consulted. Other opposition movements, particularly the SSDF, felt that the USC had slighted their long years of struggle against the Siad Barre regime, and refused to accept the legitimacy of the provisional government. The SPM and the SSDF formed a loose alliance to contest USC control of the central government and ousted USC forces from Chisimayu, Somalia's main southern city. Violent clashes throughout March threatened to return the country to civil war. Although in early April 1991, the USC and its guerrilla opponents in the south agreed to a cease–fire, this agreement broke down in the latter part of the year as fighting spread throughout those areas of Somalia under the nominal control of the the provisional government. The provisional government was continuing to hold talks on power sharing, but the prospects for long–term political stability remained uncertain.

The situation in northern Somalia was even more serious for the provisional government. The dominant SNM, whose fighters had evicted Siad Barre's forces from almost all of Woqooyi Galbeed, Togdheer, and Sanaag regions as early as October 1990, had also captured the besieged garrisons at Berbera, Burao, and Hargeysa at the end of January; they were not prepared to hand over control to the new government in Mogadishu. Like its counterparts in the south, the SNM criticized the USC's unilateral takeover of the central government, and the SNM leadership refused to participate in USC–proposed unity talks. The SNM moved to consolidate its own position by assuming responsibility for all aspects of local administration in the north. Lacking the cooperation of the SNM, the provisional government was powerless to assert its own authority in the region.

The SNM's political objectives began to clarify by the end of February 1991, when the organization held a conference at which the feasibility of revoking the 1960 act of union was seriously debated.

In the weeks following Siad Barre's overthrow, the SNM considered its relations with the non–Isaaq clans of the north to be more problematic than its relations with the provisional government. The SDA, supported primarily by the Gadabursi clan, and the relatively new United Somali Front (USF), formed by members of the Iise clan, felt apprehension at the prospect of SNM control of their areas. During February there were clashes between SNM and USF fighters in Saylac and its environs. The militarily dominant SNM, although making clear that it would not tolerate armed opposition to its rule, demonstrated flexibility in working out local power–sharing arrangements with the various clans. SNM leaders sponsored public meetings throughout the north, using the common northern resentment against the southernbased central government to help defuse interclan animosities. The SNM administration persuaded the leaders of all the north's major clans to attend a conference at Burao in April 1991, at which the region's political future was debated. Delegates to the Burao conference passed several resolutions pertaining to the future independence of the north from the south and created a standing committee, carefully balanced in terms of clan representation, to draft a constitution. The delegates also called for the formation of an interim government to rule the north until multiparty elections could be held.

The Central Committee of the SNM adopted most of the resolutions of the Burao conference as party policy.

Although some SNM leaders opposed secession, the Central Committee moved forward with plans for an independent state, and on May 17, 1991, announced the formation of the Republic of Somaliland. The new state's border roughly paralleled those of the former colony, British Somaliland. SNM Secretary General Abdirahmaan Ahmad Ali "Tour" was named president and Hasan Iise Jaama vice president. Ali "Tour"

appointed a seventeen–member cabinet to administer the state. The SNM termed the new regime an interim government having a mandate to rule pending elections scheduled for 1993. During 1991 and 1992, the interim government established the sharia as the principal law of the new republic and chose a national flag. It promised to protect an array of liberties, including freedom of the press, free elections, and the right to form political parties, and tried, albeit unsuccessfully, to win international recognition for the Republic of Somaliland as a separate country.

Politics of Disintegration

Mogadishu could not deal effectively with the political challenge in the north because the interim government of President Mahamaad gradually lost control of central authority. Even though the interim government was dominated by the USC, this guerrilla force failed to adapt to its new position as a political party. Although the USC was primarily a Hawiye militia, it was internally divided between the two principal Hawiye clans, the Abgaal and Habar Gidir. Once in power, the clans began to argue over the distribution of political offices.

Interim president Mahammad emerged as the most prominent Abgaal leader whereas Aidid emerged as the most influential Habar Gidir leader. Fighters loyal to each man clashed in the streets of Mogadishu during the summer of 1991, then engaged in open battle beginning in September. By the end of the year, the fighting had resulted in divided control of the capital. Aidid's guerrillas held southern Mogadishu, which included the port area and the international airport, and Mahammad's forces controlled the area around the presidential palace in central Mogadishu and the northern suburbs.

A United Nations–mediated cease–fire agreement that came into effect in March 1992 helped to reduce the level of fighting, but did not end all the violence. Neither Mahammad nor Aidid was prepared to compromise over political differences, and, consequently, Mogadishu remained divided. Aidid's faction of the USC comprised an estimated 10,000 guerrillas. Many of these men looted food supplies destined for famine victims and interfered with the operations of the international relief agencies. They justified their actions on the grounds that the assistance would help their enemies, the USC faction loyal to Mahammad. The proMahammad forces included an estimated 5,000 fighters. They also used food as a weapon.

MASS MEDIA

Prior to the overthrow of the Siad Barre regime in January 1991, all domestic publications and broadcasting were controlled by the government. The Ministry of Information and National Guidance published the country's only daily newspaper,

Xiddigta Oktoobar (October Star), which offered editions in Arabic, English, Italian, and Somali. The ministry also published a variety of weekly and monthly magazines. The state–run Somali National News Agency (SONNA) distributed press reports about the country to foreign news bureaus.

The ministry's Broadcasting Department was responsible for radio and television broadcasts. The two radio stations, at Mogadishu and Hargeysa, transmitted a variety of news and entertainment programs. Radio Mogadishu featured about two hours each day of programs in foreign languages, including Afar, Amharic, Arabic, English, French, Italian, Oromo, and Swahili. In 1988, the most recent year for which statistics were available, there were an estimated 375,000 radio receivers in Somalia. Television service was inaugurated in 1983; two hours of programs were broadcast daily from Mogadishu. The civil war disrupted service in the 1990s, however.

After Siad Barre's ouster, the provisional government maintained the publishing and broadcasting functions of the Ministry of Information and National Guidance. However, it had no authority over the new Radio Hargeysa, which was controlled by the SNM, and which, following the May 1991 declaration of independence, renamed the Voice of the Republic of Somaliland. The provisional government in the south announced that newspapers would be permitted to publish free of government censorship, but by mid–1991, the only new paper that had appeared was the USC's *Al Majlis* (The Council). Subsequently, publication of newspapers became impossible because the country disintegrated into civil war in late 1991 and early 1992. L brary of Congress Country Studies *Do NOT bookmark these search results.*

Search results are stored in a TEMPORARY file for display purposes.

FOREIGN RELATIONS

One of numerous foreign relief grain shipments being unloaded in Berbera port for distribution, 1991 Courtesy Hiram A. Ruiz An elderly woman from Burao, a town in northern Somalia severely damaged in the civil war, 1991 Courtesy Hiram A. Ruiz Village children near their hut Courtesy Hiram A. Ruiz The provisional government established in February 1991 inherited a legacy of problematic relations with neighboring states and economic dependence on aid from Arab and Western nations. Relations between Somalia and its three neighbors— Djibouti, Ethiopia, and Kenya—had been poisoned for more than two decades by Somalia's irredentist claims to areas inhabited by ethnic Somalis in each of these three states. The 1977–78 Ogaden War with Ethiopia, although a humiliating defeat for Somalia, had created deep suspicions in the Horn of Africa concerning the intentions of the Siad Barre regime. The continuing strain in Somali–Ethiopian relations tended to reinforce these suspicions.

Civil strife in Ethiopia and repressive measures in the Ogaden caused more than 650,000 ethnic Somalis and Oromo residing in Ethiopia to flee to Somalia by early 1978. The integration of so many refugees into an essentially agrarian society afflicted by persistent drought was beyond Somalia's economic capacity. In the absence of a peace agreement, prospects for repatriation continued to be virtually nonexistent. The Siad Barre government's solution to this major political, social, and economic problem was to make the search for generous financial assistance a focal point of its foreign policy.

Relations with Other African States

For ten years after the Ogaden War, the Siad Barre government refused to renounce its public support of the Ethiopian guerrilla organization, the Western Somali Liberation Front, and provided it with clandestine military assistance to carry out raids inside Ethiopia. The Mengistu government responded in kind by providing bases, sanctuary, and military assistance to the SSDF and the SNM. Siad Barre's fear of Ethiopian military power induced him in the early 1980s to begin a process of rapprochement with Somalia's other neighbors, Kenya and the former French territory of Djibouti. Kenya had long suspected Somalia of encouraging separatist activities among the predominantly ethnic Somali population in its Northern Frontier District. Following a 1981 summit meeting with Kenyan president Daniel arap Moi in Nairobi, Siad Barre's public renunciation of any Somali territorial claims on Kenya helped dissipate mistrust.

Beginning in 1982, both Kenya and Djibouti, apparently encouraged by Siad Barre's stated willingness to hold direct talks with Mengistu, made diplomatic efforts to mediate between Somalia and Ethiopia. It was not until 1986, however, that Siad Barre and Mengistu finally agreed to meet. This first meeting since before the Ogaden War took place in the city of Djibouti and marked the beginning of a gradual rapprochement. Siad Barre's willingness to defuse the situation along the Somali–Ethiopian border stemmed from the combined pressures of escalating guerrilla activity, overt Ethiopian military threats, drought, and the destabilizing presence of hundreds of thousands of Ethiopian refugees. Siad Barre and Mengistu held a second meeting in April 1988, at which they signed a peace agreement and formally reestablished diplomatic relations. Both leaders agreed to withdraw their troops from their mutual borders and to cease support for armed dissident groups trying to overthrow the respective governments in Addis Ababa and Mogadishu.

The peace accord failed to provide Siad Barre respite from guerrilla activity and probably contributed to his eventual demise. Anticipating the possibility of being expelled from Ethiopia, the SNM decided to relocate within Somalia itself, a decision that drastically changed the nature of the conflict in the north. Despite the termination of Ethiopian assistance, SNM guerrillas continued to defeat Siad Barre's forces with relative ease; by August 1988 they had captured Hargeysa and other northern towns. Siad Barre responded by ordering massive aerial bombing, carried out by foreign mercenary pilots, that damaged or destroyed virtually every building in Hargeysa (see Sources of Opposition , ch. 5). The brutal attack, which resulted in thousands of civilian casualties and brought both domestic and international opprobrium upon the Siad Barre regime, failed to crush the SNM. Fighting not only intensified in the north over the next eighteen months, but also spread throughout the country, forcing an estimated 800,000 Somalis to seek refuge in Ethiopia.

In March 1990, Siad Barre accused Ethiopia of having violated the 1988 peace agreement by providing continued military support to the SNM. However, by this time the Mengistu government was as beleaguered as the Siad Barre regime by armed opposition movements and was not in a position to assist any Somali rebels. Soon after Siad Barre fled Mogadishu in January 1991, Mengistu followed his example by fleeing Addis Ababa as guerrilla armies closed upon the Ethiopian capital. Throughout 1991 the new provisional governments in Somalia and Ethiopia regarded each other cautiously. Both were threatened by separatist movements and both had an interest in maintaining the integrity of internationally recognized borders. As conditions in Somalia worsened on account of civil strife, the collapse of central authority, and the disruption of food production and distribution, tens of thousands of Somalis fled to Ethiopia, creating a massive refugee situation in that country by early 1992.

Sharing land borders with both Somalia and Ethiopia, Djibouti believed it was in the long-term interests of the Horn of Africa region if both countries remained intact. Djibouti's president, Hassan Gouled Aptidon, attempted to mediate between the provisional government and the SNM and offered his capital as a neutral meeting place. In June 1991, Djibouti served as the venue for a national reconciliation conference between the USC and several other groups.

With most of Djibouti's diverse population consisting of ethnic Somalis, Aptidon's concern about Somalia's future was not entirely altruistic. The Somalis of Djibouti belonged overwhelmingly to the Iise clan, traditional rival of the Isaaqs who dominated the SNM. The Djibouti Iise tended to be suspicious of the Isaaq, believing that they discriminated against their Iise kinsmen in northern Somalia. This concern had prompted Djibouti in 1990 to assist in the formation and training of a separate Iise movement that challenged the SNM before and after the overthrow of Siad Barre. From Djibouti's perspective, a united Somalia composed of many clans afforded more protection to the Iise than a northern republic controlled by Isaaq.

Kenya was concerned about the situation in southern Somalia, which continued to be unstable throughout 1991. Somali refugees, both civilian and military, had crossed the border into northern Kenya to escape the fighting. The refugees included more than fifty close associates of Siad Barre who were granted political asylum. Since the provisional government had announced its intention to try these officials, this action had the potential to provoke political problems between Kenya and Somalia. By early 1992, tens of thousands of Somalis were being sheltered in makeshift refugee camps in northern Kenya.

Relations with Arab Countries

Somalia has a long history of cultural, religious, and trade ties with the Arabs of the Arabian Peninsula, which lies across the Gulf of Aden. Although Somalis ethnically are not Arabs, they identify more with Arabs than with their fellow Africans. Thus it was not surprising when Somalia joined the League of Arab States (Arab League) in 1974, becoming the first non-Arab member of that organization. Initially, Somalia tended to support those Arab countries such as Algeria, Iraq, and Libya that opposed United States policies in the Middle East. After its defeat in the Ogaden War, the Siad Barre regime aligned its policies more closely with those of Egypt and Saudi Arabia. Subsequently, both of these countries began to provide military aid to Somalia. Other Arab states, in particular Libya, angered Siad Barre by supporting Ethiopia. In 1981 Somalia broke diplomatic relations with Libya, claiming that Libyan leader Muammar al Qadhafi was supporting the SSDF and the nascent SNM. Relations were not restored until 1985.

Throughout the 1980s, Somalia became increasingly dependent upon economic aid from the conservative, wealthy oil–exporting states of Kuwait, Qatar, Saudi Arabia, and the United Arab Emirates. This dependence was a crucial factor in the Siad Barre regime's decision to side with the United States–led coalition of Arab states that opposed Iraq following that country's invasion of Kuwait in 1990. Support for the coalition brought economic dividends: Qatar canceled further repayment of all principal and interest on outstanding loans, and Saudi Arabia offered Somalia a US$70 million grant and promised to sell it oil at below prevailing international market prices.

Relations with the United States

Prior to the Ogaden War, Somalia had been allied with the Soviet Union, and its relations with the United States were strained. Largely because the Soviet Union sided with Ethiopia in the Ogaden War, a United States–Somali rapprochement began in 1977 and culminated in a military access agreement in 1980 that permitted the United States to use naval ports and airfields at Berbera, Chisimayu, and Mogadishu, in exchange for military and economic aid. The United States subsequently refurbished facilities originally developed by the Soviet Union at the Gulf of Aden port of Berbera. The United States Rapid Deployment Force used Berbera as a base for its Operation Bright Star exercises in 1981, and American military advisers were permanently stationed there one year later. Somali military units participated in Operation Bright Star joint maneuvers in 1985. The base at Berbera was used in the fall of 1990 during the deployment of personnel and supplies to Saudi Arabia in preparation for the Persian Gulf War.

Controversy over the Siad Barre government's human rights policies clouded the future of United States military cooperation with Somalia. Siad Barre's policy of repression in the north aroused criticism of his regime in the United States Congress, where the

Foreign Affairs Committee of the House of Representatives held extensive hearings during July 1988 on human rights abuses in Somalia. In 1989, under congressional pressure, the administration of President George Bush terminated military aid to Somalia, although it continued to provide food assistance and to operate a small International Military Education and Training program (see Foreign Military Assistance , ch. 5). In 1990 Washington revealed that Mogadishu had been in default on loan repayments for more than a year. Therefore, under the terms of the Brooke Amendment, this meant that Somalia was ineligible to receive any further United States aid. During the height of the fighting in Mogadishu in January 1991, the United States closed its embassy and evacuated all its personnel from the country. The embassy was ransacked by mobs in the final days of the Siad Barre regime. The United States recognized the provisional government shortly after its establishment. Since the outbreak of the civil war, the United States has consistently urged all parties to come together to resolve their dispute by peaceful means.

The United States government has supported the territorial unity of Somalia and as of May 1992 has refused to recognize the independence of northern Somalia proclaimed by the SNM.

Other Foreign Relations

The former colonial powers, Italy and Britain, both maintained an interest in Somalia. Italy was more influential, perhaps because it had provided extensive development aid to Somalia during the 1980s. Italy was instrumental in getting preferential treatment for Somali exports to the European Economic Community. Italy also made considerable, albeit unsuccessful, efforts to resolve the conflict between Siad Barre and his opponents. The last Italian effort, in cooperation with Egypt in November and December 1990, failed because the USC and SNM refused to meet with any representative of the Siad Barre regime. In 1986 Somalia and the Soviet Union reestablished diplomatic relations, broken during the Ogaden War.

In mid–1991 Somalia was a member of the United Nations and its specialized agencies, the Organization of African Unity, the League of Arab States, and the World Bank (see Glossary).

* * * Although no books deal comprehensively with Somali politics since the 1977–78 Ogaden War, chapters in several different studies provide an analysis of this important period. *A History of Modern Somalia* by I M.

Lewis is an indispensable starting point for gaining a deeper understanding of Somali politics. Chapters nine and ten of the 1988 revised edition deal with the Siad Barre government and are particularly helpful. Parts of chapters four, six, and seven of *Somalia: Nation in Search of a State*, by David D. Laitin and Said S. Samatar, provide insight into Siad Barre's political style, the formation of opposition movements, and the conduct of foreign relations. Chapters six, seven, and eight of Ahmed Samatar's *Socialist Somalia* examine the impact of the Ogaden War on the country's domestic and foreign relations.

Information on recent and current Somali political affairs can be found in several periodicals, including *Africa Contemporary Record*, *Africa Today*, *African Development*, *Asian and African Studies*, *Current History*, *Horn of Africa*, *Journal of Modern African Studies*, and *Revue française d'études politiques africaines*. (For further information and complete citations, see Bibliography.)

Chapter 5. National Security

Detail from bronze relief on monument in Mogadishu depicting deeds of Somali patriot Mahammad Abdille Hasan, the legendary "Mad Mullah"

A TER SOMALIA GAINED INDEPENDENCE in 1960, its military grew steadily, despite the country's status as one of the poorest states in sub–Saharan Africa. Largely under Soviet patronage, the military expanded from 5,000 troops at independence to 23,000 during the 1977–78 Ogaden War. By 1981 the armed forces had 50,000 personnel; by 1990 that number had increased to 65,000.

Until the Ogaden War, Somalia possessed one of East Africa's best equipped armed forces. However, Ethiopia destroyed much of the army's fighting capability during the 1977–78 conflict. To rebuild its military, Somalia sought assistance from China and a variety of Arab and Western countries, including the United States.

Somalia's defeat in the Ogaden War and deteriorating internal conditions lost the government much of its domestic support. As the Mahammad Siad Barre regime became more politically isolated, the president and members of his Mareehaan subclan increasingly dominated the government, the economy, and the armed forces. Growing oppression in Somalia forced many critics into exile, where they organized opposition groups. A lack of resources initially limited the exiles' opposition activity to propaganda campaigns and occasional minor guerrilla forays into Somalia.

By the late 1980s, several opposition groups had transformed themselves into relatively powerful, clan-based (see Glossary) insurgent movements. Relying on financial assistance from Somali exile communities and various foreign governments, the insurgents grew in strength and numbers. The armed forces, which eventually faced insurgencies throughout Somalia, gradually disintegrated. Finally, in early 1991 Siad Barre and many of his closest Mareehaan advisers relinquished power and fled Mogadishu. If Somalia were to have a future as a single nation, reconstituting the armed forces on a more representative basis would be essential to national unity and stability.

INTERNATIONAL SECURITY CONCERNS

From independence until the mid-1980s, Somalia's national security concerns focused largely on the threat posed by its neighbor, Ethiopia. After the Ogaden War, Ethiopia used Soviet, Cuban, and East European military and technical assistance to establish itself as the dominant power in the Horn of Africa. By the mid-1980s, Ethiopia's support of Somali insurgent groups posed a growing threat to Somalia's internal security. In early 1991, Somali-Ethiopian tensions eased as long-established governments fell in both Mogadishu and Addis Ababa. By the spring of 1992, however, it remained unclear whether relations between the two countries would be characterized by cooperation and peace, or if old arguments over the Ogaden's (Ogaadeen) status would renew the hostility between Somalia and Ethiopia.

Irredentism and the Changing Balance of Power

Somalia's defeat in the Ogaden War, Ethiopian hostility, the emergence of an alliance between Addis Ababa and Moscow, regional tensions, and periods of international isolation all resulted directly or indirectly from Somalia's unwillingness to recognize political boundaries drawn by British, French, and Italian colonists, in conjunction with Ethiopia. Since independence, successive Somali governments had sought to reincorporate those Somalis living in Ethiopia, Kenya, and Djibouti into Greater Somalia. (Under the Siad Barre regime, the five-pointed star on the Somali flag represented the northern and southern regions of the republic and the "unredeemed territories" in Kenya's NorthEastern Province, Ethiopia's Ogaden Province, and Djibouti.) In 1960–64, for example, guerrillas supported by the Somali government battled local security forces in Kenya and Ethiopia on behalf of Somalia's territorial claims. Then, in 1964, Ethiopian and Somali regular forces clashed.

By late 1964, it had become obvious that the initial campaign to unify all Somalis had failed. Ethiopian forces had established superiority over the Somalis in the Ogaden, in part because of Ethiopia's ability to conduct air raids on Somali territory. In Kenya the government relied on assistance from British counterinsurgency experts to control Somali guerrillas in what was then the Northern Frontier District (NFD). In late 1964, Kenya's president Jomo Kenyatta and Ethiopia's emperor Haile Selassie signed a mutual defense agreement aimed at containing Somali aggression. The two countries renewed the pact in 1979 and again in 1989. These factors, in combination with the opposition of the Organization of African Unity to Somali aims and defense costs that amounted to 30 percent of the national budget in the mid–1980s, forced Mogadishu to reconsider its territorial ambitions.

Under Mahammad Ibrahim Igaal, Somalia's last civilian government initiated—and Siad Barre's military regime initially continued—a policy of détente with Somalia's neighbors. During the 1970s, however, Somali military strength gradually increased as a result of Soviet support. The Soviet Union supplied the Somali National Army (SNA) with the largest tank force in subSaharan Africa, transport vehicles—including armored personnel carriers—for a largely mechanized infantry, and jet aircraft that included MiG–21 fighter–bombers. In 1974 Somalia and the Soviet Union formalized their relationship by signing the Treaty of Friendship and Cooperation. The Ethiopian army at that time remained twice as large as Somalia's 23,000–man force, but because of reduced military aid from the United States, the Ethiopians were not as well equipped. Furthermore, in 1974 Ethiopia's imperial government was headed toward collapse. In September of that year a group of military officers deposed Haile Selassie. Conflict ensued among those responsible for his overthrow, and several insurgent groups sought to secede from the erstwhile empire.

Somalia's military buildup, coincident with the turmoil in Ethiopia, temporarily altered the balance of power between the two countries. In 1976–77 Somalia attempted to take advantage of the situation by supporting a guerrilla campaign by the Western Somali Liberation Front (WSLF), a pro–Somali liberation group in the Ogaden, to seize the Ogaden from Ethiopia. By the late summer of 1977, Somali armored forces and mechanized infantry supported by aircraft had invaded the Ogaden, capturing 60 percent of the disputed territory within several weeks.

Meanwhile, the Soviet Union had started supporting the Marxist–Leninist regime that had emerged in Ethiopia while simultaneously attempting to maintain Somalia as a client state. After its attempts at mediation failed, the Soviet Union decided to abandon Somalia. In August 1977, the Soviet Union suspended arms shipments to Siad Barre's regime and accelerated military deliveries to Ethiopia. Three months later, Somalia renounced the Treaty of Friendship and Cooperation, expelled all Soviet advisers, broke diplomatic relations with Cuba, and ejected all Soviet personnel from Somalia.

Following Moscow's decision to support Addis Ababa, Ethiopia received massive amounts of Soviet arms.

Along with Soviet military advisers, about 15,000 Cuban combat troops also arrived. By early 1978, this aid had turned the tide of war in Ethiopia's favor. By March 9, 1978, when Siad Barre announced the withdrawal of the Somali armed forces from the Ogaden, the Somali military had lost 8,000 men—one–third of the SNA, three–quarters of its armored units, and half of the Somali Air Force (SAF).

For all intents and purposes, Ethiopia's victory during the Ogaden War ended Mogadishu's dream of recreating Greater Somalia. Even before the setback in the Ogaden, Siad Barre had relinquished his claim to Djibouti after 95 percent of the voters in that country indicated a preference for independence over incorporation into Somalia. In 1981 Somali–Kenyan relations improved after Siad Barre visited Nairobi and indicated that his government no longer had any claim to Kenyan territory. In December 1984, Somalia and Kenya signed a pact that pledged both governments to cease hostilities along their common frontier.

Subsequently, the level of insurgent activity along the border was minimal. However, the activities of Somali *shiftas*, or bandits and ivory poachers and the periodic influx of Somali refugees into Kenya continued to strain relations between Mogadishu and Nairobi.

The Ogaden War: Performance and Implications of Defeat

The SNA never recovered from its defeat in the Ogaden War. The battles to retake and then defend the Ogaden stripped the Somali armed forces of many troops, much of their equipment, and their Soviet patron.

For the next decade, the SNA sought unsuccessfully to improve its capability by relying on a variety of foreign sources, including the United States. The Ogaden War therefore remains the best example of the SNA's ability to mount and sustain conventional military operations.

Before the Ogaden War, the most striking feature of the 23,000–man SNA had been its large armored force, which was equipped with about 250 T–34 and T–54/T–55 Soviet–built medium tanks and more than 300 armored personnel carriers. This equipment gave the SNA a tank force more than three times as large as Ethiopia's. The prewar SAF also was larger than Ethiopia's air force. In 1976 the SAF had fifty–two combat aircraft, twenty–four of which were Soviet–built supersonic MiG21s . Facing them was an Ethiopian Air Force (EAF) of thirty–five to forty aircraft. Ethiopia also was in the process of acquiring several United States–built Northrop F–5 fighters from Iran. At the outbreak of fighting, Ethiopia had approximately sixteen F5A /Es.

As chaos spread throughout Ethiopia after Haile Selassie's downfall, Mogadishu increased its support to several pro–Somali liberation groups in the Ogaden, the strongest of which was the WSLF. By late 1975, the WSLF had attacked many Ethiopian outposts in the Ogaden. In June 1977, Addis Ababa accused Mogadishu of committing SNA units to the fighting. Despite considerable evidence to the contrary, Somalia denied this charge and insisted that only "volunteers" had been given leave from the SNA to fight with the WSLF. By late 1977, the combined WSLF–SNA strength in the Ogaden probably approached 50,000, of which 15,000 appeared to be irregulars.

After the Somali government committed the SNA to the Ogaden, the conflict ceased to be a guerrilla action and assumed the form of a conventional war in which armor, mechanized infantry, and air power played decisive roles. The SNA quickly adapted its organization to battlefield realities. The centralized Somali logistics system controlled supplies at battalion level (600- to 1,000-man units) from Mogadishu, an unwieldy arrangement given Somalia's limited transportation and communications network (see Transportation; Communications , ch. 3). To facilitate operations, the logistics center and headquarters for forces fighting in the northern Ogaden moved to Hargeysa, the SNA's northern sector headquarters. Before the war, all Somali ground forces had been organized into battalions. After the conflict started, however, the standard infantry and mechanized infantry unit became the brigade, composed of two to four battalions and having a total strength of 1,200 to 2,000 personnel.

During the summer of 1977, the SNA–WSLF force achieved several victories but also endured some significant defeats. In July 1977, it captured Gode, on the Shabeelle River about 550 kilometers inside Ethiopia, and won control of 60 percent of the Ogaden. By mid–September 1977, Ethiopia conceded that 90 percent of the Ogaden was in Somali hands. The SNA suffered two setbacks in August when it tried to capture Dire Dawa and Jijiga. The Ethiopian army inflicted heavy losses on the SNA at Dire Dawa after a Somali attack by one tank battalion and a mechanized infantry brigade supported by artillery units. At Jijiga the Somalis lost more than half of their attacking force of three tank battalions, each of which included more than thirty tanks.

Somalia's greatest victory occurred in mid–September 1977 in the second attempt to take Jijiga, when three tank battalions overwhelmed the Ethiopian garrison. After inflicting some heavy losses on Somali armor, Ethiopian troops mutinied and withdrew from the town, leaving its defense to the militia, which was incapable of slowing the Somali advance. The Ethiopians retreated beyond the strategic Marda Pass, the strongest defensive position between Jijiga and Harer, leaving the SNA in a commanding position within the region.

Despite this success, several factors prevented a Somali victory. Somali tank losses had been heavy in the battles around Dire Dawa and Jijiga. Moreover, because the EAF had established air superiority over the SAF, it could harass overextended Somali supply lines with impunity. The onset of the rainy season hampered such air attacks; however, the bad weather also bogged down Somali reinforcements on the dirt roads.

The Soviet Union's decision to abandon Somalia in favor of Ethiopia eventually turned the tide of battle in the Ogaden. From October 1977 through January 1978, about 20,000 WSLF guerrillas and SNA forces pressed attacks on Harer, where nearly 50,000 Ethiopians had regrouped, backed by Soviet–supplied armor and artillery and gradually reinforced by 11,000 Cubans and 1,500 Soviet advisers. Although it fought its way into Harer in November 1977, the SNA lacked the supplies and manpower to capture the city. Subsequently, the Somalis regrouped outside Harer and awaited an Ethiopian counterattack.

As expected, in early February 1978 Ethiopian and Cuban forces launched a two–stage counterattack toward Jijiga. Unexpectedly, however, a column of Cubans and Ethiopians moving north and east crossed the highlands between Jijiga and the Somali border, bypassing Somali troops dug in around the Marda Pass. Thus, the attacking force was able to assault the Somalis from two sides and recapture Jijiga after two days of fighting in which 3,000 Somali troops lost their lives. Within a week, Ethiopia had retaken all of the Ogaden's major towns. On March 9, 1978, Siad Barre recalled the SNA from Ethiopia.

After the SNA withdrawal, the WSLF reverted to guerrilla tactics. By May 1980, the rebels had established control over a significant portion of the Ogaden. Eventually, Ethiopia defeated the WSLF and the few small SNA units that remained in the region after the Somali pullout. In late 1981, however, reports indicated that the WSLF continued to conduct occasional hit–and– run attacks against Ethiopian targets.

Postwar Status of the Armed Forces

In the early 1980s, the Somali armed forces had to adjust to the realities of their defeat in the Ogaden War.

Somali manpower had doubled during the conflict, but the Ethiopian army had destroyed a significant amount of Somali equipment. Shortages of military hardware, inadequate maintenance, and lack of spare parts for what remained of Soviet–supplied equipment limited the effectiveness of all units. Better relations between Somalia and the United States resolved some of these problems. Between 1983 and 1986, United States military assistance to Somalia averaged US$36 to US$40 million per year (see Foreign Military Assistance , this ch.). This aid was insufficient, however, to restore the Somali armed forces to their pre–Ogaden War effectiveness.

As insurgent activity intensified during the late 1980s and the Somali government failed to develop additional sources of large–scale military assistance, the armed forces slowly deteriorated. By 1990 the Somali military was in a state of collapse. After Siad Barre fled Mogadishu in January 1991, the SNA and all related military and security services ceased to exist. Most of their military equipment fell into the hands of insurgents, clan militiamen, or bandits. The status of former military and security personnel varied. Some fled abroad to countries such as Kenya or Ethiopia; others returned to civilian life or became insurgents, bandits, or clan militia members. A small number remained loyal to Siad Barre, who took refuge in southern Somalia and then launched a military campaign to regain power. The campaign failed, however, and Siad Barre sought exile in Nigeria, where he remained in early 1992.

INTERNAL SECURITY CONCERNS

Somalia has a long history of internal instability; in some instances, clan feuds have lasted more than a century. Most of this turmoil has been associated with disagreements and factionalism between and among the major branches of the Somali lineage system, which includes pastoral nomads such as the Dir, Daarood, Isaaq, and Hawiye, and agriculturalists such as the Digil and Rahanwayn (see The Segmentary Social Order , ch. 2).

In more recent times, these historical animosities have expressed themselves through the emergence of clan–based dissident and insurgent movements. Most of these groups grew to oppose Siad Barre's regime because the president refused to make political reforms, unleashed a reign of terror against the country's citizenry, and concentrated power in the hands of his Mareehaan subclan (the Mareehaan belonged to the Daarood clan). After Siad Barre fled Mogadishu in January 1991, the Somali nation state collapsed, largely along warring clan lines.

Government Security Policy

In the aftermath of the 1969 coup, the central government acquired control of all legislative, administrative, and judicial functions. The only legally permitted party was the Somali Revolutionary Socialist Party (SRSP).

In April 1970, Siad Barre authorized the creation of National Security Courts (NSCs), which shortly thereafter tried approximately sixty people: leaders of the previous government, businessmen, lawyers, and senior military personnel who had failed to support the coup (see Courts , ch. 4). In September 1970, the Supreme Revolutionary Council (SRC) proclaimed that any person who harmed the nation's unity, peace, or sovereignty could be sentenced to death. The government also promised to punish anyone who spread false propaganda against Siad Barre's regime.

Until the early 1980s, the Siad Barre regime generally shunned capital punishment in favor of imprisonment and reeducation of actual, suspected, or potential opponents. The earlier parliamentary government had been able to hold people without trial up to ninety days during a state of emergency, but the military government removed most legal restrictions on preventive detention. After the coup, a local revolutionary council or the National Security Service (NSS) could detain individuals regarded as dangerous to peace, order, good government, or the aims and spirit of the revolution (see National Security Service , this ch. and Human Rights , this ch.). Additionally, regional governors could order the search and arrest of persons suspected of a crime or of activities considered threatening to public order and security, and could requisition property or services without compensation. In 1974 the government began to require all civil servants to sign statements of intent to abide by security regulations. Furthermore, any contact between foreigners and Somali citizens had to be reported to the Ministry of Foreign Affairs. By the late 1970s, most Somalis were ignoring this latter regulation.

The Somali government became more repressive after an unsuccessful 1971 coup. Officials maintained that the coup attempt by some SRC members had sought to protect the interests of the trading bourgeoisie and the tribal structure. Many expected that the conspirators would receive clemency. Instead, the government executed them. Many Somalis found this act inconsistent with Islamic principles and as a consequence turned against Siad Barre's regime.

During its first years in power, the SRC sought to bolster nationalism by undermining traditional Somali allegiance to Islamic religious leaders and clan groups. Although it tried to avoid entirely alienating religious leaders, the government restricted their involvement in politics. During the early 1970s, some Islamic leaders affirmed that Islam could never coexist with scientific socialism; however, Siad Barre claimed that the two concepts were compatible because Islam propagated a classless society based on egalitarianism.

In the mid–1970s, the government tried to eliminate a rallying point for opposition by substituting allegiance to the nation for traditional allegiance to family and clan. Toward this end, the authorities stressed individual responsibility for all offenses, thereby undermining the concept of collective responsibility that existed in traditional society and served as the basis of *diya*–paying (see Glossary) groups. The government also abolished traditional clan leadership responsibilities and titles such as *sultan* and *shaykh*.

By the late 1980s, it was evident that Siad Barre had failed to create a sense of Somali nationalism. Moreover, he had been unable to destroy the family and clan loyalties that continued to govern the lives of most Somalis.

As antigovernment activities escalated, Siad Barre increasingly used force and terror against his opponents.

This cycle of violence further isolated his regime, caused dissent within the SNA, and eventually precipitated the collapse of his government.

Sources of Opposition

From 1969 until the mid–1970s, Siad Barre's authoritarian regime enjoyed a degree of popular support, largely because it acted with a decisiveness not displayed by the civilian governments of the 1960s. Even the 1971 coup attempt failed to affect the stability of the government. However, Somalia's defeat in the Ogaden War signaled the beginning of a decline in Siad Barre's popularity that culminated in his January 1991 fall from power.

Before the war, many Somalis had criticized Siad Barre for not trying to reincorporate the Ogaden into Somalia immediately after Ethiopian emperor Haile Selassie's death in 1975. The government was unable to stifle this criticism largely because the Somali claim to the Ogaden had overwhelming national support. The regime's commitment of regular troops to the Ogaden proved highly popular, as did Siad Barre's expulsion of the Soviet advisers, who had been resented by most Somalis. However, Somalia's defeat in the Ogaden War refocused criticism on Siad Barre.

After the spring 1978 retreat toward Hargeysa, Siad Barre met with his generals to discuss the battlefield situation, and ordered the execution of six of them for activities against the state. This action failed to quell SNA discontent over Siad Barre's handling of the war with Ethiopia. On April 9, 1978, a group of military officers (mostly Majeerteen) attempted a coup d'état. Government security forces crushed the plot within hours and subsequently arrested seventy–four suspected conspirators. After a month–long series of trials, the authorities imprisoned thirty–six people associated with the coup and executed another seventeen.

After the war, it was evident that the ruling alliance among the Mareehaan, Ogaden, and Dulbahante clans had been broken. The Ogaden—the clan of Siad Barre's mother, which had the most direct stake in the war—broke with the regime over the president's wartime leadership. To prevent further challenges to his rule, Siad Barre placed members of his own clan in important positions in the government, the armed forces, the security services, and other state agencies.

Throughout the late 1970s, growing discontent with the regime's policies and personalities prompted the defection of numerous government officials and the establishment of several insurgent movements. Because unauthorized political activity was prohibited, these organizations were based abroad. The best known was the Somali Salvation Front (SSF), which operated from Ethiopia. The SSF had absorbed its predecessor, the Somali Democratic Action Front (SODAF), which had been formed in Rome in 1976. Former minister of justice Usmaan Nur Ali led the Majeerteen–based SODAF. Lieutenant Colonel Abdillaahi Yuusuf Ahmad, a survivor of the 1978 coup attempt, commanded the SSF. Other prominent SSF personalities included former minister of education Hasan Ali Mirreh and former ambassador Muse Islan Faarah. The SSF, which received assistance from Ethiopia and Libya, claimed to command a guerrilla force numbering in the thousands.

Ethiopia placed a radio transmitter at the SSF's disposal from which Radio Kulmis (unity) beamed anti–Siad Barre invective to listeners in Somalia. Although it launched a low–intensity sabotage campaign in 1981, the SSF lacked the capabilities to sustain effective guerrilla operations against the SNA.

The SSF's weakness derived from its limited potential as a rallying point for opposition to the government.

Although the SSF embraced no ideology or political philosophy other than hostility to Siad Barre, its nationalist appeal was undermined by its reliance on Ethiopian support. The SSF claimed to encompass a range of opposition forces, but its leading figures belonged with few exceptions to the Majeerteen clan.

In October 1981, the SSF merged with the radical–left Somali Workers Party (SWP) and the Democratic Front for the Liberation of Somalia (DFLS) to form the Somali Salvation Democratic Front (SSDF). The SWP and DFLS, both based in Aden (then the capital of the People's Democratic Republic of Yemen—South Yemen), had included some former SRSP Central Committee members who faulted Siad Barre for compromising Somalia's revolutionary goals. An eleven–man committee led the SSDF. Yuusuf Ahmad, a former SNA officer and head of the SDF acted as chairman; former SWP leader Idris Jaama Husseen served as vice chairman; Abdirahman Aidid Ahmad, former chairman of the SRSP Ideology Bureau and founding father of the DFLS, was secretary for information. The SSDF promised to intensify the military and political struggles against the Siad Barre regime, which was said to have destroyed Somali unity and surrendered to United States imperialism. Like the SSF, the SSDF suffered from weak organization, a close identification with its Ethiopian and Libyan benefactors, and its reputation as a Majeerteen party.

Despite its shortcomings, the SSDF played a key role in fighting between Somalia and Ethiopia in the summer of 1982. After a SNA force infiltrated the Ogaden, joined with the WSLF and attacked an Ethiopian army unit outside Shilabo, about 150 kilometers northwest of Beledweyne, Ethiopia retaliated by launching an operation against Somalia. On June 30, 1982, Ethiopian army units, together with SSDF guerrillas, struck at several points along Ethiopia's southern border with Somalia. They crushed the SNA unit in Balumbale and then occupied that village. In August 1982, the Ethiopian/SSDF force took the village of Goldogob, about 50 kiloeters northwest of Galcaio. After the United

States provided emergency military assistance to Somalia, the Ethiopian attacks ceased. However, the Ethiopian/SSDF units remained in Balumbale and Goldogob, which Addis Ababa maintained were part of Ethiopia that had been liberated by the Ethiopian army. The SSDF disputed the Ethiopian claim, causing a power struggle that eventually resulted in the destruction of the SSDF's leadership.

On October 12, 1985, Ethiopian authorities arrested Ahmad and six of his lieutenants after they repeatedly indicated that Balumbale and Goldogob were part of Somalia. The Ethiopian government justified the arrests by saying that Ahmad had refused to comply with a SSDF Central Committee decision relieving him as chairman. Mahammad Abshir, a party bureaucrat, then assumed command of the SSDF. Under his leadership, the SSDF became militarily moribund, primarily because of poor relations with Addis Ababa. In August 1986, the Ethiopian army attacked SSDF units, then launched a war against the movement, and finally jailed its remaining leaders. For the next several years, the SSDF existed more in name than in fact. In late 1990, however, after Ethiopia released former SSDF leader Ahmad, the movement reemerged as a fighting force in Somalia, albeit to a far lesser degree than in the early 1980s.

In April 1981, a group of Isaaq emigrés living in London formed the Somali National Movement (SNM), which subsequently became the strongest of Somalia's various insurgent movements. According to its spokesmen, the rebels wanted to overthrow Siad Barre's dictatorship. Additionally, the SNM advocated a mixed economy and a neutral foreign policy, rejecting alignment with the Soviet Union or the United States and calling for the dismantling of all foreign military bases in the region. In the late 1980s, the SNM adopted a pro-Western foreign policy and favored United States involvement in a post-Siad Barre Somalia. Other SNM objectives included establishment of a representative democracy that would guarantee human rights and freedom of speech. Eventually, the SNM moved its headquarters from London to Addis Ababa to obtain Ethiopian military assistance, which initially was limited to old Soviet small arms.

In October 1981, the SNM rebels elected Ahmad Mahammad Culaid and Ahmad Ismaaiil Abdi as chairman and secretary general, respectively, of the movement. Culaid had participated in northern Somali politics until 1975, when he went into exile in Djibouti and then in Saudi Arabia. Abdi had been politically active in the city of Burao in the 1950s, and, from 1965 to 1967, had served as the Somali government's minister of planning. After the authorities jailed him in 1971 for antigovernment activities, Abdi left

Somalia and lived in East Africa and Saudi Arabia. The rebels also elected an eight–man executive committee to oversee the SNM's military and political activities.

On January 2, 1982, the SNM launched its first military operation against the Somali government. Operating from Ethiopian bases, commando units attacked Mandera Prison near Berbera and freed a group of northern dissidents. According to the SNM, the assault liberated more than 700 political prisoners; subsequent independent estimates indicated that only about a dozen government opponents escaped. At the same time, other commando units raided the Cadaadle armory near Berbera and escaped with an undetermined amount of arms and ammunition.

Mogadishu responded to the SNM attacks by declaring a state of emergency, imposing a curfew, closing gasoline stations to civilian vehicles, banning movement in or out of northern Somalia, and launching a search for the Mandera prisoners (most of whom were never found). On January 8, 1982, the Somali government also closed its border with Djibouti to prevent the rebels from fleeing Somalia. These actions failed to stop SNM military activities.

In October 1982, the SNM tried to increase pressure against the Siad Barre regime by forming a joint military committee with the SSDF. Apart from issuing antigovernment statements, the two insurgent groups started broadcasting from the former Radio Kulmis station, now known as Radio Halgan (struggle). Despite this political cooperation, the SNM and SSDF failed to agree on a common strategy against Mogadishu. As a result, the alliance languished.

In February 1983, Siad Barre visited northern Somalia in a campaign to discredit the SNM. Among other things, he ordered the release of numerous civil servants and businessmen who had been arrested for antigovernment activities, lifted the state of emergency, and announced an amnesty for Somali exiles who wanted to return home. These tactics put the rebels on the political defensive for several months. In November 1983, the SNM Central Committee sought to regain the initiative by holding an emergency meeting to formulate a more aggressive strategy. One outcome was that the military wing—headed by Abdulqaadir Kosar Abdi, formerly of the SNA—assumed control of the Central Committee by ousting the civilian membership from all positions of power. However, in July 1984, at the Fourth SNM Congress, held in Ethiopia, the civilians regained control of the leadership. The delegates also elected Ahmad

Mahammad Mahamuud "Silanyo" SNM chairman and reasserted their intention to revive the alliance with the SSDF.

After the Fourth SNM Congress adjourned, military activity in northern Somalia increased. SNM commandos attacked about a dozen government military posts in the vicinity of Hargeysa, Burao, and Berbera. According to the SNM, the SNA responded by shooting 300 people at a demonstration in Burao, sentencing seven youths to death for sedition, and arresting an unknown number of rebel sympathizers. In January 1985, the government executed twenty– eight people in retaliation for antigovernment activity.

Between June 1985 and February 1986, the SNM claimed to have carried out thirty operations against government forces in northern Somalia. In addition, the SNM reported that it had killed 476 government soldiers and wounded 263, and had captured eleven vehicles and had destroyed another twenty–two, while losing only 38 men and two vehicles. Although many independent observers said these figures were exaggerated, SNM operations during the 1985–86 campaign forced Siad Barre to mount an international effort to cut off foreign aid to the rebels. This initiative included reestablishment of diplomatic relations with Libya in exchange for Tripoli's promise to stop supporting the SNM.

Despite efforts to isolate the rebels, the SNM continued military operations in northern Somalia. Between July and September 1987, the SNM initiated approximately thirty attacks, including one on the northern capital, Hargeysa; none of these, however, weakened the government's control of northern Somalia. A more dramatic event occurred when a SNM unit kidnapped a Médecins Sans Frontières medical aid team of ten Frenchmen and one Djiboutian to draw the world's attention to Mogadishu's policy of impressing men from refugee camps into the SNA. After ten days, the SNM released the hostages unconditionally.

Siad Barre responded to these activities by instituting harsh security measures throughout northern Somalia.

The government also evicted suspected pro–SNM nomad communities from the Somali–Ethiopian border region. These measures failed to contain the SNM. By February 1988, the rebels had captured three villages around Togochale, a refugee camp near the northwestern Somali–Ethiopian border.

Following the rebel successes of 1987–88, Somali–Ethiopian relations began to improve. On March 19, 1988, Siad Barre and Ethiopian president Mengistu Haile Mariam met in Djibouti to discuss ways of reducing tension between the two countries. Although little was accomplished, the two agreed to hold further talks. At the end of March 1988, the Ethiopian minister of foreign affairs, Berhanu Bayih, arrived in Mogadishu for discussions with a group of Somali officials, headed by General Ahmad Mahamuud Faarah. On April 4, 1988, the two presidents signed a joint communiqué in which they agreed to restore diplomatic relations, exchange prisoners of war, start a mutual withdrawal of troops from the border area, and end subversive activities and hostile propaganda against each other.

Faced with a cutoff of Ethiopian military assistance, the SNM had to prove its ability to operate as an independent organization. Therefore, in late May 1988 SNM units moved out of their Ethiopian base camps and launched a major offensive in northern Somalia. The rebels temporarily occupied the provincial capitals of Burao and Hargeysa. These early successes bolstered the SNM's popular support, as thousands of disaffected Isaaq clan members and SNA deserters joined the rebel ranks.

Over the next few years, the SNM took control of almost all of northwestern Somalia and extended its area of operations about fifty kilometers east of Erigavo. However, the SNM did not gain control of the region's major cities (i e., Berbera, Hargeysa, Burao, and Boorama), but succeeded only in laying siege to them.

With Ethiopian military assistance no longer a factor, the SNM's success depended on its ability to capture weapons from the SNA. The rebels seized numerous vehicles such as Toyota Land Cruisers from government forces and subsequently equipped them with light and medium weapons such as 12.7mm and 14.5mm machine guns, 106mm recoilless rifles, and BM–21 rocket launchers. The SNM possessed antitank weapons such as Soviet B–10 tubes and RPG– 7s. For air defense the rebels operated Soviet 30mm and 23mm guns, several dozen Soviet ZU23 2s, and Czech–made twin–mounted 30mm ZU30 2s. The SNM also maintained a small fleet of armed speed boats that operated from Maydh, fifty kilometers northwest of Erigavo, and Xiis, a little west of Maydh. Small arms included 120mm mortars and various assault rifles, such as AK–47s, M–16s, and G–3s. Despite these armaments, rebel operations, especially against the region's major cities, suffered because of an inadequate logistics system and a lack of artillery, mine– clearing equipment, ammunition, and communications gear.

To weaken Siad Barre's regime further, the SNM encouraged the formation of other clan–based insurgent movements and provided them with political and military support. In particular, the SNM maintained close relations with the United Somali Congress (USC), which was active in central Somalia, and the Somali Patriotic Movement (SPM), which operated in southern Somalia. Both these groups sought to overthrow Siad Barre's regime and establish a democratic form of government.

The USC, a Hawiye organization founded in 1989, had suffered from factionalism based on subclan rivalries since its creation. General Mahammad Faarah Aidid commanded the Habar Gidir clan, and Ali Mahdi Mahammad headed the Abgaal clan. The SPM emerged in March 1989, after a group of Ogaden officers, led by Umar Jess, deserted the SNA and took up arms against Siad Barre. Like the USC, the SPM experienced a division among its ranks. The moderates, under Jess, favored an alliance with the SNM and USC and believed that Somalia should abandon its claims to the Ogaden. SPM hardliners wanted to recapture the Ogaden and favored a stronger military presence along the Somali–Ethiopian border.

On November 19, 1989, the SNM and SPM issued a joint communiqué announcing the adoption of a "unified stance on internal and external political policy." On September 12, 1990, the SNM concluded a similar agreement with the USC. Then, on November 24, 1990, the SNM announced that it had united with the SPM and the USC to pursue a common military strategy against the SNA. Actually, the SNM had concluded the unification agreement with Aidid, which widened the rift between the two USC factions.

By the beginning of 1991, all three of the major rebel organizations had made significant military progress.

The SNM had all but taken control of northern Somalia by capturing the towns of Hargeysa, Berbera, Burao, and Erigavo. On January 26, 1991, the USC stormed the presidential palace in Mogadishu, thereby establishing its control over the capital. The SPM succeeded in overrunning several government outposts in southern Somalia.

The SNM–USC–SPM unification agreement failed to last after Siad Barre fled Mogadishu. On January 26, 1991, the USC formed an interim government, which the SNM refused to recognize. On May 18, 1991, the SNM declared the independence of the Republic of Somaliland. The USC interim government opposed this declaration, arguing instead for a unified Somalia. Apart from these political disagreements, fighting broke out between and within the USC and SPM. The SNM also sought to establish its control over northern Somalia by pacifying clans such as the Gadabursi and the Dulbahante. To make matters worse, guerrilla groups proliferated; by late 1991, numerous movements vied for political power, including the United Somali Front (Iise), Somali Democratic Alliance (Gadabursi), United Somali Party (Dulbahante), Somali Democratic Movement (Rahanwayn), and Somali National Front (Mareehaan). The collapse of the nation state system and the emergence of clan–based guerrilla movements and militias that became governing authorities persuaded most Western observers that national reconciliation would be a long and difficult process.

HISTORY AND DEVELOPMENT OF THE ARMED FORCES

Street scene, Mogadishu Courtesy Hiram A. Ruiz Mogadishu scene reflecting damage from civil war, 1991 Courtesy Hiram A. Ruiz Donkey carts passing United Nations refugee relief truck damaged in crossfire, 1991 Courtesy Hiram A. Ruiz War–damaged houses in Hargeysa, a major city in northern Somalia, 1991 Courtesy Hiram A. Ruiz S nce independence, the Somali military establishment had undergone several changes. From the early 1960s to 1977, the period when good relations existed between Somalia and the Soviet Union, the Somali military had the largest armored and mechanized forces in sub–Saharan Africa, and the SAF and the Somali navy were among the region's best. However, the outbreak of the 1977– 78 Ogaden War and the withdrawal of Soviet military advisers and technicians had a crippling effect on the Somali military. After the emergence of the United States–Somalia alliance, Mogadishu reorganized the army so that it would be based on infantry, rather than on mechanized forces. As part of this restructuring, the military's overall personnel strength grew from about 23,000—the size of the military during the Ogaden War—to approximately 50,000 in 1981, and about 65,000 in early 1990. But by late 1990, the Somali military establishment was in a state of disintegration. In large part because of dismay at Somalia's increasingly poor human rights record, foreign military assistance had been reduced to a minimum. Desertions and battlefield defeats had caused a decline in the military's personnel strength to about 10,000. By the time insurgent forces took the capital in January 1991, the Somali military had ceased to exist as a fighting force.

The Warrior Tradition and Development of a Modern Army

Historically, Somali society accorded prestige to the warrior (*waranle*—see Glossary) and rewarded military prowess. Except for a man of religion *(wadaddo) (wadad*; pl., *wadaddo* —see Glossary), and they were few in number, all Somali males were considered potential warriors. As a result, a culture of military readiness flourished throughout a long history of foreign invasion, colonial occupation, domestic conflict, and wars with neighboring countries.

Warfare always had been an important factor in relations with outsiders such as the Ethiopian Christians and the Oromo and even with other Somali clans. The lack of modern weapons, however, prevented the Somalis from successfully resisting the imposition of European colonial rule. Antagonists in intra–Somali conflicts generally belonged to groups bound by their commitment to pay or receive *diya*. Because the entire group would be considered responsible for paying *diya* to compensate for damages inflicted, and would receive *diya f* r its own losses, a war would begin only with the unanimous approval of its likely participants. A meeting of the elders of the warring groups was the usual means of restoring peace. The elders would determine which group was responsible for starting the war and would decide compensation, usually livestock, for damages incurred. The group judged responsible for starting the war normally would be the only one fined unless it emerged the victor. In a jihad (holy war) against infidels and in most conflicts against non–Somalis, such rules would not apply.

The number of warriors who belonged to each party traditionally determined the strength of rival clans and *diya*–paying groups. However, after the introduction of firearms in the Horn of Africa in the late nineteenth century, firepower became the primary determinant. Although Somalis may have used matchlock guns as early as the sixteenth century, firearms became numerous in the region only in the 1890s, when various European nations and arms merchants began supplying them to Ethiopian emperor Menelik II. Shipped through the port of Djibouti, some of these weapons fell into Somali hands and came into use against the Ethiopians and the British in Sayyid Mahammad Abdille Hasan's 1899–1920 jihad. After 1920 the Italian and British colonial governments pursued a policy of disarming Somali nomads. For several years before independence, however, nomads frequently were more heavily armed than the colonial forces responsible for maintaining public order.

In 1884 Britain declared a protectorate over northern Somaliland. During its first sixteen years, the colonial administration relied on naval landing parties, detachments from the Aden garrison, and a small local police force to maintain order. The emergence in 1900 of Mahammad Abdille Hasan (the "Mad Mullah") and his band of about 3,000 dervishes represented the first serious challenge to colonial rule in British Somaliland (see Mahammad Abdille Hasau's Dervish Resistance to Colonial Occupation, ch. 1). In response, the British deployed to Berbera the Central Africa Rifles, 2d Battalion, which included 16 British officers, 1 British warrant officer, 30 Sikh, and 862 African troops, to prevent Hasan from crossing into British Somaliland from his base in eastern Ethiopia.

After the battalion left Somalia in December 1900, Captain E J E. Swayne raised the Somali Levy, a force that included 1,000 infantry and 500 mounted men commanded by 20 British officers and 50 Punjabi *havildars* (drill instructors). Armed with Enfield rifles, swords, bayonets, and Maxim guns, the Somali Levy was one of the region's best trained military units. In 1901 the British redesignated the Somali Levy as the 6th King's African Rifles (KAR). They disbanded the unit in 1902, reactivated it in 1903, reorganized it in 1904, and converted it to an all–Indian unit in 1905, when the colonial administration started drafting Somalis into a new standing militia.

Between 1900 and 1904, the British launched four unsuccessful campaigns against Hasan. After 1904 Hasan moved to Italian Somaliland. When he returned to the British sphere in 1909, the colonial administration reinforced the 6th KAR with an Indian battalion; the standing militia and 300 police also supported military operations against Hasan. In 1910, after failing to defeat Hasan, the British relinquished control of the interior, withdrew to the coast, and disbanded the 6th KAR and the standing militia.

For the next two years, British administrators in Somaliland argued for a more assertive policy. Finally, in June 1912 the British government approved the formation of the 150–man Camel Corps, which operated within an eighty–kilometer radius of Berbera to counter Hasan's hit–and–run tactics. There also were 320 Aden troops and 200 Indians from a disbanded contingent of the 6th KAR to support the Camel Corps.

Just before the outbreak of World War I, the British reorganized the protectorate's military establishment. The Camel Corps became the Somaliland Camel Corps. The

British also increased the unit's size by enlisting 450 Somalis, with a 150– man Somaliland Indian Contingent in reserve. The authorities organized this force into two camel companies and one cavalry company; eighteen British officers seconded from the Indian and regular armies commanded the force. A 400–man Somaliland Indian Contingent (less 150 assigned to the Somaliland Camel Corps) and a temporary garrison of 400 Indian infantrymen completed the protectorate's military.

In 1920 a combined British land and air offensive—which included the Somaliland Camel Corps, Somaliland Police, and elements from the 2d and 6th KAR and an Indian battalion—finally defeated Hasan's army.

Despite this defeat, many Somalis continued to hail Hasan as a warrior hero and the source of modern Somali nationalism. In 1923 the colonial authorities attached the Somaliland Camel Corps to the KAR. The unit, whose nucleus remained non–Somali, relied on Yao askaris (East African native soldiers) from the 1st KAR to fill its ranks. In the early 1930s, the Somaliland Camel Corps consisted of one camel and one pony company, both staffed by Somalis, and one Yao mechanized infantry company.

In 1940 Italian forces overran British Somaliland, which had been defended by the Somaliland Camel Corps and five British, Indian, and African battalions. Before withdrawing from Somaliland, the British disbanded the Somaliland Camel Corps. After defeating the Italians in 1941, the British reformed the Somaliland Camel Corps and created two battalions, the 71st and 72d (Somali) KAR battalions, both of which eventually were disbanded after World War II. In 1943 the colonial authorities converted the Somaliland Camel Corps into an armored car regiment. The following year elements in this unit mutinied; as a result, the British permanently disbanded the Somaliland Camel Corps.

The history of Somalia's postcolonial armed forces began in 1941, when the British formed an irregular force known as the Somali Prisoner of War Guards. The next year, the colonial authorities renamed the unit the Somali Companies; in 1943 the British redesignated the unit as the Somaliland Scouts. During the war, the British used this force to maintain lines of communication and patrol the colony's frontiers. After 1945 the Somaliland Scouts, which never belonged to the KAR, performed internal security duties. In 1960 the British assigned the Somaliland Scouts to Somalia's independent government; the unit subsequently formed the nucleus of the SNA.

On the eve of independence, the provisional government in the Italian–administered trust territory requested permission from the United Nations (UN) Trusteeship Council to establish a national army to protect its borders. The UN agreed and, a few months before independence, the provisional government created a small army from the Somali Police Force's Mobile Group (Darawishta Poliska—commonly known as the Darawishta). At the time the trust territory joined with British Somaliland to form the Somali Republic, troops from the Darawishta combined with those of the Somaliland Scouts to form the 5,000–man Somali National Army (SNA). Its first commander was Colonel Daud Abdullaahi Hersi, who had served in the Somalia Gendarmerie, the British Military Administration's police force. He was succeeded at his death in 1965 by Siad Barre.

Even before the 1969 coup, the SNA played a central role in the foreign policy process. Although the 1961 constitution renounced war as a means of settling international disputes, it also urged the amalgamation of Somali–inhabited territories in Ethiopia, Djibouti, and Kenya into a Greater Somalia. The government also deployed the SNA in support of Somali irredentism in Ethiopia.

The SNA was battle–tested in 1964 when the conflict with Ethiopia over the Somali–inhabited Ogaden erupted into warfare. On June 16, 1963, Somali guerrillas started an insurgency at Hodayo, in eastern Ethiopia, a watering place north of Werder, after Ethiopian emperor Haile Selassie rejected their demand for self–government in the Ogaden. The Somali government initially refused to support the guerrilla forces, which eventually numbered about 3,000. However, in January 1964, after Ethiopia sent reinforcements to the Ogaden, Somali forces launched ground and air attacks across the Ethiopian border and started providing assistance to the guerrillas. The EAF responded with punitive strikes across its southwestern frontier against Feerfeer, northeaast of Beledweyne, and Galcaio. On March 6, 1964, Somalia and Ethiopia agreed to a cease–fire; at the end of the month, the two sides signed an accord in Khartoum, Sudan, agreeing to withdraw their troops from the border, cease hostile propaganda, and start peace negotiations. Somalia also terminated its support of the guerrillas.

Despite its failure to incorporate the Ogaden into a Greater Somalia, the SNA continued to enjoy widespread support. In the late 1960s, for example, most Somalis believed that the SNA was less influenced by clan divisions and corruption than the civilian sector. The military also had succeeded in integrating British– and Italian–trained units more rapidly than had civilian institutions. The armed forces, moreover, maintained contact with the people through civic action projects and public relations programs. An army–trained, quasi–military youth group called the Young Pioneers worked in several agricultural and construction projects connected with national development ventures.

The SNA's reputation soared during the early stages of the 1977–78 Ogaden War. After Ethiopia defeated Somalia, however, public support for the military waned. As opposition to Siad Barre's regime intensified, the SNA became more and more isolated. During the late 1980s, various international human rights organizations accused the armed forces of committing crimes against civilians, dissidents, and government opponents.

Costly counterinsurgency campaigns in northern, central, and southern Somalia gradually sapped the military's strength. After Siad Barre fled Mogadishu in January 1991, the SNA ceased to exist. As of early 1992, although the SNM and the USC had announced their intention to reconstitute professionally trained national armies in their respective areas of operation—northern and south central Somalia, respectively, no progress had been made toward this goal. A lack of resources and expertise, however, would almost certainly prevent both groups from achieving their objectives over the short term.

The Armed Forces in National Life

The armed forces traditionally had enjoyed considerable prestige in Somali society. The military's early popularity was reflected in the fact that its numbers were maintained without resort to conscription. Chronic manpower shortages, however, compelled the government to institute a draft in 1984 (see Manpower, Training, and Conditions of Service , this ch.). For most of its postindependence history, the military had been involved in conflicts against its neighbors or against domestic insurgent groups.

The Military and the Government

During most of Somalia's early postindependence history, the SNA stayed out of politics. The only exception occurred in 1961, when a group of British–trained officers who objected to Italian influence on the military attempted to overthrow the government. In 1969 the SNA's apolitical stance changed when Major General Mahammad Siad Barre seized power. After abolishing the National Assembly of the Republic, he established the SRC, which was made up of military and police officers. This military junta relied on the largely civilian Council of the Secretaries of State to administer many of the country's ministries.

To enhance its image, the SRC intervened in nearly every aspect of Somali society. To reduce government corruption, Siad Barre instituted a nationwide campaign to make civil servants accountable. He also appointed a police general to head the Ministry of Interior, which controlled the means of enforcing government decisions and appointing military personnel to senior positions in district and provincial offices and in Somali embassies. In 1971 the SRC ordered senior civil servants to attend a three–month course at Camp Halane, Mogadishu, where they wore military uniforms and underwent military training. The military junta also recruited young men and women into a paramilitary organization called Victory Pioneers (see People's Militia , this ch.). In the foreign policy arena, Siad Barre adopted an anti–United States stance, ordered the Peace Corps out of the country, and accused Washington of imperialism.

In 1976 the government consolidated its power by creating the Somali Revolutionary Socialist Party (SRSP), which emerged as the basis for political authority. Furthermore, Siad Barre allowed the NSS to jail or harass dissidents, suppress freedom of speech, and create an atmosphere of fear and suspicion throughout Somalia. In 1980 a constitutional amendment empowered the SRC to resolve all state security and national interest issues during a declared state of emergency.

Opposition to Siad Barre's dictatorship increased during the mid–and late 1980s (see Sources of Opposition , this ch.). An increasing number of Somalis perceived the government and the nation's armed forces as enemies of the people. Siad Barre's refusal to institute reforms and include more people in the political process eventually led to his downfall and the dissolution of the armed forces.

The Military and the Economy

Under the Siad Barre regime, the army command, in conjunction with the Ministry of Defense, annually assessed the military's needs. The Ministry of Defense then passed budget recommendations to Siad Barre, who made final budget decisions.

With the formation of the SNA, the cost of maintaining the military establishment became the largest item in the national budget. During the first decade after independence, military expenditure increased at an average rate of more than 9 percent a year; moreover, defense costs consistently exceeded the combined amounts budgeted for health and education.

Between 1961 and 1979, Somalia imported approximately US$660 million in arms. During this same period, the SNA's personnel strength increased from 4,000 to 54,000. Although precise figures were unavailable, Somalia's military expenditures totaled about US$44.5 million annually for the 1980–90 decade.

Mission, Organization, and Strength

Since independence the armed forces' mission has been to protect the country's territorial integrity from foreign aggression and to maintain internal security. In 1990 the defense establishment consisted mainly of ground forces. Organizationally it was composed of the SNA and its subordinate air, air defense, and naval elements. The military command structure extended from Siad Barre, president and commander in chief of the armed forces, through the minister of defense to commanders who exercised authority over forces stationed in the country's six military sectors.

The ground forces were organized into twelve divisions. Allocated among the divisions were four tank brigades, forty–five mechanized and infantry brigades, four commando brigades, one surface–to–air missile brigade, three field artillery brigades, thirty field battalions, and one air defense battalion.

Military equipment was a mixture of old weapons of Soviet and United States origin, none of which could have withstood an attack from the better armed Ethiopian forces. Serviceability of all types of equipment was extremely poor, largely because of inadequate maintenance capability. As a result, foreign military advisers or technicians performed nearly all maintenance tasks. Included in the SNA inventory were Centurion, M–41, M–47, T–34, and T–54/T–55 tanks; BRDM–2 and AML–90 reconnaissance

235

vehicles; BTR–40/–50/–60/–152, Fiat 6614/6616, and BMR–600 armored personnel carriers; 100mm, 105mm, 122mm, and 155mm (M–198) towed artillery; 82mm and 120mm mortars; Milan TOW anti–tank guided weapons; 89mm rocket launchers; and 106mm recoilless rifles.

The Somali Air Force (SAF), initially known as the Somali Aeronautical Corps, operated most of its aircraft from bases near Mogadishu and Hargeysa. Its mission was to support ground forces. Since the Ogaden War, the SAF's performance had been hindered by inadequate equipment, lack of spare parts, and poor maintenance. During the late 1980s, however, the SAF managed to deploy some of its fighter aircraft against rebels in northern Somalia. Some of these aircraft were kept operational by Zimbabwean contract personnel.

In 1990 the SAF was organized into three fighter ground attack squadrons equipped with J–6 and Hawker Hunter aircraft; three fighter squadrons equipped with MiG–21MF and MiG17 aircraft; a counterinsurgency squadron equipped with SF–260W aircraft; a transport squadron equipped with An–2, An–24, An–26, BN–2, C–212, and G–222 aircraft; and a helicopter squadron equipped with Mi–4, Mi–8, and Augusta–Bell aircraft.

The SAF also possessed a variety of training aircraft such as the MiG–15UTI, the SF–260W, the Yak–11, and the Cessna. The SAF used Somali Airlines aircraft to ferry troops and supplies to war zones.

The Air Defense Forces consisted of seven brigades, four of which were equipped with SA–2, SA–3, and SA–7 surface–to–air missiles, none of which were believed to be operational in early 1992. The inventories of the other three units included 20mm, 23mm, 37mm, 40mm, 57mm, and 100mm air defense guns. The Air Defense Forces also possessed P–12, P–30, P–35, P–15, and Westinghouse AN/TPS–43F radars with AN/UPX–23 and AN/UPA–59A IFF.

In 1965 the Soviet Union helped Somalia establish a navy. As part of its mission to help SNA forces maintain coastal security, the navy maintained bases at Berbera, Mogadishu, and Chisimayu, and a radar site at Merca.

In 1990 the naval inventory included two Soviet Osa–II missile–armed fast attack craft, four Soviet Mol PFT torpedo–armed fast attack craft, and several patrol craft. The Somali navy also possessed a Soviet Polnocny–class landing ship capable of carrying five tanks and 120 soldiers, and four smaller mechanized landing craft. Much of this equipment had been unserviceable since the departure of Soviet military personnel in 1977. The navy was not operational from 1991 onward.

Paramilitary forces, which reported to the president via the minister of state, supplemented the SNA. These included a 1,500– man elite border guard; the 20,000–man People's Militia; and the 8,000–man Somali Police Force (SPF), which had an air unit based in Mogadishu consisting of two Dornier Do–28D2 aircraft, neither of which was believed to be operational in early 1992 (see Somali Police Force , this ch.).

In the early 1980s, the Somali armed forces were organized and deployed to prevent an Ethiopian attack. By the end of the decade, however, the military concentrated its activities on maintaining internal security.

Antigovernment resistance originated from various clan–based guerrilla groups that defended their interests against outsiders, each other, and Siad Barre's soldiers. The availability of weapons in the Horn of Africa and the ability to obtain military aid from foreign nations and Somali expatriate communities enabled the rebels to wage a protracted guerrilla war against Mogadishu.

Manpower, Training, and Conditions of Service

Despite the social and economic benefits associated with military service, the Somali armed forces began to suffer chronic manpower shortages only a few years after independence. The government attempted to solve this problem by instituting obligatory military service in 1984. Conscription affected men from eighteen to forty years of age and lasted for two years. Opposition to conscription and to the counterinsurgency campaigns against guerrilla groups resulted in widespread evasion of military service. As a result, during the late 1980s the government normally met manpower requirements by impressing men into military service.

This practice alienated an increasing number of Somalis who wanted the government to negotiate a peaceful resolution of the conflicts that were slowly destroying Somali society. Traditionally, the Siad Barre regime had followed a policy of mixing recruits from different parts of the country in order to cultivate nationalism among the soldiers. However, as the ongoing counterinsurgencies further isolated the regime, members of Siad Barre's subclan, the Mareehaan, increasingly dominated senior military positions. As a result, by 1990 many Somalis looked upon the armed forces as Siad Barre's personal army. This perception eventually destroyed the military's reputation as a national institution.

Throughout the postindependence period, the Somali armed forces relied on reserves to help defend national security and preserve internal stability. In 1961, for example, the government created the Women's Auxiliary Corps. Qualified enlistees underwent a five–month period of basic training and instruction in typing, record keeping, and related subjects. During their two–year enlistment, Somali women worked in a variety of positions associated with administration, personnel, and military welfare. Most Women's Auxiliary Corps personnel served in army headquarters in Mogadishu or in subordinate headquarters in the field.

In 1964 border clashes with Ethiopia prompted the Somali government to authorize the organization of a reserve force. The National Assembly therefore passed legislation mobilizing about 2,000 volunteers to be trained by the army at special camps in the regional capitals. After determining that these men would not be needed in the border war, Mogadishu released them from active duty. Although they carried identity cards, these reservists received neither pay nor training and had no official status.

In 1967 the Somali authorities established a Home Guard and called up 3,000 men for six months of training.

After completing their tours of duty, they received discharges and joined a reserve pool. The government then called another 3,000 men for the next six months.

In addition to the reserve forces, irregulars also augmented the military. After its defeat in the Ogaden War, Somalia organized paramilitary units in the country's many refugee communities. Mogadishu also encouraged the creation of clan militias, especially among Daarood civilians. The SNA trained and financed both groups.

Additionally, the Somali government recruited nomads and Ogaden refugees into the WSLF, the insurgent movement that sought to regain the Ogaden from Ethiopia. The use of irregulars did little to improve Somalia's military capabilities; indeed, these groups became a political liability to Siad Barre's regime because they brutalized large numbers of civilians.

The Somali armed forces always had depended on foreign training. Many high–ranking Somali officers had served in the British and Italian colonial armies and some had received training at Italian military and police academies. From the early 1960s until 1977, the Soviet Union provided most officer training. By the mid–1970s, as many as 60 percent of all activeduty officers had received Soviet training. The SNA used Soviet methods of organization and tactics.

Beginning in the early 1980s, many Somali officers started attending one of two military schools in Mogadishu. The Siad Barre Military Academy offered general instruction, and the Ahmad Guray War College was a staff school for senior officers. Noncommissioned officers attended the General Daoud Military Academy in Chisimayu. The Weapons School provided courses in specialties such as field artillery, transportation, and communications. The Somali armed forces also maintained instruction centers for personnel from the engineering, railway, and paratroop–commando corps. Despite the existence of these academies and schools, the Somali military relied on foreign training to maintain sophisticated weapons systems and to improve the technical and leadership skills of its personnel. After the breakup of the Somali–Soviet alliance, the SNA largely depended on the United States, Saudi Arabia, France, and Italy for such training. Following the fall of Siad Barre in January 1991 and the disintegration of the armed forces, military training ceased.

FOREIGN MILITARY ASSISTANCE

Throughout its history, Somalia has had to rely on foreign sources to equip and help maintain its military establishment. During the colonial period, Britain and Italy relied on military force to consolidate their respective positions in Somalia. These two nations then established and outfitted indigenous military units to help preserve internal security in their spheres of influence.

Shortly after independence, Somalia determined that its national interests required development of a 20,000–man army. Because of its weak economy, however, the Somali government rarely has been able purchase matériel outright. Instead, it has had to depend on donor countries whose assistance has been motivated by their own national interests. Somalia initially sought support from the United States. However, Washington argued that a 5,000–man army would be sufficient to maintain Mogadishu's internal security.

Somali leadership, determined to press its irredentist claims against neighbors in the Horn of Africa, therefore looked elsewhere for military assistance.

In 1962 the Soviet Union agreed to grant a US$32 million loan to modernize the Somali army, and expand it to 14,000 personnel. Moscow later increased the amount to US$55 million. The Soviet Union, seeking to counter United States influence in the Horn of Africa, made an unconditional loan and fixed a generous twenty– year repayment schedule.

During the rest of the 1960s, the Soviet Union provided Somalia with a substantial number of T–34 tanks, armored personnel carriers, MiG–15 and MiG–17 aircraft, small arms, and ammunition. Approximately 300 Soviet military advisers deployed to Somalia to train the army, and about 500 Somali pilots, officers, and technicians received training in the Soviet Union. Until Siad Barre seized power in 1969, Somalia's Western orientation and small amounts of United States and West German aid to the Somali police force limited the impact of Soviet military assistance. After the coup, however, Siad Barre embraced scientific socialism and the Soviet Union became Somalia's major supplier of military matériel.

Over the next eight years, the Somali–Soviet military relationship prospered. In 1972 Defense Minister Andrei Grechko visited Somalia and signed an agreement to improve and modernize the port of Berbera in return for Soviet access to the facility. The Soviet Union eventually built Berbera into a base that included a missile storage facility for the Soviet navy, an airfield with runways nearly 5,000 meters long and capable of handling large bombers, and extensive radar and communications facilities. Access to Berbera gave the Soviet Union a presence in the strategically important Indian Ocean–Persian Gulf region to counter United States military activities in the area. Berbera acquired additional importance when Egypt expelled all Soviet advisers in July 1972.

After signing the 1974 Treaty of Friendship and Cooperation with Moscow, Mogadishu started taking delivery of numerous sophisticated weapon systems, including MiG-21 jet fighters, T-54 tanks, a SAM-2 missile defense system for Mogadishu, and modern torpedo and missile-armed fast attack and landing craft for the navy. Soviet military advisers increased in number to about 1,500, supplemented by approximately 50 Cubans. The Soviet Union also trained and organized the Somali army's intelligence apparatus and the NSS.

By the time Siad Barre terminated the Treaty of Friendship and Cooperation with Moscow and expelled all Soviet advisers in 1977, about 2,400 Somali military personnel had undergone training in the Soviet Union and another 150 in Eastern Europe.

Somalia also relied on the Muslim world for military assistance. Somalia's ideological ties with the Islamic world reinforced mutual interests shared with several Muslim states, most notably Egypt, Saudi Arabia, and Iran, and provided the basis for military cooperation. In the 1960s, Cairo trained the Somali army and navy.

During the Ogaden War, Egypt provided approximately US$30 million in military assistance to Siad Barre's regime. After the conflict ended, Egypt supplied ammunition and spare parts for some of Somalia's Soviet-made equipment, such as T-54/T-55 tanks and armored personnel carriers. After the 1982 renewal of hostilities between Somalia and Ethiopia, Egypt delivered T-54 and T-55 tanks, 37mm antiaircraft guns, and ammunition. Thereafter, Egypt furnished more spare parts for Somalia's Soviet-made equipment, opened its military schools to Somali personnel, and, until the late 1980s, maintained a small military training team in Somalia.

Like Egypt, Saudi Arabia provided military assistance to Somalia in an effort to keep that country stable, conservative, and pro-Western. After Somalia joined the League of Arab States (Arab League) in 1974, Saudi Arabia, supported by Iran, tried to weaken the Somali-Soviet alliance by making a US$75 million aid package contingent on a reduction of Soviet activities in Somalia. When Siad Barre rejected this condition, Riyadh withdrew the offer. When Somalia broke with the Soviet Union in 1977, Saudi Arabia rewarded Somalia by paying for old stocks of Egyptian and Sudanese weapons, which were then sent to Mogadishu.

Until Siad Barre's downfall, Riyadh provided Mogadishu with a variety of weapons, including armored and reconnaissance vehicles, small arms, and ammunition. Additionally, Saudi Arabia trained SNA personnel.

Other Middle East states also supplied military assistance to Somalia. During the Ogaden War, for example, Iraq, Iran, and Jordan provided small arms and ammunition to the SNA. In 1982 Kuwait delivered forty Centurion tanks to Somalia. The United Arab Emirates and Oman equipped the SAF with Hawker Hunter fighters and Britten Norman Defender transports. Furthermore, funds from Islamic states enabled the acquisition of numerous weapons, the most notable of which was China's F–6 fighter–bomber in 1981.

The United States and several West European countries refused to supply weapons to Somalia as long as that country remained close to the Soviet Union. Once it became clear that a rift had developed between Somalia and the Soviet Union because of the latter's warming relations with Ethiopia, Washington adopted a new policy toward Siad Barre's regime. On July 26, 1977, the Department of State announced that the United States, Britain, and France were prepared to provide arms to Somalia. Approximately one year later, however, Washington reversed itself because of Mogadishu's decision to use military force to try to incorporate Ethiopia's Ogaden region into Somalia. According to the United States and most West European countries, no military equipment would be transferred to Somalia until Mogadishu withdrew its forces from the Ogaden.

Even after the SNA evacuated the Ogaden and Siad Barre promised to respect the boundaries of neighboring states, it was more than two years before the United States provided arms to Somalia.

The United States decision to begin a military assistance program in Somalia grew out of Washington's desire to bolster its presence in the Indian Ocean–Persian Gulf region after Mohammad Reza Pahlavi, the shah of Iran, fell from power in 1979. In August 1980, Washington and Mogadishu signed an agreement whereby the former received access to Somali ports and airfields in Berbera, Mogadishu, and Chisimayu in exchange for providing US$40 million in defensive military equipment over the next two years. This equipment included three TPS–43 long–range air defense radars, twelve M–167 (towed) Vulcan 20mm air defense guns, and associated communications gear, spare parts, and training. The agreement did not become official until February 1981 because of insistence by the United States Congress on the verified withdrawal of Somali troops from the Ogaden.

Over the next few years, the United States increased its military assistance to Somalia. In 1982, for example, equipment sales and gifts amounted to US$14.3 million; on July 24 of that year, the United States responded to an Ethiopian attack on Somalia by providing the Siad Barre regime with antitank weapons, radars, air defense guns, small arms, and ammunition. In 1983 United States military aid totaled US$21.2 million; in 1984 US$24.3 million; in 1985 US$80 million, a large amount of which included air–transpor; table 155mm M–198s; in 1986 US$40 million; and in 1987 approximately US$37.1 million. For 1981–84 United States Foreign Military Sales (FMS) to Somalia included US$57.15 million in delivered matériel, US$60 million financed with a Department of Defense guarantee, and US$1.811 million in commercial exports. During this same period, the United States trained 126 Somali military personnel under the International Military Education and Training (IMET) program. The cost of the training came to more than US$2.31 million.

Somalia also participated in the United States Central Command (USCENTCOM) Operation Bright Star exercises.

After the SNM launched armed attacks in northern Somalia in late May 1988, the United States provided Somalia with US$1.4 million worth of military equipment, which consisted of 1,200 M16 automatic rifles and 2 million rounds of M16 ammunition, 300,000 rounds of 30–caliber ammunition, and 500,000 rounds of 50–caliber ammunition. Additionally, the Department of Defense donated US$1 million for a 220–bed hospital, which operated in Berbera to help victims of the conflict.

United States military aid to Somalia diminished significantly after it became clear that Siad Barre's regime had committed human rights violations against civilian populations in northern Somalia. Nevertheless, according to official United States statements, the United States maintained a security assistance program in Somalia largely to protect its access to Somali air and port facilities; strengthen the Somalis' ability to maintain military equipment of United States origin; encourage national reconciliation through greater concern for human rights and civil liberties, military restraint, and political accommodation with the opposition elements; and support private sector revitalization. Until Siad Barre's downfall, United States military aid to Somalia consisted primarily of technical assistance and IMET training.

Starting in 1978, Italy furnished more military aid to Somalia than any other Western country. This aid included several large shipments of Fiat trucks, which formed the backbone of the SNA's logistics system throughout the 1980s. Beginning in 1979, many Italian companies, assisted by government–subsidized export credits, supplied aircraft and training for SAF flight and ground crews. The aircraft included six SIAI–Marchetti SF–260W single– engine trainer/tactical support aircraft, four Aeritalia G–222 twin–engine transports, and two Piaggio 166 transports. Fiat also sold light tanks and armored cars to the SNA. By 1980 Italian exports to Somalia amounted to US$124 million. The following year, Italian foreign minister Emilio Colombo visited Mogadishu and signed a US$40 million aid package. Subsequently, Italy furnished an array of military equipment to Somalia, including armored vehicles, trucks, tanks, helicopters, small arms, and ammunition. In July 1983, Italy and Somalia signed an accord that provided for the training of Somali military personnel. In February 1985, the two countries concluded a new military assistance agreement. Apart from this cooperation, Italian naval ships regularly called at Mogadishu; in May 1986, for example, the frigates *Scirocco* and *Grecale* made a five–day visit to Somalia. In the late 1980s, Italy started rehabilitating the SNA's M–47 tanks; however, deteriorating conditions throughout Somalia prevented the completion of this program. On July 11, 1990, citing delays in the democratization and national reconciliation processes, Italy announced the withdrawal from Somalia of its fifty–six army and air force advisers and instructors.

The Federal Republic of Germany (West Germany) specialized in aid to the Somali police and security services. Bonn also trained about sixty Somali Army Special Forces personnel and maintained a technical assistance mission with the police air wing to service the Dornier Do–28s. Until 1985 West Germany had delivered vehicles and radio communications equipment valued at 68 million deutsche marks (DM). For the 1985–87 period, West German aid amounted to DM12 million. Like other Western nations, Bonn curtailed its military assistance to Somalia after the armed forces started committing human rights violations against civilians.

Cooperation between Somalia and China started before the break between Mogadishu and Moscow. It was not until 1981, however, that Beijing emerged as a major arms supplier to Siad Barre's regime. Thereafter, China supplied Somalia with an array of weaponry, including F–6 fighter–bombers in 1981, F–7 fighter– bombers in 1984, artillery, antiaircraft guns, rocket launchers, mortars, small arms, and ammunition. China also provided technical assistance to the Somali armed forces. On February 10, 1989,

Somalia and China signed an agreement transferring Somalia's territorial fishing rights to China in exchange for armament credits. Beijing continued to provide military assistance to Mogadishu until the downfall of Siad Barre's regime.

Since the mid–1980s, there had been numerous unconfirmed reports of Somali–South African military cooperation. The relationship supposedly began on December 18, 1984, when South African foreign minister Roelof "Pik" Botha visited Somalia and conducted discussions with Siad Barre. The two leaders reportedly signed a secret communiqué granting South African Airways landing rights in Somalia and the South African navy access to the ports of Chisimayu and Berbera. It was said that Somalia also agreed to sell South Africa eight MiG–21 fighters. In exchange, South Africa reportedly promised to provide Somalia with Soviet–built equipment, including tanks, captured in Angola and Mozambique. South Africa supposedly arranged to ship spare parts and ammunition for the Hawker Hunter aircraft supplied to Somalia by the United Arab Emirates, and to be responsible for the salaries of ten former Rhodesian Air Force pilots who already were in Somalia helping to train Somali pilots and technicians and flying combat missions in the north. Despite Mogadishu's repeated denials of a military link with Pretoria, rumors of a Somali– South African alliance continued to surface until the downfall of Siad Barre's regime.

The outbreak of the SNM insurgency in mid–1988 and the drying–up of traditional sources of foreign military assistance persuaded Siad Barre to seek arms from Libya. On October 7, 1988, a Libyan Arab Airlines jet reportedly delivered nerve gas to Somalia. It was widely reported that Libya had acquired the chemical weapons from Iran. Mogadishu denied these charges. No evidence surfaced to confirm the existence of Libyan–supplied chemical weapons in Somalia. However, Tripoli supplied small amounts of conventional military weapons and ammunition to Siad Barre's regime. By early 1989, it was evident that the Somali government's strategy of using Libyan–supplied weapons to defeat the SNM and other insurgent groups had failed.

STATE SECURITY SERVICES

Under the Siad Barre regime, several police and intelligence organizations were responsible for maintaining public order, controlling crime, and protecting the government against domestic threats. These included the Somali Police Force (SPF), the People's Militia, the NSS, and a number of other intelligencegathering operations, most of which were headed by members of the president's family. After Siad Barre's downfall, these units were reorganized or abolished.

Somali Police Force (SPF)

The Somali Police Force (SPF) grew out of police forces employed by the British and Italians to maintain peace during the colonial period. Both European powers used Somalis as armed constables in rural areas.

Somalis eventually staffed the lower ranks of the police forces, and Europeans served as officers. The colonial forces produced the senior officers and commanders— including Siad Barre—who led the SPF and the army after independence.

In 1884 the British formed an armed constabulary to police the northern coast. In 1910 the British created the Somaliland Coastal Police, and in 1912 they established the Somaliland Camel Constabulary to police the interior. In 1926 the colonial authorities formed the Somaliland Police Force. Commanded by British officers, the force included Somalis in its lower ranks. Armed rural constabulary *(illalo)* supported this force by bringing offenders to court, guarding prisoners, patrolling townships, and accompanying nomadic tribesmen over grazing areas.

The Italians initially relied on military forces to maintain public order in their colony. In 1914 the authorities established a coastal police and a rural constabulary *(gogle)* to protect Italian residents. By 1930 this force included about 300 men. After the fascists seized power in Italy, colonial administrators reconstituted the Somali Police Corps into the Corpo Zaptié. Italian carabinieri commanded and trained the new corps, which eventually numbered approximately 800. During Italy's war against Ethiopia, the Corpo Zaptié expanded to about 6,000 men.

In 1941 the British defeated the Italians and formed a British Military Administration (BMA) over both protectorates. The BMA disbanded the Corpo Zaptié and created the Somalia Gendarmerie. By 1943 this force had grown to more than 3,000 men, led by 120 British officers. In 1948 the Somalia Gendarmerie became the Somali Police Force.

After the creation of the Italian Trust Territory in 1950, Italian carabinieri officers and Somali personnel from the Somali Police Force formed the Police Corps of Somalia (Corpo di Polizia della Somalia). In 1958 the authorities made the corps an entirely Somali force and changed its name to the Police Force of Somalia (Forze di Polizia della Somalia).

In 1960 the British Somaliland Scouts joined with the Police Corps of Somalia to form a new Somali Police Force, which consisted of about 3,700 men. The authorities also organized approximately 1,000 of the force as the Darawishta Poliska, a mobile group used to keep peace between warring clans in the interior. Since then, the government has considered the SPF a part of the armed forces. It was not a branch of the SNA, however, and did not operate under the army's command structure. Until abolished in 1976, the Ministry of Interior oversaw the force's national commandant and his central command. After that date, the SPF came under the control of the presidential adviser on security affairs.

Each of the country's administrative regions had a police commandant; other commissioned officers maintained law and order in the districts. After 1972 the police outside Mogadishu comprised northern and southern group commands, divisional commands (corresponding to the districts), station commands, and police posts. Regional governors and district commissioners commanded regional and district police elements.

Under the parliamentary regime, police received training and matériel aid from West Germany, Italy, and the United States. Although the government used the police to counterbalance the Soviet–supported army, no police commander opposed the 1969 army coup. During the 1970s, German Democratic Republic (East Germany) security advisers assisted the SPF. After relations with the West improved in the late 1970s, West German and Italian advisers again started training police units.

By the late 1970s, the SPF was carrying out an array of missions, including patrol work, traffic management, criminal investigation, intelligence gathering, and counterinsurgency. The elite mobile police groups consisted of the Darawishta and the Birmadka Poliska (Riot Unit). The Darawishta, a mobile unit that operated in remote areas and along the frontier, participated in the Ogaden War. The Birmadka acted as a crack unit for emergency action and provided honor guards for ceremonial functions.

In 1961 the SPF established an air wing, equipped with Cessna light aircraft and one Douglas DC–3. The unit operated from improvised landing fields near remote police posts. The wing provided assistance to field police units and to the Darawishta through the airlift of supplies and personnel and reconnaissance. During the final days of Siad Barre's regime, the air wing operated two Cessna light aircraft and two DO–28 Skyservants.

Technical and specialized police units included the Tributary Division, the Criminal Investigation Division (CID), the Traffic Division, a communications unit, and a training unit. The CID, which operated throughout the country, handled investigations, fingerprinting, criminal records, immigration matters, and passports.

In 1961 the SPF established a women's unit. Personnel assigned to this small unit investigated, inspected, and interrogated female offenders and victims. Policewomen also handled cases that involved female juvenile delinquents, ill or abandoned girls, prostitutes, and child beggars.

Service units of the Somali police included the Gadidka Poliska (Transport Department) and the Health Service. The Police Custodial Corps served as prison guards. In 1971 the SPF created a fifty–man national Fire Brigade. Initially, the Fire Brigade operated in Mogadishu. Later, however, it expanded its activities into other towns, including Chisimayu, Hargeysa, Berbera, Merca, Giohar, and Beledweyne.

Beginning in the early 1970s, police recruits had to be seventeen to twenty–five years of age, of high moral caliber, and physically fit. Upon completion of six months of training at the National Police Academy in Mogadishu, those who passed an examination would serve two years on the force. After the recruits completed this service, the police could request renewal of their contracts. Officer cadets underwent a nine–month training course that emphasized supervision of police field performance. Darawishta members attended a six–month tactical training course; Birmadka personnel received training in public order and riot control. After Siad Barre fled Mogadishu in January 1991, both the Darawishta and Birmadka forces ceased to operate, for all practical purposes.

People's Militia

In August 1972, the government established the People's Militia, known as the Victory Pioneers (Guulwadayaal). Although a wing of the army, the militia worked under the supervision of the Political Bureau of the presidency. After the SRSP's formation in 1976, the militia became part of the party apparatus.

Largely because of the need for military reserves, militia membership increased from 2,500 in 1977 to about 10,000 in 1979, and to approximately 20,000 by 1990. After the collapse of Siad Barre's regime, the People's Militia, like other military elements, disintegrated.

The militia staffed the government and party orientation centers that were located in every settlement in Somalia. The militia aided in self–help programs, encouraged "revolutionary progress," promoted and defended Somali culture, and fought laziness, misuse of public property, and "reactionary" ideas and actions.

Moreover, the militia acted as a law enforcement agency that performed duties such as checking contacts between Somalis and foreigners. The militia also had powers of arrest independent of the police. In rural areas, militiamen formed "vigilance corps" that guarded grazing areas and towns. After Siad Barre fled Mogadishu in January 1991, militia members tended to join one of the insurgent groups or clan militias.

National Security Service

Shortly after Siad Barre seized power, the Soviet Committee of State Security (Komitet Gosudarstvennoi Bezopasnosti—KGB) helped Somalia form the National Security Service (NSS). This organization, which operated outside normal bureaucratic channels, developed into an instrument of domestic surveillance, with powers of arrest and investigation. The NSS monitored the professional and private activities of civil servants and military personnel, and played a role in the promotion and demotion of government officials. As the number of insurgent movements proliferated in the late 1980s, the NSS increased its activities against dissidents, rebel sympathizers, and other government opponents (see Human Rights , this ch.). Until the downfall of Siad Barre's regime, the NSS remained an elite organization staffed by men from the SNA and the police force who had been chosen for their loyalty to the president.

CRIMINAL JUSTICE

Over the centuries, the Somalis developed a system of handling disputes or acts of violence, including homicide, as wrongs involving not only the parties immediately concerned but also the clans to which they belonged. The offending party and his group would pay *diya* to the injured party and his clan. The British and Italians enforced criminal codes based on their own judicial systems in their respective colonies, but did not seriously disrupt the *diya*–paying system.

After independence the Somali government developed its own laws and procedures, which were largely based on British and Italian legal codes. Somali officials made no attempt to develop a uniquely Somali criminal justice system, although *diya*– paying arrangements continued.

The military junta that seized power in 1969 changed little of the criminal justice system it inherited.

However, the government launched a campaign against *diya* and the concept of collective responsibility for crimes. This concept is the most distinctly Somali of any in the criminal justice system. The regime instead concentrated on extending the influence of laws introduced by the British and Italians. This increased the government's control over an area of national life previously regulated largely by custom.

Penal System

The Somali Penal Code, promulgated in early 1962, became effective on April 3, 1964. It was Somalia's first codification of laws designed to protect the individual and to ensure the equitable administration of justice.

The basis of the code was the constitutional premise that the law has supremacy over the state and its citizens.

The code placed responsibility for determining offenses and punishments on the written law and the judicial system and excluded many penal sanctions formerly observed in unwritten customary law. The authorities who drafted the code, however, did not disregard the people's past reliance on traditional rules and sanctions.

The code contained some of the authority expressed by customary law and by Islamic, sharia, or religious law.

The penal laws applied to all nationals, foreigners, and stateless persons living in Somalia. Courts ruled out ignorance of the law as a justification for breaking the law or an excuse for committing an offense, but considered extenuations and mitigating factors in individual cases. The penal laws prohibited collective punishment, which was contrary to the traditional sanctions of *diya*–paying groups. The penal laws stipulated that if the offense constituted a violation of the code, the perpetrator had committed an unlawful act against the state and was subject to its sanctions. Judicial action under the code, however, did not rule out the possibility of additional redress in the form of *diya* through civil action in the courts. Siad Barre's regime attacked this tolerance of *diya*, and forbade its practice entirely in 1974.

Under the Somali penal code, to be criminally liable a person must have committed an act or have been guilty of an omission that caused harm or danger to the person or property of another or to the state. Further, the offense must have been committed willfully or as the result of negligence, imprudence, or illegal behavior.

Under Somali penal law, the courts assumed the accused to be innocent until proved guilty beyond reasonable doubt. In criminal prosecution, the burden of proof rested with the state.

Penal laws classed offenses as either crimes or contraventions, the latter being legal violations without criminal intent. Death by shooting was the only sentence for serious offenses such as crimes against the state and murder. The penal law usually prescribed maximum and minimum punishments but left the actual sentence to the judge's discretion.

The penal laws comprised three categories. The first dealt with general principles of jurisprudence; the second defined criminal offenses and prescribed specified punishments; the third contained sixty–one articles that regulated contraventions of public order, safety, morality, and health. Penal laws took into consideration the role of punishment in restoring the offender to a useful place in society.

The Criminal Procedure Code governed matters associated with arrest and trial. The code, which conformed to British common law, prescribed the kinds and jurisdictions of criminal courts, identified the functions and responsibilities of judicial officials, outlined the rules of evidence, and regulated the conduct of trials.

Normally, a person could be arrested only if caught in the act of committing an offense or upon issuance of a warrant by the proper judicial authority. The code recognized the writ of habeas corpus. Those arrested had the right to appear before a judge within twenty–four hours.

As government opposition proliferated in the late 1970s and early 1980s, the Siad Barre regime increasingly subverted or ignored Somalia's legal system. By the late 1980s, Somalia had become a police state, with citizens often falling afoul of the authorities for solely political reasons. Pressure by international human rights organizations such as Amnesty International and Africa Watch failed to slow Somalia's descent into lawlessness. After Siad Barre fell from power in January 1991, the new authorities promised to restore equity to the country's legal system. Given the many political, economic, and social problems confronting post–Siad Barre Somalia, however, it appeared unlikely that this goal would be achieved soon.

Prison System

The few prisons that existed before 1960 had been established during the British and Italian colonial administrations. By independence these facilities were in poor condition and were inadequately staffed.

After independence the Somali government included in the constitution an article asserting that criminal punishment must not be an obstacle to convicts' moral reeducation.

This article also established a prison organization and emphasized prisoner rehabilitation.

The Somali Penal Code of 1962 effectively stipulated the reorganization of the prison system. The code required that prisoners of all ages work during prison confinement. In return for labor on prison farms, construction projects, and roadbuilding, prisoners received a modest salary, which they could spend in prison canteens or retain until their release. The code also outlawed the imprisonment of juveniles with adults.

By 1969 Somalia's prison system included forty-nine facilities, the best-equipped of which was the Central Prison of Mogadishu. During the 1970s, East Germany helped Somalia build four modern prisons. As opposition to Siad Barre's regime intensified, the country's prisons became so crowded that the government used schools, military and police headquarters, and part of the presidential palace as makeshift jails. Despite criticism by several international humanitarian agencies, the Somali government failed to improve the prison system.

HUMAN RIGHTS

Center for internally displaced persons, Mogadishu, 1991 Courtesy Hiram A. Ruiz
Refugee women in camp near Luuq, western Somalia, 1991 Courtesy Hiram A. Ruiz
The constitution of 1961 in force until the October 1969 revolution protected the civil rights outlined in the United Nations Declaration of Human Rights. These included the presumption of innocence before the courts, the right of habeas corpus, the freedoms of political association, public expression, and personal liberty and movement, and the right to form labor unions and to strike. The state owned all land (outright ownership of land conflicts with Somali traditions), but developed property and improved land could be expropriated only on the basis of equitable compensation. With few exceptions, the Somali government respected these rights.

In October 1970, the Siad Barre government abolished the right of habeas corpus; however, the courts continued to recognize the presumption of innocence and to provide free legal assistance to indigent defendants in serious cases. The regime also extended equal rights to women in several areas, including inheritance. In the late 1970s, however, the government began restricting civil rights, to counter the spread of dissident elements.

This policy was criticized by the United States and several other Western nations.

In 1979, anxious to obtain United States military and economic assistance, Siad Barre promulgated a new liberal constitution. Approved by a national referendum held on August 29, 1979, this constitution stipulated the restoration of many of the civil rights that had been extinguished by the military government. The new constitution guaranteed freedom of speech, religion, and publication and the right to participate in an assembly, demonstration, or organization. The constitution also supported the inviolability of the home and the privacy of correspondence. However, these safeguards were subject to important qualifications—in the cases of freedom of expression and association by the condition that exercise of these rights "shall not contravene the constitution, the laws of the land, general morality, and public order." Furthermore, under the constitution the government was permitted to control the press, subject foreign publications to censorship, and circumscribe freedom of assembly.

The constitution stipulated that anyone deprived of personal liberty should forthwith be informed of the offense of which he was accused, and anyone detained on security grounds must be brought before a competent judicial authority without delay. Despite these provisions, the *Amnesty International Report, 1980 e* timated that the government had jailed at least 100 people on political grounds without charge or trial, among them former prime minister Mahammad Ibrahim Igaal. After the 1978 coup attempt, the Mogadishu National Security Court tried seventy–four men and subsequently ordered the execution of seventeen of them.

The defendants had access to legal representation, and close relatives were permitted to attend the trials.

However, in early 1980 the government secretly executed as many as several dozen military personnel for supporting the Somali Salvation Front (SSF) guerrilla movement.

Over the next few years, the proliferation of insurgent movements prompted Mogadishu to become increasingly oppressive. In 1982, for example, the government declared a state of emergency in northern Somalia and took steps to suppress local populations. Additionally, laws were adopted that placed civilians under the jurisdiction of military tribunals and military police. Several institutions comprised this new security apparatus, including the Mobile Military Court (MMC), the Regional Security Council (RSC), the

HANGASH (Somali acronym for military police), the NSS, and the Victory Pioneers.

Established in 1982, the MMC was composed entirely of military officers. Two years later, after the SNM had launched an offensive in the mountainous region of Sheekh and nearby Burao, the MMC assumed jurisdiction over civilians. Operating from headquarters in Hargeysa, the MMC created a network of offices throughout northern Somalia. Initially, the MMC tried small numbers of suspected opponents of the regime such as businessmen and educated people. Eventually, however, the MMC tried every variety of politically active person or group. The court prosecutor, Colonel Yuusuf Muse, quickly earned a reputation for cruelty and his insistence on the death penalty. In 1984–85 and from late 1987 until mid–1988, Muse authorized mass executions of hundreds, if not thousands, of northerners.

The RSC, which was superior to all other branches of the security system, consisted of the regional governor, the regional military commander, a military officer, the regional police commander, and the following national officials: the NSS director, the head of the SRSP, the commander of the Victory Pioneers, and the director of the Police Custodial Corps. Although it could operate anywhere in the country, the RSC confined its activities to northern Somalia. The RSC usually met weekly, but it convened more frequently during emergencies. Any quorum of six could impose long prison sentences or the death penalty. From its inception, the RSC ordered mass arrests of SNM sympathizers and other suspected government opponents and confiscated their property. The RSC often relied on the NSS to conduct interrogations and prepare arrest warrants.

Mogadishu created the HANGASH in the aftermath of the 1978 coup attempt. Its purpose was to maintain surveillance over the military and the NSS. As the government's crackdown on political activity became more severe, however, the HANGASH acquired power over civilians. Eventually, the HANGASH, which operated without legal authority, became more feared than the NSS.

The NSS, Somalia's principal intelligence agency, possessed the power to detain people indefinitely if they were suspected of having committed national security offenses. Article 5 of Law No. 8 of January 26, 1970, abolished the right to habeas corpus in national security cases and permitted access to lawyers only after the NSS had completed its investigations and had prepared charges. Over the years, the NSS used the national security rationale to justify the arrest, execution, or imprisonment of hundreds, if not thousands, of real and imagined government opponents.

The Victory Pioneers were a uniformed militia that provided security at the neighborhood level. Pioneer units, which existed in every town and village, ensured loyalty to Siad Barre's regime by encouraging people to spy on each other in the work place, schools, mosques, and private homes.

After the SNM launched a major offensive in northern Somalia in late May 1988, deterioration of the government's human rights record accelerated. The SNA used artillery shelling and aerial bombardment in heavily populated urban centers to retake the towns of Hargeysa and Burao. As a result, thousands of refugees gathered on the outskirts of these cities. After breaking into smaller groups of 300 to 500, the refugees started a ten– to forty–day trek to Ethiopia; others fled to Djibouti and Kenya. Along the way, SNA units robbed many civilians and summarily executed anyone suspected of being an SNM member or sympathizer. SAF jet aircraft strafed many refugee columns, forcing refugees to walk at night to avoid further attacks. Africa Watch reported that government forces had killed as many as 50,000 unarmed civilians between June 1988 and January 1990; most victims belonged to the northern Isaaq clan.

By 1990 security conditions had become as bad in central and southern Somalia as they had been in the north.

As a result, the government enacted harsh new measures against opposition elements. In Mogadishu, for example, SNA personnel and members of the various security agencies regularly raped, robbed, and killed noncombatant citizens. The emergence of bandit groups in the capital only exacerbated security problems in Mogadishu. On July 6, 1990, some of Siad Barre's bodyguards, the Red Berets (Duub Cas), started shooting at people who had been shouting antigovernment slogans at a soccer match. Other Red Berets, stationed outside the soccer stadium, shot into the crowd as it tried to escape the chaos inside (see Harrying of the Hawiye , ch.

1). Eventually, at least 65 civilians lost their lives and more than 300 sustained serious wounds. The authorities refused to allow families to recover the bodies of their relatives.

In the central area, which consists of Mudug, Hiiraan, and Galguduud regions, the government unleashed a reign of terror against those suspected of supporting or belonging to the United Somali Congress (USC), another insurgent group. According to Africa Watch, the SNA killed hundreds of civilians in retaliation for rebel attacks. Government troops also ambushed numerous cars, killing and injuring many of the passengers.

After robbing vehicles, soldiers usually hanged some victims on trees and then forced local inhabitants to view the bodies of what the soldiers claimed were armed bandits. Similar violence occurred at several other central and southern towns and villages, including Beledweyne, Adaddo, Gaalcaio, Doolow, Hara Cadera, Hobyo, Las Adale, and Wisil.

Apart from atrocities committed by troops in the field, prison authorities mistreated political detainees and other prisoners, despite the fact that on January 24, 1990, the government had ratified the International Covenant on Civil and Political Rights. According to Africa Watch, detainees and prisoners were held in tiny, overcrowded cells and denied medical treatment and physical exercise. Many were tortured. During Siad Barre's final months in power, the Central Prison of Mogadishu, which was intended to hold about 600 people, often contained 1,600 or more prisoners. There was also a lack of food, water, medicine, bedding, and air. Guards extorted food and money, which had been supplied by prisoners' families.

In response to growing domestic and international pressure, the government introduced a provisional constitution, effective for one year from October 12, 1990. Supposedly, the constitution would have repealed a series of repressive security laws; permitted free, multiparty elections; guaranteed individual civil rights; and transferred considerable power from the president to the prime minister, cabinet, and parliament. However, the heavy fighting which engulfed Mogadishu and other areas of Somalia at the end of 1990 prevented the new constitution from having any impact. After Siad Barre fled Mogadishu in early 1991, Somalia's human rights record further deteriorated, largely because of fighting between and among various insurgent groups and clan militias, and the attacks by bandit groups on the civilian population.

* * * Given the West's limited access to Somalia and the secrecy that surrounded security–related activities, there is no definitive study of the country's armed forces. Those interested in Somali national security affairs therefore must rely on a variety of periodical sources, including *Africa Research Bulletin, Keesing's Contemporary*

Archives, *Third World Reports*, *Africa Confidential*, and *African Defense Journal*. Other useful publications include *New African*, *Africa Events*, *Africa News*, *Focus on Africa*, and *Horn of Africa*. Two International Institute for Strategic Studies annuals, *The Military Balance* and *Strategic Survey*, also are essential for anyone wishing to understand the evolution of Somalia's security forces. The same is true of three annuals:

Africa Contemporary Record, *Africa South of the Sahara*, and *World Armaments and Disarmament*. The last is published by the Stockholm International Peace Research Institute.

Useful historical works include Malcolm McNeill's *In Pursuit of the `Mad Mullah':* *Service and Sport in the Somali Protectorate*, Douglas J. Jardine's *The Mad Mullah of Somaliland*, and H F P. Battesby's *Richard Corfield of Somaliland*. Bruce D. Porter's *The USSR in Third World Conflicts* provides an excellent analysis of the 1977–78 Ogaden War between Somalia and Ethiopia. *Somalia: Nation in Search of a State*, by David D. Laitin and Said S. Samatar, contains some useful information on the post–independence evolution of the Somali armed forces. Material on human rights practices in Somalia can be found in the annual *Amnesty International Report* and in a variety of Africa Watch reports, the most important of which is *Somalia: A Government at War with Its Own People*. (For further information and complete citations, see Bibliography.)

Printed in the United States
65363LVS00003B